"*Equity in Higher Education: Time for Social Justice* critique of the longstanding inequalities in contemp and how race, gender, social class and age continu participation in socially unjust ways. In addition – and book so compelling and exciting – the deployment social justice framework for both analysis and action ur̞~~ ~~~~ ~~~~~ ~~~~ is meant by equity. Drawing on a wealth of theoretical and empirical work, this timely and insightful book acknowledges the messiness and necessity of working in collaborative ways; its grounding in a praxis for change makes it a must-read for policymakers, academics and educators."

Carol A. Taylor, *Professor of Higher Education and Gender, University of Bath, UK*

"If you work in higher education, or if your policy work influences its directions, this profound book will compel you to reconsider and alter what you do. It puts conventional approaches to equity in higher education under pressure highlighting their deep, and sometimes subtlety seductive, structural flaws. In the spirit of positive critique, it also offers fresh and highly persuasive considerations for praxis. Enlivened by strong ethical sensibilities it provides the best of practical theory and of thought-full practice."

Jane Kenway, *Emeritus Professor, Monash University, Australia*

"What is the role of the university? This is a crucial and recurrent question in the global histories and geographies of higher education, but it is also at the heart of this important and timely book. In flagging up the urgency of social justice in higher education the book's urgent argument is that equity can only be materialized as praxis and in doing so it offers a unique framework for action in different socio-political, cultural and geographical contexts."

Maria Tamboukou, *Professor of Feminist Studies, University of East London, UK*

"Penny Jane Burke's and Matt Lumb's *Equity in Higher Education: Time for Social Justice Praxis* is an essential and challenging text for all those concerned for more socially just polices, practices and participation in higher education. They proffer original, sophisticated, multidimensional and equitable theory and methodologies for achieving these aspirational goals in the context of the climate emergency, challenges to democracy, growing inequality and corporatised universities."

Bob Lingard, *Emeritus Professor, University of Queensland, Australia*

"This book is a welcome contribution to conversations on how current higher education policies and practices are insidiously undergirded by a metaphysics of individualism. The book critiques pathologisation of individual students through deficit discourses, and taken-for-granted notions of time in higher education, providing provocations for alternative methodologies towards a theoretically-informed social justice praxis."

Vivienne Bozalek, *Emerita Professor, Women's and Gender Studies, University of the Western Cape, South Africa; Honorary Professor Centre for Higher Education Research Teaching and Learning (CHERTL), Rhodes University, South Africa*

EQUITY IN HIGHER EDUCATION

In a global context of growing inequality and socio-environmental crises, *Equity in Higher Education* considers the issues and challenges for progressing an equity agenda.

It advances a unique multidimensional framework based on theoretical and conceptual threads, including critical, feminist, decolonial, post-structural, and sociological discourses. It also provides readers with the sophisticated insights and tools urgently needed to challenge long-standing, entrenched, and insidious inequalities at play in and through higher education.

Written as a form of a pedagogical interaction, and addressing nuanced temporal and spatial inequalities, this key resource will be of value to policymakers, practitioners, educators, and scholars committed to progressive and groundbreaking approaches that can engage the ongoing challenges of transforming higher education towards more just realities.

Penny Jane Burke is United Nations Educational, Scientific and Cultural Organization (UNESCO) Chair in Equity, Social Justice and Higher Education, Global Innovation Chair of Equity, and Director of the Centre of Excellence for Equity in Higher Education, University of Newcastle, Australia.

Matt Lumb is Associate Director of the Centre of Excellence for Equity in Higher Education, University of Newcastle, Australia.

Foundations and Futures of Education

Peter Aggleton
University of New South Wales, Australia
Sally Power
Cardiff University, UK
Michael Reiss
University College London, UK

Foundations and Futures of Education focuses on key emerging issues in education as well as continuing debates within the field. The series is inter-disciplinary, and includes historical, philosophical, sociological, psychological and comparative perspectives on three major themes: the purposes and nature of education; increasing interdisciplinarity within the subject; and the theory-practice divide.

Paradoxes of Democracy, Leadership and Education
Struggling for Social Justice in the Twenty-first Century
Edited by John Schostak, Matthew Clarke and Linda Hammersley-Fletcher

Learning as Social Practice
Beyond Education as an Individual Enterprise
Edited by Gunther Kress, Staffan Selander, Roger Säljö and Christoph Wulf

Queering Higher Education
Troubling Norms in the Global Knowledge Economy
Louise Morley and Daniel Leyton

Rethinking Knowledgeable Practice in Education
Jim Hordern

Equity in Higher Education
Time for Social Justice Praxis
Penny Jane Burke and Matt Lumb

For more information about this series, please visit: www.routledge.com/Foundations-and-Futures-of-Education/book-series/FFE

EQUITY IN HIGHER EDUCATION

Time for Social Justice Praxis

Penny Jane Burke and Matt Lumb

Routledge
Taylor & Francis Group

LONDON AND NEW YORK

Designed cover image: © Getty Images

First published 2025
by Routledge
4 Park Square, Milton Park, Abingdon, Oxon OX14 4RN

and by Routledge
605 Third Avenue, New York, NY 10158

Routledge is an imprint of the Taylor & Francis Group, an informa business

British Library Cataloguing-in-Publication Data
A catalogue record for this book is available from the British Library

ISBN: 978-1-032-18969-7 (hbk)
ISBN: 978-1-032-18970-3 (pbk)
ISBN: 978-1-003-25716-5 (ebk)

DOI: 10.4324/9781003257165

Typeset in ITC Galliard Pro
by Apex CoVantage, LLC

CONTENTS

ABOUT THE AUTHORS

Penny Jane Burke is UNESCO Chair in Equity, Social Justice and Higher Education, global innovation chair of Equity, and director of the Centre of Excellence for Equity in Higher Education, University of Newcastle, Australia. With over 30 years of experience and dedication as a student-scholar-activist in the field of equity, Penny remains passionately committed to mobilising higher education as a vehicle for social justice. Through sustained engagement with research, theory, and practice, she has generated participatory methodologies for collaborative praxis with the aim of creating transformative possibilities for equity.

Matt Lumb is associate director of the Centre of Excellence for Equity in Higher Education at the University of Newcastle in Australia. He grew up on the unceded lands of Gumbaynggirr peoples on the mid-north coast of New South Wales. Moving between professional, programmatic, and academic contexts, he works with colleagues to create generative, critical, praxis-based participations with staff, students, and community members invested in reforming higher education.

ACKNOWLEDGEMENTS

We want to recognise many people for their contribution to the publication of this book.

To Peter Aggleton, Sally Power, and Michael Reiss. Your invitation as editors of the Foundations and Futures of Education book series to develop a proposal building on *The Right to Higher Education* is the reason this work exists. Thank you for your belief in and support of the project.

To the team at the Centre of Excellence for Equity in Higher Education (CEEHE) at the University of Newcastle in New South Wales (NSW): Alison Carter, Felicity Cocuzzoli, Emily Fuller, Stephanie Hardacre, Amber Hughes, Kate Mellor, Jean Parker, Julia Shaw, Ceanne Trotter, Jace Blunden, Matthew Bunn, Rhyall Gordon, and Louis Ndagijimana. We have the privilege of navigating the complexities of contemporary higher education with you every day. CEEHE is an expression of the ideas in this book, and we want to recognise your important efforts that bring these ideas to life in your praxis, care-fully, together. Julia Coffey, we see you as part of this team too and want to acknowledge your important contribution, particularly in the context of CEEHE's ongoing focus on gender-based violence. Gifty Gyamera, thank you for your ongoing partnership in building collaborative praxis with others in the Ghanaian context.

To the past and present senior leaders at the University of Newcastle, NSW. It is difficult to sustain transformative equity praxis without conditions of institutional understanding for the project. Thank you for your enduring commitment and support.

To the late Geoff Whitty CBE who was a mentor and friend to us both. Thank you for your important scholarship and support over many years, including co-directing CEEHE with Penny in its early days, and then offering your vast experience as a visiting professor.

Thank you also to our esteemed current visiting professors. Sue Clegg, for your mentorship, scholarship, and courageous advocacy over decades. Claire Cameron, for your valuable collaborations that continue to provoke new possibilities for social justice praxis. Andrew Brown, for your boundless academic energy and expertise, committed collaborative ethos, and important knowledge of institutional dynamics. You are all valuable members of CEEHE and our communities of praxis.

To Anna Bennett, our friend and colleague. Your leadership and scholarship continue to shape, defend, and build the field of equity at Newcastle and across the country. We thank you for the expertise, effort, and ethics you have brought to our collaborations over the last decade.

To Belinda Munn, who helped establish CEEHE as founding associate director and who worked tirelessly to help facilitate the possibility of an equity research-practice nexus at Newcastle. Thank you for the foundational efforts and committed advocacy in relation to equity that created programmatic contexts enduring to this day.

To all the university students, university colleagues, and community members who are part of the 'de-centred Centre' that makes CEEHE such a lively and generative hub. The work of CEEHE relies on the energy of a network of committed reformers. We treasure the relationships with you all and deeply value your contributions.

We pay special and heartfelt tribute to the student victim-survivors who are participants in the UNESCO Chair project and for the immense wisdom and knowledge they bring. We would also like to acknowledge the UNESCO Chair and CEEHE team and our community and international partners in this context – importantly, the UNESCO Chair scheme is not conceived of as the work of a lone scholar, which also reflects the values of CEEHE.

UNESCO understands that transformation can only come through collective action, cooperation, collaboration, and meaningful parity of participation in the project of change. It is only together that we can build sustainable higher education for equity.

Penny would like to thank Matt who has been an absolute partner in the project of developing CEEHE and the framework for transformative equity praxis over the past decade. Always a calming influence in a context of great challenge and deep commitment, but sustaining his contribution with precision, reflexivity, and an ethics of care, it has been significant to have such consistent and meaningful collaboration and friendship over these many years.

Matt thanks Penny for inviting him into this co-authorship, and for being such a generous collaborator for many years. It's a rare and special thing to be listened closely to, and heard, and for the questions or ideas you've shared to be met with more and better questions and ideas, and, as a result, for something to emerge that might not have existed otherwise. Penny, your scholarship, mentorship, and friendship are all treasured.

Finally, to our families for understanding the energy and focus equity work takes and for your patience and support for our commitment.

Penny is especially grateful to Metin for being such a loving and supportive advocate for her work from the very beginning when she discovered an Access to Higher Education programme and was full of the joy and promise of participating in this pathway. Penny thanks Matt, Chun, and Tian for their love and encouragement as well as lots of challenging and fruitful discussions about the work of developing equity praxis and how to engage with communities in different forms of lifelong learning inside and outside the sPace of higher education. She is grateful to Timur for many inspiring philosophical chats over cups of tea and for his wonderful film-making contributions to making the ideas of social justice praxis accessible and to Sarah and Lavender and to Djem for their love and support over the many years that Penny has been immersed in the project of equity and social justice.

Matt is especially grateful to Beth for her patience, curiosity, and humour as she enjoys (endures?) our discussions on all manner of education policy and practice. Matt thanks Hamish and Connor for their excellent questions and the hugs when everything feels a bit overwhelming in our worlds. He also wants to thank Bruce and Kerrie, Kirsty, and Jacqui (and their families) for such a stimulating, creative, intellectual environment in which he continues to learn and grow. It's precious, and a privilege, to be surrounded by folks you admire, who just happen to be family.

INTRODUCTION – TIME FOR EQUITY PRAXIS

Introduction

Equity in higher education remains a major policy agenda in many international contexts, including in Australia, the UK, across Europe, some parts of Latin America, the USA, and some parts of Asia. Advanced policy frameworks operate in Australia and the UK, with universities held accountable to equity through government agency reporting processes, evaluation regimes, and specialist funding. Despite this, higher education remains an inequitable landscape and contemporary changes towards greater marketisation, student fees, and individualisation have arguably exacerbated the unevenness of access to and participation in higher education for historically underrepresented groups. Throughout this book, we refer to representation, misrepresentation, and underrepresentation as social justice concerns that bring attention to the political relations and processes by which people, communities, and knowledges are subjugated. This book considers the issues and challenges for progressing an equity agenda by weaving together a new multidimensional framework for equity through a range of social justice theories and methodologies. The aim is to engage readers with concepts, insights, and tools from across fields of social justice, which we argue are urgently needed to challenge long-standing, entrenched, and insidious inequalities at play in and through higher education. Demonstrating the power of praxis for creating time, space, and conceptual and practical resources for transformative equity, we argue for the significance of social justice frameworks to address otherwise-ignored multidimensional inequalities. This book was written for policymakers, practitioners, educators, and scholars who are committed to progressive and groundbreaking approaches that can engage the ongoing challenges of transforming higher education towards more just realities.

DOI: 10.4324/9781003257165-1

As societies grow increasingly unequal and polarised, struggles over the right to higher education for marginalised communities become more and more urgent. Arguably, higher education is at a significant moment of transformation, with accelerated shifts towards corporatised, marketised, and commercialised forms of higher education moving steadily away from stronger social justice orientations. Debates about the purpose of higher education are rarely fully articulated, with assumptions made about its value, and largely constrained to economic terms. This is signalled through a greater focus on employability, industry, and job-readiness and the turn towards the assumed value of some disciplinary areas and not others. These are changes that have long-term social, cultural, and symbolic implications and require ongoing attention to guard against losing some of the gains long struggled for by social justice scholars and activists who have advocated for the role of higher education for the wider social good. Furthermore, equity in higher education requires a sustained commitment to challenging deeply entrenched, historical inequalities that are reproduced, often unwittingly, through taken-for-granted assumptions and practices. This book illuminates that the project to create more inclusive and equitable higher education demands a long-term commitment rather than quick, superficial fixes.

Significant inequities persist globally in relation to higher education access and participation. These are related to wider social, cultural, material, and discursive inequalities but are also produced in and through higher education itself. This is despite considerable fiscal, institutional, and human investment in widening participation initiatives that aim to create a more equitable and inclusive higher education landscape. Some countries have implemented specialised funding and explicit governance and policy systems to effect change and, while this has led to some achievement of equity agendas, stubborn inequalities still characterise these higher education systems. Commonly, these priorities are anchored in the understandings that university qualifications are necessary to contribute to the 'knowledge economies' of the present and future and to build human capital.

Inequities of access and participation endure whilst questions are increasingly raised regarding the role and purpose of higher education in contemporary societies. Notions of social mobility and employability dominate competition-based reforms of higher education, guided by a taken-for-granted 'common sense' that the systems and institutions being reformed should primarily serve economic and market interests. Higher education is, of course, deeply related to other dimensions of social life. Yet within these policy, funding, and governance arrangements, there is currently little opportunity for consideration of lived experiences, how a sense of self and personhood might matter, or indeed questions concerning who is recognised as having the right to higher education at all. Instead, a phenomenon plays out across the globe – albeit differently in relation to context – whereby policy structures are established that come to influence the ideas upon which higher education is itself and then reconstructed. This, in turn, shapes the reproduction of structural and intersecting inequalities, including those of race, class, and gender. For example, we increasingly observe how the ways in which people are located within professional fields and subjectivities prepare the terrain for the reproduction of systemic social inequalities that are also embedded within university practices.

This entrenched problem presents a complex challenge: to apprehend the contextualised ways that higher education institutions play a significant role in perpetuating privileges and social inequalities that both intersect and accumulate in and over time. A second aspect of this challenge is to identify and implement approaches and practices within higher education that can move beyond this insidious dynamic, towards institutions and systems characterised by a contribution to the creation of more socially just societies. *The Right to Higher Education: Beyond Widening Participation* (Burke, 2012) engaged this problem and argued that a multidimensional social justice framework (Fraser, 1997) would become significant for reframing this complex challenge and for bringing a critical and transformative praxis to processes of widening participation; a praxis that could intervene within deeply inequitable dynamics and forge new and more equitable kinds of higher education.

In this book, we build on Burke (2012) to show that efforts to address inequities in higher education continue to be fundamentally limited by a deficit imaginary that consistently places equity practice outside the core work of universities. We argue that inequities persist largely due to the monodimensional and individualising conceptualisations of equity across all domains of practice, including research, evaluation, policy, and programming. These tend to be characterised by approaches that seek to 'fix' or to remedy a perceived problem or 'ill' embodied by a student or category of student. The challenge of breaking from the deficit is made difficult due to prevailing conditions that hold in place a narrow and ineffective response. These are conditions of contemporary higher education (reflective of broader social conditions) that do not easily allow for a considered and 'just' reconceptualisation of equity within higher education; one that allows for a broader, positive contribution to the lives of all people or the social character of countries, regions, and educational institutions.

Taking up explicitly the challenge implied in the subtitle of *The Right to Higher Education* (Burke, 2012), this book articulates research and praxis that lies *Beyond Widening Participation* by bringing together international literature in the field of equity in higher education with empirical case studies from social justice praxis drawn from the Centre of Excellence for Equity in Higher Education (CEEHE). The book articulates cutting-edge equity work that constructs and maintains counter-hegemonic 'timescapes' (Adam, 1998) to disrupt the conditions described earlier and, through multidimensional approaches to research and practice, make recognition of different person-hoods possible. Such approaches support into existence of new institutional practices that respond to the question of the purpose of higher education in an era of troubling precarity, privilege, and pandemic. The book does not ignore historically constructed discursive formations but argues that it is also possible to make these the focus of the investigation by asking what (and how) 'the problem' is posed to be, and what values are at play – navigating between the preservation of systems of power and the preservation of knowledges that can erode these systems of power.

Those involved in higher education equity policy, practice, research, and evaluation are struggling to navigate the tense nexus of large-scale widening participation agendas and excellence imperatives. Many nation-states are investing significantly in 'equity-oriented' programmes whilst also reforming funding and evaluation regimes towards conditions that we see as directly undermining aspects of their own equity agendas. This book aims to engage readers with approaches that can generate and maintain a transformative equity praxis carefully framed by social justice theories, concepts, methodologies, and practices. The work draws together three overarching themes that offer a re/framing of equity in higher education as *transformative equity praxis*:

1) Weaving together critical, feminist, decolonial, post/structural, and socio-logical threads to offer a new multidimensional tapestry to dismantle harm-ful deficit imaginaries;
2) Understanding that methodologies matter in critically exploring transfor-mation at the personal, system and social scales;
3) Broadening the purpose of higher education for sustained and collective human and more-than-human flourishing.

Structure of the book

The book commences by setting out our aims in the context of contem-porary debates and contestations across the field of equity and widening participation in higher education. Providing examples from the UK, the USA, and Australia, where long-standing but problematic policy systems for access, equity, and/or widening participation exist, we locate these debates and contestations in relation to questions regarding the purpose(s) of higher education and the underpinning assumptions regarding access, diversity, inclusion, and belonging. Returning to a key question "who is recognised as having the right to higher education?" we will problematise the current equity agendas, imbued as they are with *deficit*, a concept that will sustain our critique of hegemonic forms of equity and widening participation policy and practice.

In Part One – Recontextualising and Reframing Equity – we trouble the assumed purpose of widening participation in higher education as articulated (both implicitly and explicitly) in contemporary policy discourses, to analyse how higher education institutions support social reproduction and to reclaim the potential of higher education for a more broadly valuable process of social justice transformation. Drawing on bodies of work across social justice fields, this section aims to illuminate, and make accessible, relevant theoretical and conceptual tools for those grappling with the challenges of developing 'equity-generating' research, evaluation, policy-formation, and academic and professional practices.

In Chapter 1, the book commences by setting out our aims and articulating our stance on higher education equity. We do this in conversation with publications that strive to broaden ideas about the purpose of higher education, including its role in addressing the 'urgent issues of our times' (UNESCO, 2022), and the sustainable development goals (e.g. McCowan, 2019), with an emphasis on social justice considerations. We also critique hegemonic policy discourses that continue to 'neoliberalise' higher education, to consider the effects of these on how equity is discursively constructed across higher education internationally. Underpinning this is a key question: Who is recognised as having the right to higher education?

Chapter 2 sets out germinal social justice work to interrogate the hegemonic logics currently underpinning equity agendas. Drawing examples from both policy and literature, this chapter aims to illuminate how monodimensional and atheoretical explanations profoundly narrow, limit, and ultimately sabotage commitments to develop equitable higher education. This is exacerbated by the deficit imaginaries that tend to underpin equity policies and practices. Drawing from Nancy Fraser's groundbreaking multidimensional social justice framework (e.g. Fraser, 1997, 2003, 2009), we demonstrate the salience of her framework for reshaping the equity agenda by dislodging persistent and harmful deficit imaginaries that currently drive equity policy agendas. The overarching aim of the chapter is to make these multidimensional concepts accessible to those striving towards generating more equitable higher education spaces. The chapter looks closely at the idea of 'neoliberalism', to reiterate how equity and widening participation agendas and governance infrastructures in different nation-state contexts demonstrate a close alignment with, if not co-production of, neoliberal commitments to competition, markets, and 'enterprise'.

Chapter 3 builds on our call to bring social justice theoretical insights in to inform transformative equity praxis. Weaving together an ensemble of conceptual threads, this chapter seeks to embolden readers to reorient towards a confidently uncomfortable position in relation to the equity contexts in which we are all entangled. We assert the importance of this discomfort as an ethical responsibility when it comes to navigating the fraught, political territories of equity, social justice, and higher education. Although readers will be differently situated in relation to the conceptual ensemble we introduce, and acknowledging the limitations of space a single chapter affords, we see the chapter as an entrée of sorts, a beginning point for continued pursuit in readers' own contexts of research, practice, and policymaking, the bringing together of conceptual ensembles of your own. Indeed, we understand this ongoing process of meaning-making from different perspectives, locations, and orientations as a crucial dimension of social justice for transformative equity praxis.

Equity tends to be located at the peripheries of higher education, external to core academic practices such as teaching and learning. Chapter 4 interrogates this 'peripherisation' of equity by considering its relation to the pedagogical dimensions of higher education experience. The peripherisation of equity tends to focus on the remediation of 'disadvantaged students' who are seen to lack the capability to succeed. This remedial approach, entrenched in deficit imaginaries, fails to grapple with complex power dynamics at play across and within taken-for-granted pedagogical and disciplinary practices. It also frames the problem of equity at the level of the individual student constructed through the discourse of disadvantage. Whilst decontextualising their experiences from the multidimensional inequalities, students navigate in the struggle to be recognised as university students (Threadgold, Burke and Bunn, 2018). To deepen conceptions of equity in higher education, this chapter draws from the insights of critical, feminist, and decolonising pedagogies to illuminate the relational, affective, and embodied formations of identity and knowledge, knowing and being known in and through spaces of higher education (e.g. Zembylas, 2013; Bozalek et al, 2014; Luckett, 2016). The chapter aims to translate these theoretical insights for the purpose of embedding equity in higher education teaching practices.

In Part Two – Methodologies for Transformative Equity Praxis – we build on an argument developed in *The Right to Higher Education* (Burke, 2012) that methodology matters for equity. Methodology is conceptualised as an ethical-political-epistemological-ontological complex, framing the ways that method becomes animated in space-time. The case is made for care-full methodological consideration in equity research, but just as importantly in programmatic practice, evaluation, and policymaking. We advocate for resisting the quick jump-to method as has become part of the institutional machinery of producing evidence. Through methodological approaches, knowledge is re/produced whilst values are re/author/ised and positions of knowing are re/asserted. Research and evaluation in the field of equity and widening participation are tied to methodological frameworks, often underpinned by and reproductive of deficit. We think about this first in relation to the timescapes of higher education, which tend to reassert hegemonic time-frames and methodologies, including an ongoing focus on measurement for producing evidence-based policy and practice. This section interrogates this hegemonic preoccupation with evidence-based policy and practice, which emphasises that which is measurable and observable, perpetuating a privileging of positivist-oriented methods and metric-centred performatives, hiding from view the always interpretive processes of knowledge formation. In this section, we also convey a methodological framework for social justice praxis, (PPoEMs: Praxis-based, Pedagogical, Ethically Oriented Methodologies) for developing communities of praxis, opening new sPaces for collective interrogation, building response-abilities with Others, and acting with an ethics of care.

Time is a significant yet taken-for-granted discourse in our collective and contested (re)imagining(s) of contemporary higher education. Chapter 5 explores how discourses such as 'time management' play out in contexts often characterised by uncertainty and precarity, with increasing numbers of staff on temporary, casual and/or fixed-term contracts, with continual uncertainties around the funding of higher education, with greater moves towards marketised constructions of the purpose of higher education, with corporate notions reshaping pedagogical orientations. Rejecting hegemonic understandings of time, we see time as an intersecting form of social difference. With Adam's (1998) notion of 'timescapes', we show how spatio-temporal relations re/produce inequalities in subtle ways through taken-for-granted structures, discourses and practices. Sharma's 'power-chronographies' (2014) reinforce a balanced space-time approach to understanding differential and relational temporalities as power relations. These conceptual tools help show how 'our time' and our experience of 'our time' rely on Others and their labours. This relational focus shows the need for an ethics that can build participation across different differences to apprehend and resist 'mis/time/framing'.

Evaluation has become an essential condition of policymaking and social programmes. In Chapter 6, we look at how evaluation has become an effective form of modern governance practice that readily takes up problem constructions developed by those in positions of relative authority. Our argument is that this dynamic has concerning consequences for equity if the value systems of those authorised to frame evaluation are not aligned with the diverse interests and desires of underrepresented people and communities. This chapter also offers a sustained analysis of how policy and programme evaluation has become an effective tool for re-embedding neoliberal commitments and rationalities, helping to remake higher education in ways that are arguably anathema to notions of fairness and justice. Drawing on Fielding (2001), we argue there are important distinctions to be made between the *accountabilities* that new managerial techniques and neoliberal economic frameworks facilitate, and different approaches we would advocate for that resonate with reciprocal *responsibility* to one an/Other. Evaluation is about values and valuing. In this chapter, we argue for resisting an 'axiologically bereft' metric-only fixation that characterises hegemonic equity policy and programme evaluation.

Given our argument built up across this section that methodology matters for equity, in Chapter 7, we build on prior work developing 'Pedagogical Methodologies' (Burke, Crozier and Misiaszek, 2017; Burke and Lumb, 2018) to offer a new framework in PPoEMs. This methodological framework has been developed to 'stay with the trouble' (Haraway, 2016) within the social institution of higher education that holds a unique and powerful position in the production, legitimation, and dissemination of knowledge. This is a framework that responds to questions we see as urgent. Questions such as: as we negotiate new twenty-first-century forms of the production of knowledge, whilst apprehending and situating past bodies of knowledge, how might we open new temporalities, spatialities, and relationalities for transformative possibilities? What role might higher education play in generating decolonial, social justice praxis to address the urgent issues of our times; the human and more-than-human crises that knowing differently and collectively could enable us to act in the world response-ably? This chapter urges us all to resist the jump directly to the method, as has arguably become part of the institutional apparatus of producing evidence. We explain how PPoEMs draws from the theoretical perspectives outlined so far in this book, bringing together feminist, decolonial, post/structural, and sociological insights for communities of praxis, opening sPace for solidarity, compassion, response-ability, and an ethic of care.

In Part Three – Social Justice Transformation through Equity Praxis – we articulate explicitly the possibilities provided by a new approach to equity and widening participation in higher education; constructed via critical, feminist, Freirean, and post/structural commitments (Burke, 2012). Building on the section above, we show how ethical methodological frameworks can engage participants across differences and power in the research/practice nexus, opening up access to theoretical, methodological, and conceptual tools to illuminate and examine the complexity of inequalities, as well as then translate these insights for policy and practice. This final section identifies and demonstrates what is possible in contemporary higher education by drawing together case studies from international literature and from work conducted in the Australian context including at the CEEHE.

Throughout this book, we argue against monodimensional, deficit imaginaries, which contribute to a vicious cycle of equity interventions unwittingly perpetuating insidious inequalities. In Chapter 8, we offer the ideas of an equity spectrum to bring attention to the different, contested, and often overlapping perspectives that come into play in the complex timescapes of higher education, as an institution that both reproduces and transforms unequal relations. We reiterate the imperative of continuously thinking-with the challenges and dynamics we are negotiating, and this might mean navigating different positionalities across the spectrum at any one time, or at different times in which we are working-with others across and with relational differences. We present two case studies to illustrate how we, in the CEEHE, put these ideas to work through ongoing reflection/action as part of our sustained, collective, social justice praxis. The first case study details a praxis-based project, situated within the UNESCO Chair in Equity, Social Justice and Higher Education at the CEEHE; a project attending to the overlooked question of how experiences of gender-based violence (GBV) over the life course impact higher education equity. The second case study details a praxis-based project of counter-hegemonic evaluation at the CEEHE, whereby methods of evaluation practice are animated with and through a sustained focus on methodology, responding to the ethical dilemma of valuing across difference, adopting sPaces of *care-full* evaluation. These case studies reach beyond superficial, one-dimensional and decontextualised solutions, instead digging into the challenge of higher education equity work in often overwhelming times.

The book concludes in Chapter 9 by considering ways of restructuring equity in higher education. We reiterate how critical, praxis-based re/framings of 'the problem' offer a powerful force for transforming higher education for equity and social justice. Working within the messy site of struggle and contestation that is the research/practice/policy nexus in contemporary higher education calls for meta-theoretical commitments that have sophisticated, creative, and conceptual rigour. We argue that praxis-based approaches can open up critical time, space, and resources for collaborative, reciprocal, reflexive, and ethical ways of reframing equity and widening participation around broadly valued social purposes.

References

Adam, B. (1998) *Timescapes of Modernity: The Environment and Invisible Hazards.* London: Routledge.
Bozalek, V., Leibowitz, B., Carolissen, R., and Boler, M. (2014) *Discerning Critical Hope in Educational Practices.* London: Routledge.
Burke, P.J. (2012) *The Right to Higher Education: Beyond Widening Participation.* London and New York: Routledge.
Burke, P.J., Crozier, G., and Misiaszek, L.I. (2017) *Changing Pedagogical Spaces in Higher Education: Diversity, Inequalities and Misrecognition.* London: Routledge.
Burke, P.J., and Lumb, M. (2018) 'Researching and evaluating equity and widening participation: Praxis-based frameworks', in Burke, P.J., Hayton, A., and Stevenson, J. (Eds) *Evaluating Equity and Widening Participation in Higher Education.* London: Trentham Books Limited, 11–32.
Fielding, M. (2001) 'OFSTED, inspection and the betrayal of democracy', *Journal of Philosophy of Education*, 35(4), 695–709. https://doi.org/10.1111/1467-9752.00254
Fraser, N. (1997) *Justice Interruptus: Critical Reflections on the "Postsocialist" Condition.* London and New York: Routledge.
Fraser, N. (2009) *Scales of Justice: Reimagining Political Space in a Globalizing World.* New York: Cambridge University Press.

Haraway, D. (2016) *Staying with the Trouble: Making Kin in the Chthulucene*. Durham, NC: Duke University Press.

Luckett, K. (2016) 'Curriculum contestation in a post-colonial context: A view from the South', *Teaching in Higher Education*, 21(4), 415–428. https://doi.org/10.10 80/13562517.2016.1155547

McCowan, T. (2019) *Higher Education for and Beyond the Sustainable Development Goals*. Cham: Palgrave Macmillan. https://doi.org/10.1007/978-3-030-19597-7

Sharma, S. (2014) *In the Meantime: Temporality and Cultural Politics*. Durham, NC: Duke University Press.

Threadgold, S., Burke, P.J., and Bunn, M. (2018) *Struggles and Strategies: Does Social Class Matter in Higher Education*. Report prepared for the Centre of Excellence for Equity in Higher Education, University of Newcastle, Australia.

UNESCO (2022) *Knowledge-Driven Actions: Transforming Higher Education for Global Sustainability*. Paris, France: UNESCO. https://doi.org/10.54675/YBTV1653

Zembylas, M. (2013) 'Critical pedagogy and emotion: Working through "troubled knowledge" in posttraumatic contexts', *Critical Studies in Education*, 54(2), 176–189. https://doi.org/10.1080/17508487.2012.743468

PART ONE

Recontextualising and reframing equity

Contemporary discourses continually reassert the purpose of higher education in narrow economic terms, with equity largely regarded as a peripheral consideration. Widening participation in higher education is seen primarily as supporting the imperatives of nation-state and market economies, and equity interventions are developed in the context of job-readiness and employability agendas. Equity is thus increasingly framed by the imperatives of neoliberalism, with its focus on marketising, commercialising and corporatising higher education. Indeed, these neoliberal ideas about the purpose of higher education and the problem of equity have become part of a common sense; there is no alternative to the neoliberal hegemonic order.

Part One rejects this hegemonic 'misframing' of higher education and recontextualises the problem of equity in relation to entrenched social, cultural, and political inequalities in which policy-formation and programmatic development is produced in the interests of neoliberalism. We trouble the idea that there is no alternative. Rather, we aim to ignite our collective imagination by recontextualising higher education in relation to the urgent crises of our times, and as rooted in the widening of inequalities that exacerbate social and environmental urgencies. In reframing higher education as a social institution with the power to reproduce and transform inequalities, Part One elaborates on the significance of social justice theories and concepts to enable us to 'stay with the trouble' (Haraway, 2016) of equity work, not least by understanding the complicity of higher education in reproducing multidimensional injustice.

Drawing from policy and literature to illuminate how monodimensional, apolitical, and atheoretical equity frameworks profoundly narrow, limit, and ultimately sabotage commitments to develop equitable higher education, Part One traces the important insights of feminist, decolonial, critical, post/

DOI: 10.4324/9781003257165-2

structural, and sociological theory in the process of reframing equity. Nancy Fraser's groundbreaking multidimensional social justice framework (e.g. Fraser, 1997, 2003, 2009), together with post-Freirean, feminist and decolonial theories, are put to work as resources for reimagining higher education for equity and social justice. Through weaving together the insights from bodies of social justice theory, Part One argues that hegemonic equity policies and practices are embroiled in persistent and harmful deficit imaginaries that construct the problem of equity in the bodies of people and communities navigating multidimensional injustice. A key aim of Part One is to illuminate, and make accessible, relevant theoretical and conceptual material for those grappling with the challenges of developing 'equity-generating' research, evaluation, policy-formation, and academic and professional practices to dislodge the deficit imaginaries that sustain inequalities.

Throughout Part One, we assert the importance of dis/positions of uncertainty and discomfort as an ethical response-ability to the complexity of equity work, which inevitably involves navigating the fraught, inequitable, and political territories of higher education. Part One is offered as an initiation for sustained engagement in readers' own contexts of research, practice, and policymaking, which will require the bringing together of different conceptual ensembles in relation to thinking-with and making-with Others in the specific contexts in which readers are situated. Equity is reframed as an ongoing process of meaning-making from different perspectives, locations, and orientations as a crucial dimension of transformative equity praxis.

References

Fraser, N. (1997) *Justice Interruptus: Critical Reflections on the "Postsocialist" Condition*. London and New York: Routledge.
Fraser, N. (2003) 'Social justice in the age of identity politics: Redistribution, recognition and participation', In Fraser, N., and Honneth, A. (Eds) *Redistribution or Recognition? A Political-Philosophical Exchange*. London and New York: Verso.
Fraser, N. (2009) *Scales of Justice: Reimagining Political Space in a Globalizing World*. New York: Cambridge University Press.
Haraway, D. (2016) *Staying with the Trouble: Making Kin in the Chthulucene*. Durham, NC: Duke University Press.

1

CONTEXTUALISING EQUITY

Introduction

In this chapter, we aim to ignite our collective imagination about the role and purpose of higher education by considering how contested perspectives differently frame equity, some of which grossly narrow the scope of policy and practice in harmful and inequitable ways. We begin by explicitly articulating our stance on higher education equity in conversation with counter-hegemonic efforts to broaden ideas about the purpose of higher education. In doing so, we strongly contest the idea that higher education is primarily about building human capital to strengthen national economies, an idea that has increasingly shaped higher education policy, funding regimes and widening participation agendas. We see this as an impoverished framing that negates the many ways higher education might be situated socially. We also see it as an irresponsible framing, given the multi-dimensional, multi-scalar socio-ecological crises facing our more-than-human communities across the globe. To build the foundation for this book, we examine the hegemonic policy discourses that are grounded in neoliberal frameworks and the implications of these for *misframing* access, equity, and widening participation. We briefly trace the emergence of neoliberal policy agendas that have arguably undermined commitments to equity, particularly educational justice movements that have struggled towards the transformation of higher education systems by tackling social and institutionalised discriminatory structures and practices.

Higher education is a powerful social institution that has the potential to contribute to transformative change in society, including reducing inequalities, building gender equity, generating more peaceful societies, and protecting the right to higher education for all. However, higher education's power

DOI: 10.4324/9781003257165-3

is too often reproductive of social, cultural, and political inequalities, which are entrenched in its historical and contemporary formations, structures, and systems. Throughout this book, we inter-weave a range of social justice theories, concepts, and practices to develop a new multidimensional framework for equity in and through higher education. Our aim is to offer conceptual and practical resources to support what we call *transformative equity praxis*, an idea we take up in more detail in Chapter 2 and later in the book.

It is important to recognise that higher education is never neutral or separate from complex social relations of power; higher education is immersed in a range of complex power dynamics, including its role in producing and legitimating knowledge and who is recognised as knowing. Indeed, we argue that the politics of knowing and knowledge have extensive implications beyond higher education, not only for mobilising the interests of neoliberalism but also relatedly for the pernicious forces of neocolonialism and patriarchy, in which unequal cultural value orders are put to work in ways that impact claims to personhood. Anti-colonial and feminist scholars have illuminated the manipulative strategies over decades in which some groups have been 'Othered', negated, pathologised, misrecognised, and ultimately dehumanised. The co-option of equity through populist, corporate, and neoliberal discourses effectively neutralises and sanitises what are struggles over status, value, and personhood as well as access to resources, opportunities, and privileges, afforded through university access and participation. While common-sense arguments that not everyone is 'right' for higher education seem on the surface straightforward, those who have a position to decide who has the right to higher education and on what terms, have themselves been university educated. There is then a fundamental political injustice of misrepresentation that is obscured. Thus, questions of representation are vital to our focus in this book – who influences and decides the terms of participation matters, and this is never an apolitical act.

Equity then should not simply be about recruiting and supporting students from disadvantaged backgrounds into higher education, although it is often the main premise of equity policy and practice. This focus is one part of a much more complex project, which we argue must involve reimagining higher education as a force for social justice. This must include attention to the politics of knowledge and knowing, and connected methodological frameworks, as a key dimension of equity work. In this book, we set out our vision for working towards equity in and through higher education, through the lens of social justice praxis, and we provide detailed insight into the imperative of this praxis-based approach.

To be precise, we argue that contemporary and hegemonic structures for higher education, built on an ongoing agenda to marketise, commercialise, and corporatise higher education, are not sustainable. It is also profoundly inequitable and unjust. The problem that equity is placed on the peripheries of universities *and* constructed within the constraints and limitations of hegemonic and contemporary structures means that much of the investment in equity fails to make any long-term and sustainable change. Efforts to generate equitable higher education are significantly undermined when the structural and discursive forces of inequality are concealed from view through sanitised and neutralised language that prevents getting to the root of the issue of equity, tackling ongoing forces of injustice and relations of inequality. Furthermore, the failure of governments in most nation-state contexts to provide comprehensive public funding, together with the increasing pressure on individuals to take on substantial levels of student debt, has the perverse outcome of widening inequality rather than building equity. In this book, we present an alternative vision for equity in, through, and beyond higher education that puts social justice theory and action at the heart of the long-term project to build equitable and inclusive higher education systems, structures, and practices.

Contesting 'equity'

Equity in higher education is a contested terrain with intersecting and competing discourses at play. These include struggles over access to higher education that played out over the twentieth century in relation to the politics of class, gender, and race. This led to what some have described as the 'access movement' with national strategies emerging in the second part of the 1900s. Examples we draw from in this chapter include the development of Access to Higher Education programmes in the UK, 'Enabling' programmes in Australia, and a US policy scape to expand access to higher education. These examples share a commitment to transforming higher education systems and structures through creating new, high-quality pathways to higher education for working-class and Black and ethnic minority communities and for women. An underpinning aim across these examples is to support a national commitment to equal opportunities, to a sense of fairness, and to the belief that everyone should have access to higher education. Key characteristics of the access movement include providing access to 'powerful knowledge', whilst simultaneously engaging students with critical forms of knowing and critique to dismantle unequal power relations at play in (and beyond) education. Germinal thinkers such as Paulo Freire were highly influential in their struggles to develop critical, anti-racist pedagogies that aimed to identify and overturn oppressive social relations. These access frameworks have been subjected to multiple waves of political struggle and hegemony yet have survived into the 2020s although not without significant challenges and some diminishing of the overarching commitment to social justice transformation. The legacy of the challenges faced, including the ongoing peripherisation of access programmes, which we discuss in detail in Chapter 2, remains a thread throughout the many discourses that have emerged since the 1960s and 1970s when these programmes were initially established. The access movement has brought attention to the historical legacy of classism, sexism, and racism, which remains concealed from view in hegemonic accounts of equity even though these legacies continue to be entrenched in higher education systems, structures, and practices. In this chapter, we examine these examples to consider the impact of neoliberalism on social justice-oriented equity agendas.

One particularly powerful force in undermining the progressive strands of the access movement has been the rise of neoliberalism and its timely intersection with discourses of access and equity, creating new policy commitments such as widening participation in the 1990s. We explore the entanglement of equity with neoliberalism in more detail in the next chapter, but one important thread we want to introduce here is how neoliberalism has been highly effective in erasing classed, gendered, and racialised inequalities from the view of public discourse and instead reframing concerns with access and equity in economic and market terms. Widening participation in higher education emerged as part of a broader neoliberal agenda to strengthen the national economy, to create innovation for business and industry, to maximise human capital for the 'knowledge economy', and to produce 'employable' individuals for advancing capitalist agendas.

As these neoliberal imperatives have achieved greater hegemony and common sense in higher education policy, leadership and management, the commitment to redressing systemic, structural, and social inequalities has eroded. Rather, the focus has shifted from transforming relations of inequality to transforming disadvantaged individuals so that they might become successful in the context of neoliberal, neo-colonial, and neopatriarchal imperatives. This not only grossly ignores the multidimensional injustices that reproduce intergenerational poverty, trauma, and suffering but also reframes higher education as a project of individual investment in self-advancement and reduces its potential contribution to the wider social good. Although we will examine what the 'social good' might mean from different perspectives, we make the argument here that the major achievement of neoliberalism in narrowing the purpose of higher education in market terms has produced, in turn, narrow conceptions of equity, which are most harmful to those experiencing social inequalities and multidimensional injustices. The implication of neoliberal hegemony for equity in higher education is profound. It enables sanitised, neutralised, and apolitical policies and practices to obscure the representation of experiences of exclusion from and marginalisation in higher education, exclusion, and marginalisation that is experienced beyond entry to higher education for many students navigating complex, multidimensional inequalities. Neoliberal hegemony in education creates conditions which have been described by some (Fielding, 2001) as 'axiologically bereft', endlessly facilitating frameworks that contain no value-sets beyond implicit market logics. A premise of our book is that these not only are matters for what happens in higher education but also have broader ramifications for the kinds of societies and futures to which higher education is contributing.

The phenomenon of EDI (which stands for Equity, Diversity and Inclusion; also formulated as DEI in some contexts) is a thriving formation within but also beyond higher education. This formation thrives within contemporary neoliberal governmental regimes of truth that constantly recondition our current political practices. We worry that EDI appears to be an exemplary vehicle for the gathering together of complex histories of struggle and counter-hegemonic thought, for the defanging of their iterations and intents, and for having the facilitation of new structures and practices in which only certain professionalisms are considered reasonable. Wolbring and Lillywhite (2021) describe how EDI as a term and suite of initiatives came to inhabit UK universities in different ways, having arrived via the Athena SWAN (Scientific Women's Academic Network) charter developed by Advance HE. Indeed, the opening statement regarding EDI on the Advance HE website is imbued with perspectives and commitments that arguably narrow and close down so many possibilities through which EDI separately or together might be explored: "The best talent is highly mobile, and institutions perceived as not being diverse, or failing to take EDI seriously, are likely to be avoided by individuals or groups who believe they might be disadvantaged" (Advance HE, 2023: np). In this book, we aim to bring such narrow conceptions of EDI into relief, interrogating the implications of neoliberal hegemony, and its intersection with other political forces of injustice and oppression, to consider possibilities for recontextualising and reframing equity in higher education through social justice praxis.

Transformative equity

Transformation is regularly represented in positive terms; as a progressive process towards creating greater equity. It appears to be progressive in another sense too, in a presumed linearity of development towards the aims of equity agendas. However, transformation is a complex process, with multi-directional possibilities as it is shaped by competing and contested influences and dynamics. Different political forces are at play at any given moment, creating a range of competing possibilities, directions, and discourses, even while it may appear that there is a collective understanding of what is being aspired towards through shared vocabularies describing the social phenomenon.

In this section, we trace the contested political forces at play that have shaped and reshaped access to higher education policies, commitments, and practices over time in ways that are not predictable or directly knowable. Rather, it is generative to analyse the transformational forces and processes to bring to light the discursive formations of access that produce competing meanings about what 'access' is, who it is for and why it is understood to be important.

These meanings have considerable influence on the formation of policy and practice and who has a voice in defining questions of access. We start our analysis in the UK context with the rise of the access movement in the late 1970s.

Enabling transformative pathways

The second half of the nineteenth century saw increasing numbers of students from underrepresented communities gain access to higher education across different international contexts. This was an outcome of several different efforts, including state policy and intervention as well as educational movements, rooted in counter-hegemonic philosophies. These travelled globally, so that the influence of educational philosophers such as Paulo Freire in Latin America, together with social movements such as the women's and civil rights movements, had profound impact on the development of adult and access education in countries such as England, Australia, and the USA. Over the 1970s and 1980s, Access Education emerged in Britain with a strong political commitment to redressing the social and educational inequalities entrenched in the elitism of higher education (Burke, 2001: 12–13). Access to Higher Education, introduced by the UK's Department of Education and Science in 1978 as a pilot across seven local education authorities (LEAs), aimed to widen educational access and participation for those social groups experiencing historical, structural, and cultural exclusion from degree-level study (Benn, Elliott and Whaley, 1995: 2; Fieldhouse, 1996: 73; Thompson, 1980). The 1978 LEA pilot schemes were developed to enable ethnic minority and working-class groups to participate in higher education and to ensure that these groups would then have a strong presence in key professional fields. Thus, from its initiation, there were different intentions at play; for many access educators, the aim was to dismantle elitism and reform curriculum whilst for the LEAs the overarching concern was to ease growing class and racial tensions in society by creating the conditions for greater representation of working class and ethnic minorities in professions such as teaching, social work, and nursing. By 1994, there were 1000 Access to Higher Education programmes with over 30,000 students, most of whom were mature women students (Fieldhouse, 1996). Thompson describes Access Education as a commitment to

> developing a distinctive social theory of knowledge derived from a politically committed analysis and theory of power which leads to a form of pedagogy that is concerned to democratise knowledge making and learning, in ways that redefine the very parameters of what counts as higher education.
> *(Thompson, 2000: 10)*

Access Education was identified as a 'radical movement' (Williams, 1997: 43) in its aim to "challenge the dominant canons and discourses in operation within and without academia" (Kennedy and Piette, 1991: 35). Motivated by an overarching commitment to transform higher education by placing marginalised groups at the centre of knowledge reconstruction, the Access Movement was characterised by student-centred approaches to teaching and learning, the negotiation with students in relation to course content and pedagogy, encouragement of students to follow their own interests, and community-led organisation of Access courses (Kennedy and Piette, 1991: 35). Access to Higher Education was generally practitioner-led, but with a strong student-centred ethos, and was committed to the contexts of its local communities and situated outside of central state sponsorship (Corrigan, 1992). Its student-centred approach led to experimental approaches to curriculum development in response to the needs and interests of local communities (Diamond, 1999: 186; Maxwell, 1996: 112). Burke (2001) describes the Access Movement as:

> A project committed to engaging groups, who have been historically and socially excluded from re/defining and producing knowledge and re/constructing theory, in participating in and contributing to ontological, epistemological, theoretical, methodological and pedagogical questions, debates and developments. Furthermore, [Access Education is] a site of possibility for creating spaces for the mobilisation of counter-[hegemonic] discourses that are collectively constructed.
>
> *(Burke, 2001: 25)*

Yet Thompson warned over 20 years ago that neoliberal assertions about the importance of widening participation, combating social exclusion, and recognising social capital were undermining the capacity to address the contexts of inequality in which Access Education was situated (Thompson, 2000: 8). As neoliberalism crept in, "the incorporation of Access policymakers into the decision-making processes of the dominant agencies" significantly reshaped Access Education (Diamond, 1999: 184). Diamond explains:

> In less than a decade the most public exponents of Access were no longer the day-to-day practitioners, but those who were mainly concerned with the administration of systems and organisations.
>
> *(ibid.)*

By the late 1990s, Access to Higher Education was centralised by the New Labour government's appointment of the UK Quality Assurance Agency for Higher Education to oversee its operations, with a preoccupation on standards, pulling the focus away from meeting the needs of local communities to developing a standardised and regulated national system of access pathways. The use of accreditation bodies and policy instruments to standardise and instrumentalise higher education under the guise of quality has become an increasingly common process, with the result often that 'quality' comes mainly to correspond with the labour market relevance of programmes of study (Brøgger and Madsen, 2022) and forms of 'employability' imbued primarily with industry's interests. This concern with standards and standardisation coincided with moral panics emerging about the dumbing down of higher education (Burke, 2002: 80–81). The abuse of the term quality, weaponising social ine/quality for the maintenance of patterns of privilege and participation, is a predictable aspect of conservative politics yet higher education appears a particularly acute site for these dynamics.

Over time, Access to Higher Education became less associated with community-led and student-centric approaches, to a mainstream pathway to higher education. Access Education became increasingly vocationalised, instrumentally oriented, and utilitarian, losing its counter-hegemonic political agenda (Barr, 1999 cited in Burke, 2001: 32). As shifts in funding from student grants to student loans emerged, discipline-based Access to Higher Education aiming to build pathways to the social sciences, arts, humanities, and natural sciences closed, with increasing numbers of courses with a vocational focus, such as Access to Social Work and Access to Nursing. The growing cost of studying in higher education closed avenues for students from underrepresented groups to pursue degree pathways that did not have a specific vocational focus, creating new inequalities in the system in terms of student 'choices'. The marketisation of higher education was taking hold with consequences for approaches to equity concerned with social justice and transformation. A global context helped to accelerate this dynamic, in which international organisations such as the Organisation for Economic Co-operation and Development (OECD) and the World Bank were increasingly involved in shaping the governance apparatus guiding formal education systems, including the imagined purpose of access and participation. In the UK, a narrow instrumentalism in terms of the reason to build equity was beginning to gain hegemony and became expressed through New Labour's discourse of widening participation and its insistence that 'education is the best economic policy' available (reiterated recently by the Tory prime minister Sunak at the Conservative conference 2023).

In contrast, access pathways in Australia, known as 'Enabling Education', have continued to benefit from public funding, sustaining opportunities for students to have unrestricted access to curriculum-rich pathways into higher education characterised by a strong commitment to inclusive pedagogical expertise and practice. Bennett et al (2016) identify the following as central components of Enabling Education: recognises students' existing knowledges; is embedded in care-full pedagogical relationships; provides access to discipline-based concepts rather than decontextualised facts, skills, or literacies; makes connection with the contexts of students' lives; draws from pedagogies that enable a sense of connection with the curriculum; its assessment is committed to students' development, designed to support students' understanding of their relevance and meaning; recognises and values the diversity of aims and outcomes of engaging in enabling education while extending students' expectations; non-completion is not seen as failure but as engagement in lifelong learning; and time spent in learning must be contextualised in relation to the many external and personal challenges students are navigating. Enabling approaches are caring and flexible and are committed to transition students into and through courses, pointing out that different expectations and approaches may exist in other contexts (Bennett et al, 2016).

> Educators aim to provide access to powerful knowledges through dialogical learning of university discipline concepts. Understanding of disciplinary concepts and theories is more important than recounting individual facts or formulas.
>
> *(Bennett et al, 2016: 9)*

A key example of these ongoing commitments is the Open Foundation programme at the University of Newcastle in NSW, established in 1974 and still providing open access to the social sciences, arts, and humanities as well as the full range of natural sciences. Students access these programmes without student fees and benefit from a solid pedagogical and curricular foundation to support their transitions to an undergraduate degree upon completion of their pathway. Open Foundation is firmly rooted in the local communities surrounding the University of Newcastle and the programme has served over 60,000 students in the 50 years since its inception. Open Foundation was the case study for identifying the key characteristics of Enabling Education in the work cited earlier by Bennett et al (2016). However, there is a dearth of research that captures the significance of Enabling Education to equity in higher education due to the structural conditions in which Enabling staff are employed, often on teaching-only contracts and as casual staff. In this context, we argue with Bennett et al (2016: 14) that much of the rich pedagogical expertise around equity that has been generated by Enabling Education has not been a focus of research and scholarship of teaching and learning in higher education and thus has been overlooked. This lack of attention to the significance of Access and Enabling expertise in both the UK and Australia is a major loss for equity in higher education in building pedagogical and curricular expertise for equity.

Unequal transformation: higher education exacerbating inequalities

Suzanne Mettler (2014) has provided a sharp analysis of a higher education crisis in the USA that begins with a clear policy agenda rooted in a mid-twentieth-century American value system that higher education should be accessible to all. Access is central to this policy agenda, initially with a strong framework of redistribution through providing significant grants to cover the costs of study for students facing socioeconomic inequalities. Higher education policy was grounded in a cultural belief in the mutual benefit that a university education should provide in support of the 'American dream'. This 'dream' aspires towards the ideal that every American should have access to improved employment prospects with the promise of increased income over a graduate's lifetime. However, the 'dream' encompasses a broader set of ideals beyond individual economic gain, placing belief in higher education to improve health and wellbeing, to enhance civic participation, to expand representation in the public sphere, and to carry mutual benefit to the individual, wider community, and society overall. Thus, most Americans agree that the government needs to increase investment in the higher education system, as evidenced in a 2012 poll (Mettler, 2014: 67–68), a public commitment to higher education that has held constant over decades. This is distinctive from the unfavourable public view on the redistribution of wealth, while Americans "consistently support the idea that everyone, regardless of their social group, should have an equal chance to achieve" through access to higher education (ibid.).

Despite this strong public consensus, Mettler's analysis illuminates that the contemporary higher education system is not only in crisis but also directly exacerbating inequality (Mettler, 2014: 70). This, she argues, is largely due to outdated policy that is unable to address the political dynamics of the present day. However, the underlying issues that contribute to widening inequalities are regularly distorted by deficit assumptions that the core problem is an individual lack of ability or motivation to succeed in higher education. She contests these assumptions by pointing out that "even among individuals with the same academic credentials, those from the less advantaged families are less likely to gain college degrees" (2014: 47). Indeed, the focus on access as enrolment, and the absence of a broader conceptualisation of access, is part of the problem. Mettler's analysis uncovers that among those who enrol in higher education degree programmes, only about 47 per cent are complete. Although more students are starting a higher education programme, less are graduating, reflecting socioeconomic inequalities. She demonstrates in quantitative terms the staggering inequalities that are overlooked by a focus on deficit imaginaries. Ninety-seven per cent of students from high-income groups complete their degrees by age 24, which is a 42 *per cent improvement since 1970*. On the other hand, only 23 per cent of students from the lowest income quartile complete their degrees by age 24, which is an improvement of *only 1 per cent since 1970* (Mettler, 2014: 46).

Mettler illuminates the unintended consequences in which higher education policy has not kept pace with political change, leading to the current malfunctioning of the higher education system. Without due maintenance,

updating and rerouting of higher education policies formed by earlier generations, higher education "not only fails to mitigate inequality but it exacerbates
it, creating a deeply stratified society" (Mettler, 2014: 12). She locates the
problem in the rise of partisan polarisation in which political parties are far
less likely to cooperate across party lines than in the past. This polarisation
has been accompanied by "an asymmetric quality", in which the Republican
party has veered more sharply to the right while the Democrats have remained
centre-left (Mettler, 2014: 19). This has undermined a cooperative two-party
political system leaving "little incentive to care for and upgrade existing policies" (ibid.). Polarisation has emerged with the rise of plutocracy, with politi-
cians and legislators increasingly more responsive to the needs and interests of
powerful industries and wealthy families and less concerned with those of the
majority of Americans (ibid.). The combined rise of polarisation and plutocracy has contributed to the stagnation of the value of Pell Grants, which were
established in 1972 with the aim of widening access to higher education by
providing funds to low-income students (Mettler, 2014: 6). Further, attention
to grants have been overshadowed by a focus in the new political order on
student loans, as the conditions of polarisation and plutocracy made it more
straightforward for policymakers to increase student loans, thus avoiding any
complicated budget deliberations regarding cost-of-living adjustments to Pell
grants. These dynamics promoted the escalation of student loan borrowing
and the deterioration of grants, allowing poorer students to become more and
more indebted (Mettler, 2014: 26). This is echoed in Caitlin Zaloom's (2021)
insightful and critical analysis of the highly complex, and strikingly messy, system of financing higher education in the USA. Zaloom reinforces the point
that "government support for higher education was once transformative, ful-
filling cultural ideals of access and opportunity", while now she argues that
"families bear the financial responsibility for college" and are "compelled to
borrow heavily for college, because providing children with quality education
is a sacred value" in American culture (Zaloom, 2021: 190).

The new political order outlined in both Zaloom's and Mettler's intricate
analyses has enabled a widening gap to develop between different and dispa-
rate forms of provision, further disadvantaging students navigating multidimensional inequalities (Mettler, 2014: 14). Part of the problem that Mettler
uncovers are the benefits and costs that are concealed by the commercialisation of higher education including what she calls the misleading 'sticker price'
of higher education. She explains:

> The advertised prices of attending [elite institutions] may actually under-
> state the value of what many of them offer to their students. Some devote far
> greater resources to students than even their full-paying students contrib-
> ute. The most selective colleges spend up to $92,000 per student while the
> least selective colleges spend approximately $12,000 per student. Students

attending the wealthiest 10 percent of institutions pay just twenty cents per every dollar spent on them, whereas at the other end of the spectrum, students contribute seventy-eight cents per dollar.

(Mettler, 2014: 15)

The US higher education system is constituted of private non-profit, public non-profit, and private for-profit institutions. Private non-profit institutions consist of a mainly affluent student body, have high graduation rates, produce a disproportionate share of executive corporate and government leaders, and are positioned to invest significantly in funding programmes and in creating the conditions for high-quality teaching and learning experiences. Again, the quantitative profile Mettler provides is illuminating. For example, the student-staff ratio tends to be 18 to 1 in private non-profits in contrast to 57 to 1 in community colleges. Further, obtaining a degree from a private non-profit institution tends to offer substantial rewards, including 45 per cent higher earnings than other higher education graduates. In comparison, and in the context of increasingly constrained state funding, public non-profit institutions have aimed to delicately balance decreased budgets with high-quality provision. The student-staff ratio varies across public non-profits from 22 to 1 in flagship public institutions and 28 to 1 in public four-year colleges. Mettler points to the impact of diminishing resources on public non-profits, with many institutions turning to online teaching to reduce costs. Mettler questions the efficacy of online teaching suggesting that a large proportion of online students are likely to drop out of their courses compared to those studying in person, with evidence suggesting that the greatest negative impact is endured by African American, male, and educationally disadvantaged students (Mettler, 2014: 15). This raises questions about pedagogical knowledge and expertise in relation to questions of equity, which are explored in more detail in Chapter 4.

A key aspect of the widening of inequality Mettler attaches to the significant growth in private for-profit institutions. Students in private for-profits tend to borrow significantly to enable their studies, with larger levels of student debt associated with the private for-profit sector as compared to the non-profit sector. Yet, despite this burden of student debt, there is little evidence to suggest that graduating from a private for-profit institution enhances graduate income, Mettler warns. Indeed, many such graduates experience higher rates of unemployment compared to graduates in similar fields from non-profit institutions. Additionally, the debt that private for-profit students accumulate remains a significant burden even if they gain employment.

What we can say with certainty, however, is that even if graduates of for-profits fare as well as others in the job market, they face greater challenges given the much higher debt levels they have assumed in acquiring their education.

(Mettler, 2014: 16–17)

Importantly, Mettler argues that the exacerbation of inequalities is not only about graduate employment outcomes. But also at stake are the benefits that higher education affords society and individuals, including the democratic value, to enable full participation of all citizens and the right to exercise a political voice. "The nation's growing concern about student loan debt and about the value of a college degree blind us to what has really gone wrong in higher education", Mettler argues, noting that the disparities in completion rates and the state of play in which "those born on the margins of society have little hope of improving their circumstances" reflects a "demise of opportunity and the emergence of a society with caste-like characteristics" (Mettler, 2014: 17).

Mettler's key argument is the need for significant policy reform that acknowledges a fundamental shift in the political arena. Zaloom reinforces this strongly in her plea for systemic transformation at the government level:

> Our social policies and institutions do not need to trap families in moral conflict. With careful thought and political will, government support for higher education can resolve the dilemma and enable young adults to make their educations and their lives as they see fit.
>
> *(Zaloom, 2021: 191)*

Both Zaloom and Mettler point to the core problem as located in higher education policies that have not been reconsidered in the contemporary policy scapes. Mettler argues that this has produced a "caste system in which students from different socioeconomic backgrounds occupy distinct strata, and their experiences within those tiers end up making them increasingly unequal" (Mettler, 2014: 64). Indeed, Mettler's thesis is aligned to ours in this book; the underlying problem is a political misframing of the issues, leading to overlooking the predominant sources of inequality and instead focusing narrowly on institutions and individuals. "The problem is that the political system" is dysfunctional and "paralysed by polarization", with the government taking on "the character of a plutocracy as lawmakers join forces across party lines to represent the advantaged and neglect the needs of ordinary Americans" (Mettler, 2014: 64). Clearly both Mettler's and Zaloom's analyses are focused on the specificities of the US higher education system. However, there is much to learn from this context-specific study of higher education in a largely globalised system, in which commercialisation, marketisation, corporatisation, austerity measures, plutocracy, populism, political polarisation, and widening inequalities characterise a growing number of national systems. The misframing of the problem of equity in higher education through the narrowing of a focus on individual deficiencies ignores broader systemic inequalities and contributes to the 'caste-like' outcomes Mettler points to. Indeed, the fundamental problem is political and, as we will show throughout this book, is multidimensional. This requires a reorientation to equity through social justice praxis and sustained reflection/action processes that enable apprehension of the contemporary conditions that produce, reproduce, and exacerbate inequalities in, through, and beyond higher education.

Contemporary conditions

The shifting orientations, attentions, and standardisations described earlier across three nation-state contexts of access to higher education have played out in a global context shaped by international organisations and structures established (with contrasting agendas) to help reconstruct education systems following the Second World War. These organisations and structures (UNESCO, the OECD, and the World Bank) have themselves been increasingly shaped by the rise of neoliberalism and New Public Management (NPM), albeit differently and to different degrees. Taking account of these international organisations and their role in creating the conditions for policy and practice-making initiatives in different nation-state contexts helps to analyse the different problems and possibilities that projects of equity hold in those contexts. These global structures operate directly and indirectly to frame educational policy directions by creating arenas for public policymaking that are imbued with particular intentions, whilst remaining silent on many problems and possibilities. We see it is important to recognise these macro contexts and to engage with them with a critical sociological imagination because we value the notion of "an educational and cultural climate that encourages challenge and change, real empowerment and emancipations and not just a woolly tolerance of plurality of voices, where the critical voices remain enclosed within the confines of cultural ghettos" (Clark and Ivanic, 1997: 56).

The World Bank, the OECD, and UNESCO are highly political architectures yet are understood commonly as scientific and neutral forces. This denial of their political character helps to ensure that the philosophies guiding them can readily go to work 'steering at a distance' projects of access and participation for different groups and to shape the conditions of formal education provision in different contexts. Elfert and Ydesen (2023) have analysed the different positions and influences these three often competing international organisations have played over recent years and summarise them thus in relation to their influence on education systems. Following the Second World War, UNESCO was created with a mandate to help frame global education thinking, guided by idealist-humanistic imaginaries. The OECD, established as more of an advisory structure, has become influential through programmes such as the Programme for International Student Assessment (PISA), and is currently extending its reach to low-income countries; an example of the way in which neo-colonialism operates through education in these contemporary conditions (Lingard, 2022) and through which narrowed ideas regarding 'quality' education are normalised on the international stage, demanding competition and standardisation in which measurable aspects of 'core subjects', corporate practices, and only some (test-based) accountabilities are explicitly valued (Sahlberg, 2016). From the 1970s onwards, the World Bank has gained steady influence over education policymaking and programming in so-called developing contexts. In Elfert and Ydesen's analysis (2023), UNESCO has largely played the role of idealist, with different humanisms and post-humanisms at play over its history. UNESCO's focus is on norm-setting, capacity-building, and coordination, guided historically by a human rights agenda.

In this analysis, the OECD is characterised by a focus on scientific expertise around benchmarking, indicators, measurement, and their influence therefore being more towards forms of evidence and persuasion. The World Bank's influence is clearly facilitated by finance, with loans and the conditions tied to them, feeding a form of governance seen as befitting the moniker 'the master of coercion'.

> While the idealistic-humanistic ideology dominated the thinking about education in the first decade after WWII, in the 1950s a counter-agenda emerged with "the marriage of two social sciences, economics and education" (UNESCO, 2003, p. 4), from which the concept of "human capital" derived, which is still the dominant paradigm underpinning education policies worldwide. This tension between the humanistic and economistic approach to education runs like a thread through the relationship of the three IOs and global governance of education to this day.
>
> *(Elfert and Ydesen, 2023: 42)*

Earlier in this chapter we named the risk that comes with calls for transformation. If, as the above analysis helps to confirm, a 'human capital' imaginary dominates the framing of formal education's purpose within our contemporary rationality of capitalism (i.e. neoliberalism), then what forms of transformation can we readily expect to unfold? What can we expect higher education to become? And what of higher education's role in relation to the multidimensional, multi-scalar socio-ecological crises facing our more-than-human communities across the globe? In taking up an analysis of higher education's role in responding to, and/or reproducing social inequalities, we want to take care when using the sign of 'crisis'. As the late Lauren Berlant noted with the term 'crisis ordinariness', articulating how the crisis is largely embedded in the ordinary, taken up as a term to help narrativise the navigation of what feels overwhelming. The notion of crises can be adopted by different political forces to transform and this includes calls to further commodify, standardise, instrumentalise, and marketise higher education under the banner of 'progress'. One aim of this book however is to contribute to a growing field of what might loosely be referred to as 'Critical University Studies' (e.g. Bozalek and Zembylas, 2023; Williams, 2015; Boggs and Mitchell, 2018). We do so in this book by resisting an over-valorisation of what higher education is, or has ever been, and by rejecting a naive interpretation of what participation in contemporary higher education can achieve through simplistic 'inclusion'. Instead, we want to ask what types of higher education institutions might help constitute, and become constituted by, anti-misogynist, anti-racist, anti-colonialist, and culturally plural societies. Tristan McCowan, for example, has argued for the 'developmental university', an institution oriented by service to society, particularly those people historically and currently most disadvantaged by social inequality. Service that facilitates participation in the development research and engagement guided by a focus on public good (McCowan, 2019)

> [the role of the university] . . . is not only a calculating machine for generating answers to problems that are facing us, but a creator of new ideas, of new forms of thinking that have not yet been experienced. Our problem is not just that we do not have the right answers, but that we do not have the right questions.
>
> *(2019: 307)*

This analysis helps us to remember that the TINA affect, that There Is No Alternative, is something we ourselves consent to within a particular increasingly globalised hegemony. This is one way we are each complicit in reproducing inequality and injustice. We are complicit in subtle and monstrous ways that demand we move beyond simple moralising and towards an uncomfortable acceptance that we are always already complicit in conditions that facilitate endless unjust acts (Bozalek and Zembylas, 2023). This discomfort can move us towards seeing 'business as usual', or even something approximating the usual, as grossly insufficient, and immoral. Certainly, the business of contemporary universities must not be taken as acceptable if we are serious about producing more just social contexts, within and through higher education institutions. As UNESCO have recently asserted:

> 'Business as usual' is neither sufficient nor acceptable to ensure that people fully exert their right to higher education within free, peaceful, and fair societies. UNESCO urgently calls for substantive changes that help with reimagining our futures and defining clear paths for improving educational experiences and outcomes for all. These paths must involve all stakeholders who have concern with HED.
>
> *(UNESCO Beyond Limits, New Ways to Reinvent HE, 2022: 11)*

The call to embed transformative commitments within the ethos of redeveloping higher education, and with an explicit human-rights principle at play, is a call to which this book is firmly located. In doing so, we build on decades of action and reflection in relation to who is seen to have *The Right to Higher Education* (Burke, 2012). We also want to foreground commitments for transformation which generatively trouble the liberal humanism on which the human rights agenda is founded. The rights agenda in education has helped point out that high-quality education should be for everyone, not just for the most privileged. A crude form of the rights agenda however risks facilitating an overly individualised educational imaginary: a humanism that is individualistic rather than a more-than-humanism that is political, democratic, and collective. Biesta (2022) has argued that, instead of working back towards different humanistic visions, there needs to be a striving for the emancipation of education itself from duty to learn agendas and towards an ongoing right to learn in high-quality contexts throughout a person's life. This is a transformation at odds with the types of higher education reforms often couched in the language of equity yet deeply imbued with market logics and individualised imaginaries of the social. This is a transformation that requires critical counter-hegemonic action and reflection. In this book, we offer frameworks for social justice praxis designed to create contexts for counter-hegemonic practice. The commitments guiding this work we characterise as *feminist, critical, decolonial, post/structural,* and *sociological.* In the next section, we introduce and articulate these commitments.

Commitments for transformation

Centring feminist histories of thought and theorisation in the context of a book on higher education is part of an ongoing project of acknowledging that processes of education (formal or informal) are never neutral acts but instead always a site of struggle over meaning-making and knowledge. Within a book that provides an analysis of the effect of neoliberal capitalism on higher education, and highlights the consequences and possibilities for equity, it is, of course, important to remain focused on how capitalist societies have sexism hardwired 'into their DNA' (Arruzza, Bhattacharya and Fraser, 2019). It is problematic to speak of one coherent feminist set of commitments though, with incredibly diverse literatures demonstrating how biases and inequalities in relation to gender are manifest in all societal institutions and, therefore, why "it is necessary to explore how meanings, particularly representations of gender, are mobilised within the operations of power to produce asymmetrical relations amongst subjects" (McNay, 1992: 35). A *feminist, critical, decolonial,* and *post/structural sociology* brings in gender concerns certainly but just as importantly foregrounds the immense contribution of feminist orientations, theorisations and politicisations that have all too often been marginalised through, for example, citation practices playing out in patriarchal systems of privileged publication. In addition to taking up feminist concepts such as the importance of 'situated knowledges' within justice-oriented projects, following Haraway, we want to echo an urgent need for making and recognising new forms of 'kin' as we connect questions of equity and social justice in higher education to bigger questions of intersecting crises and injustice that fold back on, into, and onto one another, in intricate ways. As Haraway (2016) puts it:

> If there is to be multispecies ecojustice, which can also embrace diverse human people, it is high time that feminists exercise leadership in imagination, theory, and action to unravel the ties of both genealogy and kin, and kin and species.
>
> *(Haraway, 2016: 102)*

Throughout this book, histories of feminist thought, activism, philosophy, and scholarship are drawn upon, including those histories that have engaged with, challenged, and built beyond Foucault, following the likes of Lois McNay, Nancy Fraser, Patti Lather, Johanna Oksala, and Catriona McLeod in critiquing and developing aspects of Foucault's oeuvre. For example, in taking up the notion of 'practices of the self', feminists have taken on and worked through Foucault's offerings to navigate contemporary concerns regarding difference, discipline, and the body. Central to the feminist theory taken up in this thesis is a post/structural analysis of power that can facilitate understanding of relations within and across both micro- and macro-level politics.

> It is the constitution of knowledge claims as 'truth' that is linked to systems of power: those who have the power – institutionally as well as individually – to determine and legitimise 'truth' also have the power to determine dominant discourses. This exercising of power happens so thoroughly, so powerfully, and so ideologically, that the political nature of discourses becomes hidden.
>
> *(Burke and Jackson, 2007: 6)*

The term, concept and history of 'feminist' theory and methodology, of course, continues to be a dynamic field of thought and debate. In this book, a 'feminist' approach is used in close concert with 'critical' and 'post/structural' theories of embodiment that help to draw in subjectivity and practice, to bring attention to the ways inequalities are experienced and felt through complex formations of personhood (Burke, 2012).

Criticality, criticism, and critique are foregrounded throughout this book as generative and 'positive' characteristics, necessary for critical social justice praxis that holds any potential to engage and transform structural inequities within higher education institutions. It is important to explain what we mean by taking up these terms, and to ask, for example: How it is that 'generative critique', 'optimistic criticality', or 'critical hope' can really do justice to, and within, our contemporary moments? And: What forms of criticality are productive of social justice praxis in a globalised context that continues to see the rise of right-wing and authoritarian populist discourse that challenge the hard-won fights regarding the rights of women, LGBTQI+ communities, immigrants, and minorities? (Burke et al, 2022). This is a book that acknowledges a perennial problem of social justice projects; a problem that emerges in terms of initiatives that advocate transformation, because, immediately, the question must be asked: on whose terms, on whose time, and on what values should 'transitions' towards new arrangements 'form', and why? As a starting point, perhaps critical orientations are about showing how the supposedly self-evident should not be considered so. Mbembe has recently argued that criticism is still a useful tool for building paths for tomorrow (Mbembe, 2023). Following Foucault (1981), we might argue that criticism can be constructed as the pointing out of assumptions rather than as it is often viewed and/or received, as asserting that things are not 'correct' as they stand.

> Practicing criticism is a matter of making facile gestures difficult. . . . In these circumstances, criticism (and radical criticism) is absolutely indispensable for any transformation. A transformation that remains within the same mode of thought, a transformation that is only a way of adjusting the same thought more closely to the reality of things can merely be a superficial transformation. On the other hand, as soon as one can no longer think things as one formerly thought them, transformation becomes both very urgent, very difficult, and quite possible.
>
> *(Foucault, 1981: 155)*

We see critical perspectives, as part of a critical praxis, helping to make the familiar strange-enough, arbitrary-seeming-enough, re-thinkable enough, to help deconstruct and reconstruct the conceptualisations guiding hegemonic forms of practice. We must always be cautious when seeking some moralising, asking always what does it currently mean to 'be critical'? For Butler (2003), 'critical' denotes an approach that asks about unacknowledged assumptions and unwitting consequences rather than imposing a literal read. We see a critical orientation to equity as about anticipation of different imaginaries, diverse spaces of debate, new possibilities of action/reflection, and important dynamics in the pursuit of *Time for Social Justice Praxis*.

A *post/structural* feminist understanding of power imbues our work:

> The crossover between feminist theory and poststructuralism has been especially vibrant and productive. The poststructuralist philosophical critique of the rational subject has resonated strongly with the feminist critique of rationality as an essentially masculinist construct.
>
> *(McNay, 1992: 2)*

Working within the messy site of struggle and contestation that is the research/practice nexus in contemporary higher education calls for a set of meta-theoretical commitments that have both creative and conceptual rigour. Contemporary contexts of higher education require methodological foundations able to grapple with a complex social milieu of formations generating meaning in subtle and insidious ways. We want to pay attention to the ways in which denoting that "the stroke (/) in post/structuralism signifies the negotiating of structuralism and poststructuralism in our work" (Burke, Crozier and Misiaszek, 2017: 53). This important distinction gives us a starting point for thinking about the difficult entanglement of the material, the structural, the discursive, the affective, and the symbolic in a generative manner that has important consequences for the methodologies that guide research and practice in contexts of equity and/or widening participation. In working to continue to develop Pedagogical Methodologies (e.g. PPoEMs, see Chapter 7), we come, for example, to appreciate the important influence that feminist post/structural concepts such as *gendered subjectivity* (Butler, 1999) bring to the ongoing project of building more socially just participation in the many and varied contexts of higher education. One contribution (explored in more depth further in the text) is how post/structural orientations offer an explanatory framework for the normalising processes that establish discourses which in turn facilitate 'true' (and performative) statements that function through the repetition of legitimated institutional practices and performatives.

> Each society has its regime of truth, its general politics' of truth: that is, the types of discourses which it accepts and makes function as true; the mechanisms and instances which enable one to distinguish true and false statements, the means by which each is sanctioned; the techniques and procedures accorded value in the acquisition of truth; the status of those who are charged with saying what counts as true.
>
> *(Foucault, in Rabinow, 1984: 73)*

These multi-scale politics of truth are operations of power and are evident in the ways in which equity and widening participation practitioners are inscribed in policy and programming texts. The critical feminist post/structuralism taken up in this text understands power however as complex, generative, fluid, dynamic, and unpredictable; an account that rejects the notion that power only stems from 'the top' in contemporary times. Structures clearly matter, yet a more 'capillary' conception of power helps us see how patriarchy is (re) formed differently across diverse contexts and practices, and in relation to political forces such as colonialism, capitalism, neoliberalism, globalisation, and neoconservatism (Burke, 2012).

Feminist sociological orientations to social justice praxis help to avoid the construction of the problem of inequalities and their relation to equity in higher education as an overly individualised set of dynamics. It is important to note, of course, that there are contested feminist sociological perspectives, including differences in terms of the conceptualisation of gender and in political orientations. A feminist sociology of participation in higher education might foreground how exclusive institutions such as traditional universities were radically biased against the recognition and inclusion of women. As we make this call for sociological imagination as part of transformative equity praxis, we recognise Gillborn's reminder, following the likes of Apple, Ball, Delamont, and others, that "there is no such thing as *the* sociology of education. There are competing (and excluding) versions and constructions of the discipline, even within a single time period in a single nation state" (Gillborn, 2005: 487). Indeed, some sociologies help us to understand how, for example, epistemic violence runs much deeper than patterns of participation, into the very fundamentals of society. And we must be careful here too, of course, that the historical exclusion of women's standpoints inhabits certain sociologies too.

> The French philosopher Auguste Comte, the founder of positivism and a figure as influential as Darwin, gave close attention to the social function of women in the first-ever 'treatise of sociology', his System of Positive Polity (1851). Women were, in his view, an important base for the coming utopian society – but only if they remained in their proper sphere as comforters and nurturers of men.
>
> *(Connell and Pearse, 2014: 55)*

One of the seductive characteristics of the contemporary capitalist order is to create the conditions in which it is easiest to stay boxed in and not 'look around'. The consumption of cultural hegemony guides us away from paying attention. The ongoing neoliberal transformation of our institutions and selves requires inattention and a de-valuing of situatedness. We see bringing a sociological imagination to equity praxis as a potentially radical and relational act.

> to develop a sociological imagination is to attempt to see and listen on both of these horizons simultaneously, to pay attention to both the insights and the blindness in the accounts of the people who live the consequences of our uncertain world, and at the same time have the humility and the honesty to reflect on our own assumptions and prejudgements.
>
> *(Back, 2007: 12)*

The sociological imagination we understand as a crucial dimension of exercising social justice praxis as it opens new questions and ways of being in the world. It brings attention to the dimensions of higher education that are overlooked, ignored, glossed over, and overshadowed by the power of hegemonic frameworks. In this book, we invite readers to exercise their imagination by engaging with the questions we raise and by crafting their own questions.

Transformative equity praxis requires a stance of uncertainty and unknowing and our capacity to imagine is important in countering the hegemonies seeped in the authoritative posture of being certain. We will use questioning as a tool to put these ideas in motion through the book and in dialogue with you, our reader. It is our aim then not to provide solutions but to engage in a collective act of critical questioning, activating our capacity to imagine new possibilities.

Conclusion

In this chapter, we have started a process of engaging our collective imagination about the role and purpose of higher education. We have started to trace the contested perspectives, over space and time, that differently frame access, equity, and widening participation drawing on examples from three different national contexts to illustrate competing views, framings, and discourses. We have extended this initial exploration to a global context shaped by international organisations and structures established (with contrasting agendas) to help reconstruct education systems following the Second World War. Through these examples, we have pointed to the danger of narrowing the problem of building equity, especially through harmful deficit discourses that individualise what is a problem of social proportions. In particular, we have troubled neoliberal systems of higher education, intent on marketising, commercialising, and economising higher education as irresponsible and unethical in the context of the multidimensional, multiscale socio-ecological crises facing our more-than-human communities across the globe. We have sketched the *feminist critical, decolonial, post/structural*, and *sociological* frameworks that we will draw from throughout this book.

In the next chapter, we take these ideas further by focusing on theories of social justice to challenge hegemonic discourses and to advance transformative equity praxis. Unsettling the deficit imaginaries that tend to frame hegemonic discourses of equity and the formation of policy and practice, we engage more extensively with social justice theories, with a particular focus on Nancy Fraser's multidimensional social justice framework (e.g. Fraser, 1997, 2009, 2013; Fraser and Honneth, 2003). We invite consideration of how Fraser's framework might contribute to dislodging deficit imaginaries that are deeply embedded in contemporary equity policy agendas. The aim of the chapter will be to establish social justice as the foundation for reimagining equity in higher education, building on this in later chapters, by demonstrating that when woven together with other key social justice insights, including those oriented to action, a multidimensional framework for transformative equity praxis can challenge inequalities in, through and beyond higher education.

References

AdvanceHE (2023) *The Importance of EDI in Higher Education*. AdvanceHE. www.advance-he.ac.uk/guidance/governance/governance-and-edi/importance-edi-higher-education

Arruzza, C., Bhattacharya, T., and Fraser, N. (2019) *Feminism for the 99%: A Manifesto*. London: Verso.

Back, L. (2007) *The Art of Listening*. Oxford: Berg Publishers.

Barr, J. (1999) *Liberating Knowledge: Research, Feminism and Adult Education*. Leicester: NIACE.

Benn, R., Elliott, J., and Whaley, R. (1995) 'Introduction: Women and continuing education- where are we now?', in Benn, R., Elliott, J., and Whaley, P. (Eds) *Educating Rita and Her Sisters: Women and Continuing Education*. Leicester: NIACE.

Bennett, A., Motta, S.C., Hamilton, E., Burgess, C., Relf, B., Gray, K., and Albright, J. (2016) *Enabling Pedagogies: A Participatory Conceptual Mapping of Practices at the University of Newcastle, Australia*. Newcastle, NSW, Australia: Centre of Excellence for Equity in Higher Education, University of Newcastle.

Biesta, G. (2022) 'Reclaiming a future that has not yet been: The Faure report, UNESCO's humanism and the need for the emancipation of education', *International Review of Education*, 68, 655–672. https://doi.org/10.1007/s11159-021-09921-x

Boggs, A., and Mitchell, N. (2018) 'Critical university studies and the crisis consensus', *Feminist Studies*, 44(2), 432–463. https://doi.org/10.15767/feministstudies.44.2.0432

Bozalek, V., and Zembylas, M. (2023) *Responsibility, Privileged Irresponsibility and Response-ability*. Cham: Palgrave Macmillan. https://doi.org/10.1007/978-3-031-34996-6

Brøgger, K., and Madsen, M. (2022) 'An affirmative-diffractive re-reading of the policy instrumentation approach through agential realism and the accreditation instrument', *Journal of Education Policy*, 37(6), 925–943. https://doi.org/10.1080/02680939.2021.1938239

Burke, P.J. (2001) *Access/ing Education: A feminist post/structuralist ethnography of widening educational participation*. London: Institute of Education, University of London.

Burke, P.J. (2002) *Accessing Education: Effectively Widening Participation*. London: Trentham.

Burke, P.J. (2012) *The Right to Higher Education: Beyond Widening Participation*. London and New York: Routledge.

Burke, P.J., Coffey, J., Gill, R., and Kanai, A. (Eds) (2022). *Gender in an Era of Post-Truth Populism: Pedagogies, Challenges and Strategies*. London: Bloomsbury Academic.

Burke, P.J., Crozier, G., and Misiaszek, L.I. (2017) *Changing Pedagogical Spaces in Higher Education: Diversity, Inequalities and Misrecognition*. London: Routledge.

Burke, P.J., and Jackson, S. (2007) *Reconceptualising Lifelong Learning: Feminist Interventions*. London: Taylor and Francis.

Butler, J. (1999) *Gender Trouble: Feminism and the Subversion of Identity*. London: Routledge.

Butler, J. (2003) 'Values of difficulty', in *Just Being Difficult? Academic Writing in the Public Arena*. Redwood City: Stanford University Press, 199–216. https://doi.org/10.1515/9781503624009-014

Clark, R., and Ivanic, R. (1997) *The Politics of Writing* (1st ed.). London: Routledge. https://doi.org/10.4324/9780203351741

Connell, R., and Pearse, R. (2014) *Gender: In World Perspective*. Cambridge: Polity Press.

Corrigan, P. (1992) 'The politics of access courses in the 1990s', *Journal of Access Studies*, 7(1), 19–32.

Diamond, J. (1999) 'Access: The year 2000 and beyond- what next?', *Journal of Access and Credit Studies*, 1, 183–191, Summer.

Elfert, M., and Ydesen, C. (2023) 'UNESCO, the OECD and the World Bank: A global governance perspective', in *Global Governance of Education: Educational Governance Research*. Cham: Springer. https://doi.org/10.1007/978-3-031-40411-5_2

Fieldhouse, R. (1996) 'Historical and political context', 'The nineteenth century' and 'An overview of British adult education in the twentieth century', in Fieldhouse, R. (Ed) *A History of Modern British Adult Education*. Leicester: NIACE.

Fielding, M. (2001) 'OFSTED, inspection and the betrayal of democracy', *Journal of Philosophy of Education*, 35(4), 695–709, November. https://doi.org/10.1111/1467-9752.00254

Foucault, M. (1981/1988) 'Practicing criticism', In Kritzman, L.D. (Ed) *Michel Foucault: Politics, Philosophy, Culture – Interviews and Other Writings 1977–1984*. London: Routledge.

Fraser, N. (1997) *Justice Interruptus: Critical Reflections on the "Postsocialist" Condition*. London and New York: Routledge.

Fraser, N. (2009) *Scales of Justice: Reimagining Political Space in a Globalizing World*. New York: Cambridge University Press.

Fraser, N. (2013) *Fortunes of Feminism: From State-Managed Capitalism to Neoliberal Crisis*. New York: Verso Books.

Fraser, N., and Honneth, A. (2003) *Redistribution or Recognition? A Political-Philosophical Exchange*. New York: Verso.

Gillborn, D. (2005) 'Education policy as an act of white supremacy: Whiteness, critical race theory and education reform', *Journal of Education Policy*, 20(4), 485–505. https://doi.org/10.1080/02680930500132346

Haraway, D. (2016) *Staying with the Trouble: Making Kin in the Chthulucene*. Durham, NC: Duke University Press.

Kennedy, M., and Piette, B. (1991) 'From the margins to the mainstream: Issues around women's studies on adult education and access courses', In Aaron, J., and Walby, S. (Eds) *Out of the Margins*. London, New York and Philadelphia: The Falmer Press.

Lingard, B. (2022) 'Relations and locations: New topological spatio-temporalities in education', *European Educational Research Journal*, 21(6), 983–993. https://doi.org/10.1177/14749041221076323

Maxwell, B. (1996) 'Open college networks; are they still for adult learners?', *Adults Learning*, 111–112, January.

Mbembe, A. (2023) *Public Lecture to UNESCO Conference: Transforming Knowledge for Just and Sustainable Futures*. www.unesco.org/archives/multimedia/document-6002

McNay, L. (1992) *Foucault and Feminism: Power, Gender and the Self*. Cambridge: Polity Press.

McCowan, T. (2019) *Higher Education for and Beyond the Sustainable Development Goals*. Cham: Palgrave Macmillan. https://doi.org/10.1007/978-3-030-19597-7

Mettler, S. (2014) *Degrees of Inequality: How the Politics of Higher Education Sabotaged the American Dream*. New York: Basic Books.

Rabinow, P. (1984) 'Truth and power', in *The Foucault Reader*. New York: Pantheon Books.

Sahlberg, P. (2016) 'The global educational reform movement and its impact on schooling', in Mundy, K., Green, A., Lingard, B., and Verger, A. (Eds) *Handbook of Global Education Policy*. Chichester, West Sussex: Wiley-Blackwell, 180–196.

Thompson, J. (1980) 'Adult education for a change', in Thompson, J. (Ed) *Adult Education for a Change*. London: Hutchinson.

Thompson, J. (2000) 'Introduction', in Thompson, J. (Ed) *Stretching the Academy: The Politics and Practice of Widening Participation in Higher Education.* Leicester: NIACE.

UNESCO (2022) *Beyond Limits: New Ways to Reinvent Higher Education.* Working Document for the World Higher Education Conference, 18–20 May. UNESCO, Paris, France.

Williams, J. (1997) *Negotiating Access to Higher Education: The Discourse of Selectivity and Equity.* Buckingham: The Society for Research into Higher Education and Open University Press.

Williams, J. (2015) 'The need for critical university studies', in Hutner, G., and Mohamed, F. (Eds) *A New Deal for the Humanities: Liberal Arts and the Future of Public Higher Education.* Ithaca, NY: Rutgers University Press, 145–159. https://doi.org/10.36019/9780813573267-011

Wolbring, G., and Lillywhite, A. (2021) 'Equity/equality, diversity, and inclusion (EDI) in universities: The case of disabled people', *Societies,* 11(2), 49. https://doi.org/10.3390/soc11020049

Zaloom, C. (2021) *Indebted: How Families Make College Work at Any Cost.* Princeton: Princeton University Press.

2

FROM DEFICIT IMAGINARIES TO SOCIAL JUSTICE REFRAMING

Introduction

Building on the contextual and theoretical insights from Chapter 1, this chapter focuses on theories of social justice to challenge hegemonic equity discourses and to advance what we call transformative equity praxis. There is a large and extensive body of work on social justice that has the capacity to interrogate the dominant logics currently underpinning equity agendas. If left in place without interrogation, these dominant logics ensure that, despite significant nation-state-level investment in equity, persistent inequalities are unchallenged, reproduced, and sustained. Drawing examples from both policy and literature, this chapter aims to illuminate how monodimensional, apolitical, uncritical, and/or atheoretical explanations profoundly narrow, limit, and ultimately sabotage commitments to develop more equitable higher education. This dynamic is exacerbated by deficit imaginaries that tend to frame hegemonic discourses of equity and the formation of policy and practice. We shift attention to in-depth engagement with social justice theories, with a focus on Nancy Fraser's groundbreaking multidimensional social justice framework (e.g. Fraser, 1997, 2003, 2009, 2013). We demonstrate the possibility of this multidimensional conceptualisation for reframing equity by dislodging persistent deficit imaginaries that currently drive equity policy agendas, and that are difficult to apprehend with a monodimensional orientation. The aim of the chapter will be to establish social justice as the foundation for reimagining equity in higher education, making Fraser's multidimensional conceptualisation of social justice (redistribution, recognition, and representation) accessible to those striving towards generating inclusive higher education spaces. In later chapters, we build on this foundation to illustrate that when woven together

DOI: 10.4324/9781003257165-4

with other key social justice insights, including those oriented to action, a multidimensional framework for transformative equity praxis can be put to work to challenge inequalities in, through and beyond higher education.

We introduce the concept of *transformative equity praxis* to signal an institution's responsibility to challenge injustices that interact and overlap, and to make a distinction between this approach and what we call *deficit imaginaries* of equity. Transformative equity praxis supports commitments to generate equitable access to and participation in higher education but challenges the hegemonic deficit, remedial, and utilitarian frameworks that characterise much policy and practice. In doing so, we seek to build praxis-based, pedagogical, ethically oriented, methodologically rigorous research-informed practice and practice-informed research. Transformative equity praxis demands close attention to historical, institutionalised, and insidious injustices across multiple contexts. It requires rigorous social justice methodologies across theory/practice (praxis). It is guided by praxis to enable dialogic reflection/action-action/reflection and is embedded institutionally to avoid (re)situating equity at the peripheries of higher education. The aim is to transform the institutional and discipline-based structures, cultures and practices that perpetuate exclusion. Transformative equity praxis brings to light the problem of monodimensional framing.

The problem of monodimensional framing of equity in higher education

Equity in higher education is largely framed through a monodimensional lens, which lends itself well to deficit imaginaries and which we aim to contest. By monodimensional, we are pointing to the tendency to focus on a single thread of theory, practice, or identity, ignoring the complex tapestry of equity work and fixing the gaze on the individual constructed through a singular, homogenising categorisation. The categorisation produces *pathologising* discourses in relation to notions of merit, reducing a person's value to only measurable attributes through individualisation, datafication, and dehumanisation and through the misrecognition of being seen only through the lens of disadvantage. Monodimensional frameworks are a useful device for governments and institutions to settle on instrumentalist, technicist, utilitarian, and remedial policies that aim to 'fix' the individual, pulling attention away from power, inequalities, and oppressive relations. Such frameworks hold in place perceptions that higher education is a neutral site in which social inequalities are external to its formation and thus equity is largely seen as transforming individuals to realise their innate potential through raising their aspirations or by providing remedial support to prepare them for 'success' (as narrowly defined, which we discuss in more detail throughout the book).

Let's take gender equity as a key example of monodimensional framing of equity, which tends to focus on issues such as getting more women into Sciences, Technologies, Engineering and Mathematics (STEM) subjects. The emphasis is on a singular equity categorisation and the analytical gaze focuses on quantifying at the level of the decontextualised individual unit; for example, how many female students are taking STEM subjects and how many women academics have an academic or leadership position in STEM fields. These questions are significant, and need to be asked and explored, as they help identify unequal patterns of participation in higher education. Yet, we want to take issue with the monodimensional focus, which tends to limit understanding of what are complex and multidimensional issues of gender injustice (Fraser, 2013). Within a monodimensional framing, institutions might strive towards gender equity by simply collecting quantitative data on the constitution of STEM areas in the university and in relation to ratios of men to women. We call this a form of 'datafication', in which a complex social problem is reduced to collecting quantitative data that is seen to measure and/or represent equity 'progress'. Indeed, the problem is often formulated in terms of simply getting the measurement apparatus right. This is often accompanied by qualitative data brought in to represent 'the stories' of those involved, and to defend a 'mixed method' claim. Of course, the collection of data can be useful to illuminate patterns, yet, within a monodimensional framework, it is unable to fully grapple with multiple forms of maldistribution, the histories of power relations, and the ways difference is discursively constructed to (re)privilege traits associated with hegemonic masculinities.

Furthermore, the datafication of gender equity through a monodimensional, atheoretical, and deficit framework has several significant flaws and problems. It not only reinforces exclusionary, binary constructions of gender but also overlooks the ways that gender injustice intersects at the micro level of formations of difference (e.g. the ways personhood is formed in relation to structural inequalities and differences across, for example, age, class, gender, race and sexuality) *and* at the macro level of structural inequalities (e.g. the ways that intersecting political dynamics such as neoliberalism, neocolonialism, misogyny, (hetero)sexism and neopatriarchy are built into the structures of social institutions). It fails to comprehend the complexities of intersections; the ways differences play out in relation to gendered identities and experiences and how these differences are formed in relation to the institutional structures in place and hegemonic discourses and practices at play. Important questions to address in relation to institutional structures might include how equity is located at the university (at the centre or the peripheries?); who has influence and representation (executive leaders, equity experts, academics, students from underrepresented groups, marginalised community representatives?) and through what mechanisms (committees, working groups, units, research, evaluation, participatory projects?). Hegemonic practices might include the ways that STEM research is undertaken, assessed, and produced, inevitably underpinned by taken-for-granted values and assumptions and exclusive histories and temporalities. These might include the expectation to participate in particular research rhythms, spaces and routines that exclude those navigating competing and contradictory spaces and temporalities. For many women, for example, this might mean being torn between the expectations and demands of caring and academic work (Moreau and Robertson, 2019).

A monodimensional framing of gender equity thus ignores the macro-level power dynamics that are tied to hegemonic discursive formations, such as the processes of recognition as a legitimate and successful scientist, technologist, engineer, or mathematician. This effects students and staff and illuminates how processes of (mis)recognition are ongoing, fluid, and dynamic forms of struggle. Yet, what is continuously erased from view through uncritical monodimensional, atheoretical, and deficit framings are the ways institutional patterns of cultural value operate to misrecognise bodies associated with difference and outside of the hegemonic discourses of being a scientist, technologist, engineer, or mathematician. Also obscured is how this relates to questions of (mal)distribution and (mis)representation. This ignores key theoretical insights that personhood is formed through doing and is performative (Butler, 1999) so that neoliberal, neocolonial, and hegemonic masculinist practices are not apprehended or critiqued. Rather, the emphasis is on changing the attitudes and attributes of the individual constructed as deficient. Examples that emerge and remerge in gender equity discourse include building confidence and assertiveness skills. The judgments underpinning the taken-for-granted value of these attributes are hidden from view and re-presented as objective. Who would be against the idea of building confidence? Or being more assertive about their needs and interests? Or to be resilient in the context of everyday challenges? These discourses of confidence, assertiveness, and resilience seem logical in the face of disadvantage and there is a common sense that is appealing as a potential solution to the problem of gender inequity. Yet, without attention to the gendered power relations that discursively form 'confidence', 'being assertive', and 'resilient', the hegemonic order and injustices are left unexamined and unnoticed, while the individual's supposed deficiencies become the focal point for equity interventions. The solution to engage individuals with remedial training to boost confidence and learn to be more assertive or resilient seems straightforward. Neoliberalism, which emphasises individual agency as central to 'success', works together in insidious ways with neopatriarchies to sustain gender injustices that intersect with other political dynamics at the macro level. Yet, without the tools of social justice theories, it becomes almost impossible to identify the complex, insidious, workings of multidimensional injustices.

Despite these insights about gender equity, which emerge from feminist analyses, equity policy and practice more broadly continue to construct categorisations that reinforce monodimensional framing. These commonly include the categorisations, usually treated separately, of low socioeconomic status, culturally and linguistically diverse, regional, rural, and remote, people with a disability, and black and ethnic minority. We understand the importance of these categorisations in mapping patterns of admissions, transition, retention, attrition, and completion for groups that have been identified as historically underrepresented in higher education. These categorisations help to create formulas for governments to calculate specialised funding to support higher education institutions with their equity and widening participation initiatives. These categorisations often provide an important device for strategies of redistribution. However, redistribution can itself become a monodimensional focus if absent of attention to questions of recognition and representation. A common challenge in university equity contexts are processes of targeting (to facilitate redistribution of, for example, material resources and/or opportunities) that necessitate a process of qualification by the redistributor of recipients in ways which endlessly risk misrecognition through misrepresentation, or as a colleague of ours recently put it, 'representational violence' (Bunn, 2021). A key dilemma with monodimensional strategies is these homogenising effects that enable an ignore-ance of lived and embodied experiences of higher education (including the sense of having no relationship to higher education at all), in which structural inequalities impact personhood, and the right to higher education, but in fluid, dynamic, and multidimensional ways.

We argue for the need to grasp the complexity of multidimensional inequalities in higher education. Critical theorists have argued that the field of equity in higher education, including considerations of access and widening participation, have largely been atheoretical (e.g. Archer and Leathwood, 2003; Burke, 2002, 2012). We argue that similarly troubling is work that significantly reduces the analysis of equity by focusing on a single dimension of a theorist's body of work. In the equity and widening participation literature, this is most characterised by work that claims to draw from Bourdieu but then applies a thin layer of analysis from one part of his work, most often cultural capital (Webb et al, 2017; Burke et al, 2023). This not only misleads the presentation of what equity in higher education is, reinforcing deficit discourses that focus on the perceived deficiencies of individuals from underrepresented communities, seen to 'lack cultural capital'. But it also greatly distorts Bourdieu's critical and complex theorisation of the social reproduction of class inequalities through the fields of education. The point to make here is not only does this garble theorisation of equity but it also risks harmful policy formation, rooted in deficit discourses that de-mean and de-value those personhoods and communities who are already systemically marginalised and excluded. We therefore want not to advocate simply for 'the use of some social theory' in equity research that can guide policy and practice; instead, we advocate for the considered use of tools of important critique (including social theory) that can enrich spaces of dialogue across difference by offering explanatory possibility for the way in which assumptions (and presumptions) tend to be guiding the frameworks implicitly and explicitly at play.

We attend to the problematic nature of one-dimensional analyses, particularly emphasising the ways this exacerbates deficit imaginaries. In drawing on the sociological language of imaginaries, we suggest that deficit is more problematic than avoiding certain language or making minor refinements to an equity initiative. Rather, we must understand that the problem is in the very *framing* of equity, what Nancy Fraser identifies as a key form of social injustice: *misframing* (Fraser, 2009), a form of 'political death'. In trying to illuminate the ills of misframing, we have drawn on the metaphor of the Ames Room to reveal the significance of misframing for equity in higher education.

> The Ames Room illusion is a heavily distorted physical construction commonly used in film-making and set construction that misleads the subject into accepting a particular 'reality' through a forced perspective or lens. The illusion can lead to unsettling experiences as underlying assumptions support the subject to deal with ambiguity and 'make sense' of improbable arrangements. Stepping away from the compulsory physical viewpoint reveals the concealed dimensions of the experience, yet, as the subject steps back to the forced perspective, the assumptions return effortlessly and the illusion holds again, even with this new 'knowledge' of the deceit.
>
> *(Lumb and Burke, 2019: 216)*

In writing together and adopting this metaphor, we were attempting to provide a tool for discussion in our given context about a perplexing dilemma much deliberated in critical social theory and practice, that of whether it is possible for agents to make a form of 'break' from a surrounding epistemic apparatus, and if so, to what extent. Specifically, this metaphor was about asking whether and how an individual or group can 'remember' or hold on to ruptures made in the dominant imaginaries, glimpses perhaps of alternative ways of being 'in the true' that are often constructed as unreasonable within mainstream equity discourse.

It is popular in contemporary times to be against deficit language or models in equity networks in higher education. Yet *deficit imaginaries* – aligned so fruitfully as they are with neoliberal discourses of meritocracy to individualise the problem of equity, erasing from view long-standing, deeply entrenched inequalities – recirculate so readily back to guide the premise of much equity programming. In part, because the market logics guiding what is seen as reasonable and legitimate use of equity resources demands a deficit framing that orients itself towards demonising individuals who do not currently 'fit'. The notion of meritocracy conceals that exclusion is not about an individual's deficiencies but about the persistent working of complex relations of power and structural, institutionalised, and discursive inequalities.

Deficit framing and the persistence of the myth of meritocracy

The discourses of meritocracy individualise and instrumentalise equity and widen participation agendas by ignoring the social, economic, cultural, and political inequalities that profoundly shape judgements of merit. Meritocracy is a discursive framing that identifies key attributes, seen as objective and value-free, to assess a person's right to higher education. By discursive framing, we draw on Foucault's concept of discourse in which power/knowledge are inextricably linked in ways that profoundly frame social meanings, problems, and practices (Foucault, 1990). Discourses of potential and capability significantly frame understandings of meritocracy, which construct notions of 'deservedness' of access to and participation in higher education. However, what is missing is a critical consideration of the social contexts, institutional structures, power relations, and cultural patterns of value and micro-politics that intersect to create the complex conditions in which merit is judged and assessed.

The discourses of aptitude and capability are central to national assessment systems, such as the Australian Tertiary Admissions Rank, the UK's General Certificate of Education Advanced Level and the American Scholastic Aptitude Test. These systems, framed by meritocracy, tend to disregard the multidimensional inequalities at play in the construction of *who is recognised* as having the right to higher education. What merit means and how it is judged across time and space has been extensively researched and shown to be fluid, dynamic, and tied to unequal relations of power. Karabel's (2006) meticulous study of "the hidden history of admission and exclusion" is an outstanding example, providing a close examination of the exclusionary power of meritocracy embedded in national assessment systems. He traces in fine detail how the definition of 'merit' fundamentally changed multiple times over twentieth-century America (Karabel, 2006: 4). Such work illuminates that what is often absent are explicit discussions about the relationship between assessment and the historical struggles over the right to higher education, who is seen to belong, and how merit, aptitude, potential, and capability are discursively produced in ways that perpetuate deeply embedded inequalities (Burke, 2012). Meritocratic discourses powerfully shape – and limit – our pedagogical imaginations about possibilities to challenge exclusion and strategies to generate inclusion through *social justice principles*.

Discourses of meritocracy, which produce deficit imaginaries, actively reduce complex social and cultural histories and relations of inequality to rigid technologies of discipline and control that work to embed intensified forms of individualism. The problem is profoundly misframed by redirecting the focus away from social injustices to individual bodies re/class/ified through pathologising discourses and deficit imaginaries. Pathologising discourses of widening participation gained momentum over decades of policy and practice focused on correcting or fixing the perceived deficit and flawed attitudes of 'the disadvantaged' in order to meet their (socially constructed) special needs and to provide help to enable the individual to fit into the broader hegemonic university cultures and values. This largely framed institutional discourses of 'inclusion'. These discursive misframings largely constructed widening participation as interventions, to be performed by equity practitioners with the aim to change the attitudes of targeted disadvantaged young people.

Deficit imaginaries underpin a wide and often subtle number of areas through which students from marginalised backgrounds are framed. This notion of deficit imaginaries shows how the deficit is not a superficial problem around avoiding the language of 'lack'; it is formed through the way we imagine or think about what 'the problem' of equity 'is' (Burke, 2020). This subsequently pervades much of the way equity policy is formed and implemented, establishing through privileged ways of perceiving social realities with an inability or insensitivity towards the struggles, experiences, and forms of knowledge that students from diverse backgrounds retain (Medina, 2012). In terms of knowledge, there is a continuing dynamic between what is seen as legitimate knowledge, and subsequently, the ability for people holding this knowledge to determine what is and is not appropriate for higher education. Subsequently, this positions marginalised people and knowledges through deficit, since they do not reflect forms of knowledge institutionally legitimised as part of higher educational value.

Towards a multidimensional framework for social justice

In engaging the metaphor of the Ames Room to illustrate the harmful misframing of equity through monodimensional perspectives, we look to Nancy Fraser's *multidimensional* social justice framework as offering powerful conceptual tools to *reframe* equity in higher education. Indeed, a growing body of international research draws from Nancy Fraser's social justice framework as a compelling way to reframe equity in higher education (Burke, 2002; Chan, 2005; Burke, 2012; Molla and Gale, 2015; Msigwa, 2016; Oyarzún, Franco and McCowan, 2017; Burke, Crozier and Misiaszek, 2017; Bozalek, Holscher and Zembylas, 2020). Fraser's framework is pioneering in bringing attention to the multilayered, interrelated dimensions of redistribution, recognition, and representation for social justice.

Fraser's multidimensional framework offers social justice insights to reframe 'equity' by pointing to the inter-related dimensions of redistributive, recognitive, and representative justice (Molla and Gale, 2015; Burke, Crozier and Misiaszek, 2017; Oyarzún, Perales Franco and McCowan, 2017; Bozalek,

Holscher and Zembylas, 2020). This multidimensional analysis brings close analytic attention to a key taken-for-granted term used repeatedly in access, equity, and widening participation discourses: *participation*. Indeed, the focus on participation tends commonly to be framed in quantitative terms; for example, how many students from low socioeconomic status backgrounds gained entry to university in a specific year. Fraser's multidimensional social justice framework substantially deepens engagement with questions of participation by examining the implications of *who participates* in key processes of influence and decision-making and *on what terms*.

> For me, parity is not a matter of numbers. Rather, it is a qualitative condition, the condition of being a peer, of being on a par with others, of interacting with them on an equal footing. . . . In each arena, therefore, the meaning of parity must be tailored to the kind of participation at issue.
>
> *(Fraser, 2013: 166)*

This carries significance for equity in higher education when conclusions, recommendations, and decisions are being formed in direct relation to, and with implications for, communities who have not had access to those processes. When adopting a more explicit multidimensional approach, this more hidden, subtle underrepresentation, and in many cases misrepresentation, of personhoods and communities who have been excluded from participation in policy formation and development of equity practice can be made more visible. Instead, it is much more common to see those occupying positions of power and influence to continue to shape equity discourse and related policy, strategy, and practice that carry significant implications for the groups targeted by but simultaneously excluded from such processes. The potential to skew and/or distort knowledge and understanding that informs equity policy and practice has been largely ignored by an absence of attention to questions of representation across the dimensions of research, evaluation, policy, and practice. Fraser's concept of representation, especially when brought together with her interrelated concepts of redistribution and recognition, thus broadens and deepens the ways we engage questions of *parity of participation*. This extends frameworks of *proportional* participation (categories of participation counted through quantitative methods) to include *representational* participation that incorporates related redistributive and recognitive forms of equity. A multidimensional reframing of parity of participation is focused on ensuring all people participate as partners, interacting as equal peers (Bozalek and Boughey, 2020), which offers the potential for a greater depth of analysis to the formation of access, equity, and widening participation strategies and for facilitating parity of participation in shaping the right to higher education.

Building from this analytical depth, Fraser's framework helps to shed light on the significant demands of high-quality equity practice, which involves holding together social and economic justice (redistribution), cultural and symbolic justice (recognition), and political justice (representation) as part of a long-term process of striving towards parity of participation. "Only a framework that integrates the two analytically distinct perspectives of distribution and recognition can grasp the imbrication of class inequality and status hierarchy in contemporary society" (Fraser and Honneth, 2003: 4). Status hierarchy in Fraser's model refers to an "order of intersubjective subordination derived from institutionalised patterns of cultural value that constitute some members of society as less than full partners in interaction" (Fraser, 2003: 49). The notion of misrecognition as a form of status subordination sheds light on the ways that institutionalised cultural value patterns have discriminatory effects on the differential positioning of people (McNay, 2008). Recognition is shaped by complex relations of power that operate at the micro level of practice (e.g. in a particular local programme of outreach or study) in ongoing connection to the meso level of the institution (e.g. a school, college, or university) and macro level of society (e.g. the wider structures, systems and cultures that form and reproduce hierarchical differences and inequalities). Personhood and participation are formed through *relational processes of recognition*, which require processes of mastery and submission. That is, to be recognised as a university student, the person must master the ways of being and doing, and submit to those, which is often experienced as a form of symbolic violence (Burke, 2017). Thus, power inequalities are sustained through the recognition (and misrecognition) of who is seen as a 'worthy', 'capable', and 'successful' student in higher education, and profoundly shapes inclusion, exclusion, and the terms of participation available in any educational context. However, this major site of the reproduction of inequality in higher education is hidden through monodimensional methods that distort not only research findings but also the policy and practice that is informed by those findings. Misrecognition is an important concept for understanding, for example, the ways that candidates from underrepresented backgrounds in higher education might not be recognised as 'worthy' applicants due to the institutionalised cultural value patterns in different universities, disciplines, subjects, and/or courses (Karabel, 2006).

Close consideration of the often-fraught relationship between redistributive, recognitive, and representative justice in equity policy and practice (Burke, 2012) brings attention to challenges and complexities that otherwise are unnoticed and neglected. Redistribution is essential to ensure that equity resources are not being maldistributed to those who already have access to those resources, with the unintended consequence of further deepening forms of social and economic privilege. Redistributive equity requires ensuring that students from underrepresented backgrounds have equal access to a range of material resources, including funds to cover all costs of study, for example, the necessary technologies, books, childcare, safe and secure housing, and nutritious food. Redistribution also requires access to high-quality education, information, guidance, and advice. This demands methodological rigour in developing ethical depth to ensure that equity funding and other forms of material support are redistributed to those who otherwise would not have access to those resources and that institutions are fully accountable for those processes of redistribution. This is always a complex process and requires more than formulaic or even the oft sought-after 'scalable' approaches. Methods for redistribution must be robust enough to address concerns with recognition and must have the capacity to be responsive to context and formations of difference.

Holding together the dimensions of distribution and recognition with representation requires ethically driven policy considerations of the design of methods used to determine how to target equity resources. This includes consideration of how policy categorisations (such as low socioeconomic status) might on the one hand aid processes of redistribution but on the other deepen forms of misrecognition through the deficit and pathologising constructions of those associated with those categorisations. Representation "furnishes the stage on which struggles over distribution and recognition are played out" (Fraser, 2009: 17). A focus on the political dimension of representation enables critical attention to the (mostly implicit) criteria around who is seen to belong and matter in higher education and on what terms, broadening debates about inclusion by considering who can make claims for distributive and recognitive justice. Bringing attention to these relational dynamics illuminates why monodimensional frameworks are utterly ineffective in eradicating inequalities, despite decades of efforts to build equity in higher education. In Chapter 8, we explore some examples that we argue exemplify the approaches for which we are advocating.

Thus, as part of a methodological rigour reframed by social justice imperatives, attention must be paid to the challenge that without attention to recognition, processes of redistribution can often intensify inequalities within cultural, discursive, and political dimensions. This does not suggest that redistribution should be abandoned; a large body of international research reinforces the imperative of ensuring access to material and educational resources through equity frameworks. Furthermore, macroeconomic questions about the funding of higher education, and its impact on reproducing complex inequities when driven by neoliberal market imperatives, remain paramount. However, Fraser's multidimensional theory uncovers the complex and important work of developing methodologies for the redistribution of funding and resources that are appropriately nuanced to address the interrelated dimensions of recognition and representation. As we have pointed out earlier, this is important because redistribution often produces misrecognition in ways that generate personal sensibilities of unworthiness or not belonging, and misrepresentation in which exclusion from participation occurs despite admission to university study. Those personal experiences are related to symbolic inequalities as located in histories over who is perceived as 'deserving' or having the right to higher education, tied to constructions and judgements of talent, potential, merit, capacity, and capability that appear to be objective and value-free but are in fact shaped by privileged values, assumptions, and perspectives (Karabel, 2006; Burke and McManus, 2009; Ingram and Allen, 2019).

An example of this is the aim to redistribute widening participation resources to low socioeconomic groups. This poses a conundrum for holding together the social justice dimensions of redistribution and recognition. It is crucial to develop a method to appropriately and ethically distribute widening participation resources that have been specifically made available by the state or institution to alleviate socioeconomic inequalities. In doing so, however, policy categorisations are formed that potentially reinforce cultural inequalities of institutional value and of status subordination. The naming of an individual as low socioeconomic status itself is arguably a form of misrecognition, reducing personhood to a stigmatising policy categorisation. This poses challenges too for equity policies of affirmative action. A person who receives an equity scholarship (a form of redistribution) might simultaneously be seen as actually 'undeserving' of participation in higher education due to problematic meritocratic assumptions. Furthermore, even when there are attempts to level the playing field through equity strategies, the assessment of what counts as potential, talent, and ability often perpetuates the social injustice of misrecognition.

A case of misrecognition

A potent example of misrecognition emerges from the research project *Art for a Few* which examined admission practices in the UK field of art and design (Burke and McManus, 2009). The research involved observations of 80 live selection interviews across five UK higher education institutions. The case of Nina (pseudonym), a young black woman from an inner-city area applying for a BA Fashion course, reveals that selection interviews in the admissions process operate as a profound space of misrecognition, where knowing how to perform potential is connected to the embodiment and enactment of 'appropriate' forms of personhood in the context of the field of practice. Nina was asked the standard interview question of what influenced her artwork and her interview was cut short after she responded 'hip-hop'. She was also denied the opportunity to complete her admissions test. The observation of the post-interview process involved a discussion of Nina's perceived inappropriate influences, her immaturity because she wanted to remain living at home, and her supposed lack of 'fashion flair'. Nina's rejection was formally noted as due to her 'weak' portfolio, although her portfolio had been ranked as good/average in the pre-interview assessment process. The selection interview immediately after Nina's involved a male, white, middle-class candidate.

He cited famous contemporary artists as his influences, was dressed in expensive, designer clothing, and claimed he would 'definitely be leaving home as it's all part of the university experience'. Despite having significantly poorer qualifications than Nina, including having failed secondary school art, he was offered a place.

The case study illuminates how power works within social, cultural, and institutional contexts to undermine a sense of legitimate personhood, value and mattering. It is important to identify the interconnection of misrecognition to maldistribution, as the embodied person is judged in the interview situation not only in terms of discursive recitations but also in terms of the kind (and quality) of clothing worn by the applicant. This reveals more subtle processes of inequality that are generated at the material, subjective, experiential, and emotional levels and yet are not explicitly articulated and/or observable in any straightforward, measurable, or quantifiable way. This illustrates the urgent need for methodologies that help bring hidden, intersecting, and multidimensional inequalities to the surface to build more nuanced and sophisticated equity frameworks. Fraser's work offers powerful tools of analysis to develop more carefully conceived and nuanced strategies that address "mutually irreducible dimensions of justice" (Fraser and Honneth, 2003: 4). In the example of *Art for a Few*, this enabled an analysis that illuminated how the location of the admission tutors in entrenched communities of practice, with shared sets of taken-for-granted assumptions about talent and potential, led to the misrecognition of candidates such as Nina. The interrelationship of the material and subjective embodiment of the judgements cast on applicants brings to light how multidimensional injustices play out often without the apprehension of those engaged in exclusive practices.

However, a focus on praxis helps to ensure that these points are not only abstract, conceptual considerations. Rather, extensive engagement with those situated within the field of practice of equity is as important as the process of analysing the data. With a commitment to praxis, we held workshops about the insights emerging from the research with art and design educators across the country to encourage those in positions of exercising institutional assessment of applicants to reflect on how these insights might transform their practice. However, we encouraged colleagues to engage with the research beyond our dissemination workshops, strengthening communities of practice by transforming these into communities of praxis.

This led one programme team, responsible for one of the most selective fine arts programmes in England, to dig deep into their assumptions and taken-for-granted practices. Engaging with the research, they looked closely at their admissions, pedagogical and assessment practices, and a newly emerged perspective that deeply concerned them. They realised they had no representation from the immediate schools, colleges, and communities in their local area and the student profile was homogenous – mainly White, middle-class students from across more affluent areas in England. The programme team started to work closely with the Widening Participation Unit, local schools and colleges, and developed regular programme team meetings to collectively reform the ways they thought about what counted as potential, talent, and capability. Working with the analysis provided by *Art for a Few*, they interrogated their values, perspectives, and assessment practices – in addition to analysing quantitative patterns. Through this, they developed an inclusive capacity to accommodate diverse artistic expressions that better represented the University's underrepresented local communities.

Sustaining this commitment to the transformation of the programme over time, their student profile has dramatically shifted to a highly diverse student constituency with strong representation from the institution's immediate local communities. The curriculum developed organically as new artistic expressions emerging from their now diverse student communities were recognised, valued, and represented. The programme team effectively developed what we call a *community of praxis* in which they exercised ethical reflexivity through social justice perspectives bringing new forms of practice to play and thus transforming the programme. We unpack this idea of communities of praxis in greater detail in Chapter 7.

A multidimensional framework for equity enables a shift away from deficit imaginaries and remedial practices. Returning to our critique of how Bourdieu's use of the concept of 'capital' is often misunderstood and/or superficially applied, the problematic use of cultural and/or social capital misframes the problem as simply the need for remediating the (assumed) lack of it. This monodimensional approach fails to grapple with the arbitrary nature of the institutionalised legitimation of forms of culture that ensure the ongoing marginalisation of the cultures of historically excluded groups (including, e.g., Aboriginal and Torres Strait Islander cultures in the Australian context). A multidimensional perspective understands that redistribution, recognition, and representation are always interrelated. This requires rigorous research attention to whose cultures, identities, and histories are given status, value, and legitimacy in higher education. By generating knowledge that addresses these complex questions, strategies to create equitable and inclusive policies and practices in higher education become possible. However, engaging further with Fraser's critique of monodimensional framings of social justice might help shed light on the problematic relationship between neoliberalism and equity in higher education.

The entanglement of neoliberalism and equity

Drawing on Fraser's critique of the relationship of second-wave feminism to neoliberalism (2013: 209–226), we turn now to consider how equity policy and practice have developed alongside, and in worryingly close concert with, neoliberal agendas for globalised, corporatised higher education. We begin by introducing Fraser's analysis of how the multiple dimensions of injustice that second-wave feminism helped to foreground (socioeconomic, cultural, and political) became separated from one another and from a sustained critique of capitalism, and how this separation arguably dove-tailed neatly with the rise of neoliberalism as the rationality of contemporary capitalism. We then build from Fraser's critique by taking a closer look at how 'neoliberalism', and 'neoliberalisation' more precisely, is an ongoing and highly adaptive or 'flexible' process of state and global transformations that produces advanced social governance arrangements as new forms of power over and through human populations, always of course impacting the more-than-human relationalities of which society inevitably is part. As we have argued previously (Burke, 2012), equity and widening participation agendas and governance infrastructures in different nation-state contexts are produced at scale through discourses of individualisation, choice, mobility, aspiration, and entrepreneurship, demonstrating a close alignment with, if not co-production of, neoliberal commitments to competition and 'enterprise'. We close the chapter by returning to our call for multidimensional conceptions of social justice, *as transformative equity*, in higher education, and we make the case for sustained forms of generative critique.

Fraser's critique of second-wave feminism stems from the idea that this movement was responding to 'state-organised capitalism' when this form had already been replaced by neoliberalism.

> In a fine instance of the cunning of history, utopian desires found a second life as feeling currents that legitimated the transition to a new form of capitalism: post-Fordist, transnational, neoliberal.
>
> *(Fraser, 2013: 211)*

By 'state-organised capitalism', Fraser refers to socioeconomic contexts such as the postcolonial developmental states and OECD welfare states in the post–World War era. In these contexts, second-wave feminism erupted in the 1970s and Fraser points to four key aspects that define the political character of 'state-organised capitalism' that second-wave feminism moved against. These characteristics are: *Economism* (public political power regulating economic markets); *Androcentrism* (an imagined ideal citizen/worker who was a male breadwinner); *Etatism* (a reliance on professional experts to design policies and bureaucracies to implement them); and *Westphalianism* (linked to the Bretton Woods framework for regulation wedded to political spaces bounded largely by territorial nations). Fraser's critique of second-wave feminism was not that an existing liberalism with an overly economistic set of critiques did not need correction, but that 'the cultural turn' was taken, by some, too firmly into the arena of identity politics. Fraser is also careful to note that in challenging an overly economist construction of justice, many second-wave feminists did not ignore the importance of distributive justice and the power of political economy critique to the idea of women's emancipation. Instead, Fraser's critique claims:

> The cultural changes jump-started by the second wave, salutary in themselves, have served to legitimate a structural transformation of capitalist society that runs directly counter to feminist visions of a just society.
>
> *(Fraser, 2013: 211)*

Fraser asks whether a richer paradigm (balancing recognition and redistribution) might have been achievable, reasoning that much was lost through a 'dangerous liaison' with neoliberal commitments. As we have noted earlier in this chapter, Fraser uses 'participatory parity' to identify a political framework through which we can establish claims for recognition and redistribution. In Fraser's conception, this "enables a non-identitarian feminist politics that can adjudicate conflicts between claims centered on gender and those focused on other, cross-cutting axes of subordination" (Fraser, 2013: 166). Ultimately, Fraser seeks to elaborate how neoliberalism incorporated and reworked second-wave feminist critique, particularly the problem of the family wage, to promise a form of emancipation via waged labour, in the service of capital.

> The movement's most advanced currents saw their struggles as multidimensional, aimed simultaneously against economic exploitation, status hierarchy, and political subjection. To them, moreover, feminism appeared as part of a broader emancipatory project, in which struggles against gender injustices were necessarily linked to struggles against racism, imperialism, homophobia, and class domination, all of which required transformation of the deep structures of capitalist society.
>
> *(Fraser, 2013: 217)*

It is an unsettling notion that second-wave feminism might have provided ingredients to support the rise of neoliberalism. Fraser introduces this possibility by drawing on Boltanski and Chiapello (2005) who, in naming a *New Spirit of Capitalism*, sought to identify the "ideology that justifies people's commitment to capitalism, and which renders this commitment attractive" (2005: 162). Fraser draws on this work to argue that aspects of second-wave feminism provided something of a 'new spirit of neoliberalism' through, for example, discourses of emancipation and empowerment; forms which then positioned many women's lives directly into the service of restless capital.

Whilst acknowledging and drawing on Fraser's critique, we want also to hold open a space for ongoing criticality (of) ourselves in developing our ongoing analyses in the contexts of equity and higher education. It is important to hold ourselves response-able for exercising uncertainty in relation to 'counter-hegemonies'. Here, we want to consider whether neoliberalism dovetailed attractively with aspects of second-wave feminism because that is exactly what, as a form of contemporary power, neoliberal governance has emerged to do exceptionally well; to create the conditions for globalised state-sanctioned ongoing processes of restricting how *freedom* can be understood and/or practiced. We will return to these questions further below but wanted first to offer a moment of summary to help understand how we might take up Fraser's important critique regarding two very different challenges to traditional authority (feminism and neoliberalism) that have arguably converged and interacted in complex ways in recent decades.

> What should we conclude from my story? Certainly not that second-wave feminism has failed *simpliciter*. Nor that it is to blame for the triumph of neoliberalism. Surely not that feminist ideals are inherently problematic; nor that they are always already doomed to be resignified for capitalist purposes. I conclude, rather, that we for whom feminism is above all a movement for gender justice need to become more historically self-aware as we operate on a terrain that is also populated by our uncanny double.
>
> *(Fraser, 2013: 224)*

Before we turn to analyse how Fraser's critique offers an analysis of the ways in which equity and widening participation in higher education have proliferated across the globe, we want to briefly elaborate on an articulation of neoliberalism.

Articulating neoliberalism and neoliberalisation

Neoliberal ideas have "established themselves as the main answer to the crisis of Keynesian welfare state and lasting stagflation" (Giannone, 2016: 497). The term 'neoliberalism' has come to be used in many ways in the social sciences to describe variously: an ideological hegemonic project, a form of governmentality, policies and programmes, and a state form (Ward and England, 2007). In relation to higher education, many have identified how an ongoing neoliberalisation has produced effects in recent decades such as an ongoing intensification of strongly valuing individualisation, choice, market security, and minimal government (Slaughter and Leslie, 1997). In conceptualising neoliberalism as an ongoing process, we can bring together different ways the term has been used (and arguably abused) to identify both its adaptive globalising homogenising capacity and the context-specific impacts it has had, and continues to have, as a contemporary rationality of capitalism, deeply effective in truth-making through market and economic calculus (e.g. Foucault, 1990). Foucault in his later work progressed his focus from power/

knowledge towards governmentality and biopolitics, shifting his 'productive' conceptualisation of power to consider the subject and subjectivation in new ways. For our purposes here, it is enough to say that Foucault was interested to track and understand through his archaeological and genealogical methods the way in which capitalism and liberalism endured related and unrelated crises. In relation to liberalism, he tracked its development as an enduring form of political rationality from the classical liberalism of the eighteenth century, through to the social welfarism and economic Keynesianism of the post-war period, and towards the neoliberalism of the last four decades. His project involved trying to understand what it was to be a neoliberal subject, an entrepreneurial self, and helps us to understand how people would become measured and valued in terms of their effect on 'the market' as a new way of structuring freedom.

Neoliberalism is not necessarily just another form of liberalism, however. And whilst often associated with 'free markets' and 'free trade', it is also no retreat of the state towards laissez-faire conditions unencumbered by economic intervention by state authority. We would agree with those who point to the ways it is instead a form of highly sophisticated intervention that works to frame all human activity within a financial system (Olssen and Peters, 2005). Fraser (2009) uses the term 'neoliberalism' to "designate an ideological complex that presents the financialised capitalist regime as natural, just, efficient, and prosperity generating, destined to secure the greatest happiness of the greatest number" (Fraser, 2015: 175). It is this enduring presence of the process of neoliberalisation that signifies an increasingly globalised victory of market rationality now inscribed in state's laws across the planet as a regulatory function. This victory has successfully embedded a particular set of rules of law using market logics to exert something of a distributed, de-centred, and permanent vigilance; a process that continues to refunction states to facilitate new forms of social power, in the interest of capital. Foucault (1978/2001) helped to show how the steady embedding of rules of (primarily economic) law formalised actions in which the only real agents must now be individuals or enterprises. In this way, markets have ceased to be sites of jurisdiction but instead sites where 'truth' is produced as part of the art of government, to verify or falsify governmental practices. In Chapter 6, we will extend this argument to show how contemporary *governmentality* exercises complex forms of power that have the population as its target, political economy as its major form of knowledge, and an emphasis on security as its essential technical instrument (Burchell, Gordon and Miller, 1991). With 'the market' now serving as the mechanism by which 'correct' policy measures are to be differentiated from the 'incorrect' ones, objects or subjects of principle that emerge from anywhere except the internal logic of the market have no meaning. They are simply 'outside the true'. In these conditions, what is now endlessly naturalised is a process of dispensing rewards that offer the promise of a rhetorical freedom but within conditions in which a supremely seductive sleight of hand has fundamentally reformulated the limits of legitimate practice and relation.

While 'classical' and 'neo' liberal discourse have clear similarities, it is important also to work with and through their distinct differences. We do so now to help identify ways in which neoliberal commitments have shaped the rise of equity and widening participation agendas in recent decades.

> Whereas classical liberalism represents a negative conception of state power in that the individual was taken as an object to be freed from the interventions of the state, neoliberalism has come to represent a positive conception of the state's role in creating the appropriate market by providing the conditions, laws and institutions necessary for its operation.
>
> *(Olssen and Peters, 2005: 315)*

Neoliberalisation tends to reformulate policymaking in higher education towards a dominant imaginary (Lumb and Bunn, 2021) in which an idealised competitive and enterprising archetype individual is reified. This is a distinct shift from classical liberalism which saw imagined individuals characterised by autonomous human agency practising forms of freedom.

From neoliberalised equity to transformative equity praxis

Formal equity agendas and nation-state infrastructures designed to deliver 'widening participation' have developed in multiple contexts across the globe in recent decades. This has coincided with the most recent phases of the victory of neoliberalism as the rationality of globalised contemporary capitalism. As Gyamera and Burke (2018) have written, "Neoliberalism has been extensively critiqued by scholars of higher education for the ways it is steeped in economic imperatives, silencing complex inequalities and power relations (e.g. Rose, 1999; Bauman, 2005)" (Gyamera and Burke, 2018: 450). We draw here on Fraser's critique of second-wave feminism to analyse the character and growth of equity and widening participation projects in different contexts. Certainly, the rhetoric accompanying mostly national equity policy projects maintains close kinship to the sort of advanced neoliberal governance which holds the market as inviolable that celebrates individual entrepreneurialism and the importance of autonomous private enterprise. A question, therefore, we want to consider across this book is whether and how (monodimensional) equity conceptualisations within higher education projects tend towards aligning with and/or reproducing and accelerating a spirit of neoliberalism, and whether and how (multidimensional) equity conceptualisations within higher education projects might resist, disrupt, and even counter this dynamic.

We have argued in earlier accounts that 'widening participation' emerged in the UK in the late 1990s as a neoliberalisation of earlier social movements that had struggled for access to a transformed higher education system foregrounding critical perspectives emerging from communities historically marginalised from knowledge-production (Burke, 2001). This was sometimes referred to as the 'Access Movement' (see Chapter 1), characterised by a strong framing around redistributive and recognitive justice. However, struggles for access (often led by feminist-activism) coincided with the rise of neoliberalism, in which access as social transformation became overshadowed by an increasingly economic-oriented policy-scape. Education was now seen as the "best economic policy we have" (former Prime Minister Tony Blair quoted in Ecclestone, 1999 and cited in Burke, 2001: 45).

We can turn to some of the hegemonic discourses that are regularly re-cited in the formation of equity and widening participation policy and practice over the past two and a half decades. As the marketisation of higher education has taken hold through the rise of neoliberalism, equity has become detached from analysis of, and efforts to redress, social inequalities. Instead, equity is absorbed by concerns with aspiration-raising as the primary strategy for designing and implementing equity interventions aiming to recruit disadvantaged young people (mature students are usually not the subject of neoliberal equity policy) into higher education. This market-oriented approach is rooted in economic-imperatives and budget-balancing pressures, as public funding of higher education has been eroded and largely replaced with student loan arrangements that are based on the promise of graduate employability. Thus, aspirations recognised in the hegemonic order are those that progress neoliberal imperatives to expand human capital and ensure citizens are 'job-ready'. The welfare-to-work agenda has increasingly animated equity policy as neoliberalism has reshaped the timescapes of higher education towards markets, business, industry, and commercialisation. The pursuit of higher education as a space to engage with bodies of knowledge has been increasingly replaced with a skill-based agenda for employability. This is now so explicit and widely accepted as to be legislated in the Australian higher education system. The Job-Ready Graduate Package emphasises that demand for higher education is driven by the aspiration of individuals to develop "job-relevant skills to help them to re-enter the workforce" (Department of Education, Skills and Employment, 2020: 5). The legislation is designed to "make it cheaper for students to study in areas of expected job growth" with "additional opportunities to reskill and upskill" and provides "additional funding for partnerships between universities and business that improve workforce participation and productivity". The social justice imperatives of parity of participation in all aspects of social life, including mobilising higher education to address the multidimensional, multi-scale socio-ecological crises facing our more-than-human communities across the globe, are eclipsed by the neoliberal hegemony that education is an economic policy that improves market competitiveness. This ignores that these global development patterns framed by neoliberalism contribute to deepening already existing gross inequalities and threaten the existence of humanity (WCCES, 2024). Instead, a relentless focus on neoliberal imperatives for market-based, individualised success is at the heart of higher education reform. The forms of freedom that higher education might offer then are reduced to be/com/ing a successful subject of the market through private investment in higher education, particularly by investing in re-skilling and up-skilling in subjects deemed to be of value by the market economy. This de-politicises the privileging of epistemologies associated with natural sciences, technologies, engineering, and mathematics and conceals the power dynamics by which social science, humanities and arts faculties (and knowledges) are marginalised. That this reinstates the exclusion of Indigenous, Black, Southern theories, most especially those associated with feminist orientations, is not considered. In these ways, equity has been fully expropriated by the neoliberal imaginary, and critical theories, research and methodologies outside the hegemonic order are either re-crafted to align with the neoliberal imaginary or rendered obsolete. There are numerous examples of how critical concepts have been misframed by neoliberalised versions of equity, but one particularly salient example is the way 'intersectionality', first coined by Kim Crenshaw (1989), has been mobilised for neoliberal agendas.

As a critical conceptual framing, 'intersectionality' has been developed over decades of feminist theorisation to bring to light the ways difference is systematically organised and produced through social relations, entrenched in political and economic structures, policies, and practices (Mirza, 2015). Intersectional theory enables analysis of how a person is situated in, and affected by, the institutional power relations that reproduce inequalities at the micro level. It captures the ways in which racism, sexism, and classism are combined in specific historical junctures to create experiences of oppression and disadvantage that cannot be fully captured when systems of inequality are viewed as separate entities. By offering a critique of both monodimensional anti-sexist *and* anti-racist approaches, intersectionality calls for a consistently broadened framework that seeks to encompass all structures of injustice relevant to any given situation. One of the key insights of intersectionality is that oppressive systems (such as colonialism, patriarchy, and neoliberalism) should always be understood as connected and interrelated. In drawing attention to the connection between oppressive systems, intersectionality encourages us to take ever broader structural, historical, and global views of injustice and points to the systemic nature of inequities:

> Intersectionality's focus on the interconnectedness of categories of race, class, gender, sexuality, ethnicity, nationality, age, and ability sheds new light on how social inequities articulate with global social phenomena.
> *(Hill Collins, 2019: 22)*

However, while the critical theorisation of intersectionality focuses on structural inequalities, neoliberal misframings of intersectionality have been put to work in many institutional settings to merely replace a "single-axis analysis" (Crenshaw, 1989 cited in Nichols and Stahl, 2019: 1261) of disadvantage with a narrow, bidimensional focus at the individual level. This approach is quite antithetical to the core of intersectionality as a critical concept for praxis. This misframing of intersectional theory through "inadequate additive models" (Mirza, 2015) fails to address the "micro-institutional practices that feed into the systemic institutional structures that maintain endemic patterns of racist exclusion in higher education" (Mirza, 2018: 111).

Conclusion

In this chapter, we have articulated the harm of monodimensional, deficit misframings of equity, embedded in neoliberalised higher education systems. Neoliberalisation has eclipsed critical, feminist, decolonial, post/structural praxis, manipulating concepts developed for transformative social justice into utilitarian, individualised, economically oriented regimes of truth. Agendas for equity have become vacuous, reductive technologies for progressing the neoliberal order, whilst leaving in place insidious power relations rooted in histories of colonialism, imperialism, and patriarchy. This reproduces multidimensional injustices of maldistribution, misrecognition, and misrepresentation, furthers the exploitation of more-than-human resources, and ultimately leads to widening inequalities and planetary devastation. It is a tragedy that equity in higher education contributes to such processes. Sustainability itself is reduced to largely utilitarian orientations and is often driven by the rewards of being ranked more favourably than others in global prestige cultures. Prestige itself is not linked to ethical-political deliberations but to the promise of economic prosperity for individual institutions, people and careers. Power is not part of the grammar of neoliberal equity. That this state of play does not significantly progress equity is a gross understatement. Indeed, we argue that bizarrely the neoliberal equity agenda furthers injustice and the multidimensional, multi-scale crises that most immediately threaten the well-being and flourishing of those confronted by the intensification of injustice and inequality, so neatly covered up by the manipulative discourses of neoliberal equity.

However, our book is situated in the critical hope that through collective praxis, and by bringing to light the ongoing harms of hegemonic framings of equity, the movement towards social justice transformation becomes increasingly possible. Indeed, there are already many examples of social justice praxis collectives across the globe, and we understand the CEEHE to be one such example, from which we will draw in Chapter 8. It is our position that higher education has the capacity to play a substantial role in invigorating new frameworks, imaginaries, and ways of knowing for our collective wellbeing and flourishing. Our post-Freirean, feminist, decolonial stance to critical hope, situated as it is in a multidimensional reframing of equity, refrains from idealistic or overly romantic notions of social justice. Instead, we are hoping to generate time, space, and critical resources with others as a collaborative commitment to critically reflexive and sustained engagement across redistribution-recognition-representation with a sense of response-ability to more-than-human flourishing in, through, and beyond higher education. Such flourishing though must accept the partiality of what we can 'know' about what it is to 'flourish', recognising the ever-importance of contextual thinking and doing. Thus, we aim to reframe the purpose of higher education as sustaining knowledge-with and making-with through collective, dialogic processes of criticality, questioning, and reflexivity, embedded in orientations to humility, uncertainty, and solidarity across and with difference. We take these ideas up in Chapter 3, exploring in more detail an ensemble of conceptual tools for critical social justice praxis.

References

Archer, L., and Leathwood, C. (2003) 'Identities, Inequalities and Higher Education', in Archer, L., Hutchings, M., and Ross, A. (Eds) *Higher Education and Social Class: Issues of Exclusion and Inclusion.* London: Routledge Falmer, 171–191.

Bunn, M. (2021) 'Writing representations to life: Higher education and the production of equity realities', *Access: Critical Explorations of Equity in Higher Education*, 9(1), 10–21.

Boltanski, L., and Chiapello, E. (2005) 'The new spirit of capitalism', *International Journal of Politics, Culture, and Society*, 18(3–4), 161–188. www.jstor.org/stable/20059681

Bozalek, V., and Boughey, C. (2020) '(Mis)framing higher education in South Africa', in Bozalek, V., Holscher, D., and Zembylas, M. (Eds) *Nancy Fraser and Participatory Parity: Reframing Social Justice in South African Higher Education.* Abingdon: Taylor and Francis.

Bozalek, V., Holscher, D., and Zembylas, M. (2020) *Nancy Fraser and Participatory Parity: Reframing Social Justice in South African Higher Education.* Abingdon: Taylor and Francis.

Burchell, G., Gordon, C., and Miller, P. (1991) *The Foucault Effect: Studies in Governmentality.* Chicago: University of Chicago Press.

Burke, C. (2017) 'Graduate blues': Considering the effects of inverted symbolic violence on underemployed middle class graduates', *Sociology*, 51(2), 393–409. https://doi.org/10.1177/0038038515596908

Burke, P.J. (2001) *Access/ing Education: A Feminist Post/Structuralist Ethnography of Widening Educational Participation.* London: Institute of Education, University of London.

Burke, P.J. (2002) *Accessing Education: Effectively Widening Participation.* London: Trentham.

Burke, P.J. (2012) *The Right to Higher Education: Beyond Widening Participation.* London and New York: Routledge.

Burke, P.J. (2020) 'Contradiction and collaboration in equity and widening participation: In conversation with Geoff Whitty', in Brown, A., and Wisby, E. (Eds)

Knowledge, Policy and Practice in Education: The Struggle for Social Justice. London: University College London Press.

Burke, P.J., Bunn, M., Lumb, M., Parker, J., Mellor, K., Brown, A., Locke, W., Shaw, J., Webb, S., and Howley, P. (2023) *International Literature Review of Equity in Higher Education: Dismantling Deficit in Equity Structures by Drawing on a Multi-dimensional Framework*. A research report prepared for the Australian Government Department of Education Skills and Employment National Priority Pool Program. Newcastle, NSW, Australia: University of Newcastle.

Burke, P.J., Crozier, G., and Misiaszek, L.I. (2017) *Changing Pedagogical Spaces in Higher Education: Diversity, Inequalities and Misrecognition*. London: Routledge.

Burke, P.J., and McManus, J. (2009) *"Art for a Few": Exclusion and Misrecognition in Art and Design Higher Education Admissions*. A report for the National Arts Learning Network. London: NALN.

Butler, J. (1999) *Gender Trouble: Feminism and the Subversion of Identity*. London: Routledge.

Chan, A.S. (2005) 'Policy discourses and changing practice: Diversity and the university-college', *Higher Education*, 50(1), 129–157. www.jstor.org/stable/250 68092

Crenshaw, K.W. (1989) *Demarginalizing the Intersection of Race and Sex: A Black Feminist Critique of Antidiscrimination Doctrine, Feminist Theory and Antiracist Politics*. University of Chicago Legal Faculty. https://scholarship.law.columbia.edu/faculty_scholarship/3007

Department of Education, Skills and Employment (2020) *Standing Committee on Education and Employment Submission from the Department of Education, Skills and Employment to the Senate Standing Committee on Education and Employment*. www.education.gov.au/download/8098/job-ready-graduates-package-submission-standing-committee-education-and-employment/12236/document/pdf

Foucault, M. (1978/2001) 'Governmentality', in Faubion, J.D. (Ed) *Power: Essential Works of Foucault, 1954–1984*. London: Allen Lane.

Foucault, M. (1990) 'On power', in Sheridan, A. et al (Trans), Kritzman, L.D. (Ed) *Michel Foucault: Politics, Philosophy, Culture: Interviews and Other Writings 1977–1984*. New York: Routledge.

Fraser, N. (1997) *Justice Interruptus: Critical Reflections on the "Postsocialist" Condition*. London and New York: Routledge.

Fraser, N. (2009) *Scales of Justice: Reimagining Political Space in a Globalizing World*. New York: Cambridge University Press.

Fraser, N. (2013) *Fortunes of Feminism: From State-Managed Capitalism to Neoliberal Crisis*. New York: Verso Books.

Fraser, N. (2015) 'Legitimation crisis? On the political contradictions of financialized capitalism', *Critical Historical Studies*, 2(2), 157–189.

Fraser, N., and Honneth, A. (2003) *Redistribution or Recognition? A Political-Philosophical Exchange*. New York: Verso.

Giannone, D. (2016) 'Neoliberalization by evaluation: Explaining the making of neoliberal evaluative state', *Open Journal of Socio-Political Studies*, 9(2), 495–516. https://doi.org/10.1285/i20356609v9i2p495

Gyamera, G.O., and Burke, P.J. (2018) 'Neoliberalism and curriculum in higher education: A post-colonial analyses', *Teaching in Higher Education*, 23(4), 450–467. https://doi.org/10.1080/13562517.2017.1414782

Hill Collins, P. (2019) *Intersectionality as Critical Social Theory*. Durham, NC: Duke University Press.

Ingram, N., and Allen, K. (2019) ' "Talent-spotting" or "social magic"? Inequality, cultural sorting and constructions of the ideal graduate in elite professions', *The Sociological Review*, 67(3), 723–740. https://doi.org/10.1177/003802611 8790949

Karabel, J. (2006) *The Chosen: The Hidden History of Admission and Exclusion at Harvard, Yale and Princeton.* Boston and New York: Mariner Books.

Lumb, M., and Bunn, M. (2021) 'Dominant higher education imaginaries: Forced perspectives, ontological limits and recognising the imaginer's frame', in Brooks, R., and O'Shea, S. (Eds) *Reimagining the Higher Education Student.* London: Routledge.

Lumb, M., and Burke, P.J. (2019) 'Re/cognising the discursive fr/Ames of equity and widening participation in higher education', *International Studies in Sociology of Education*, 28(3–4), 215–236. https://doi.org/10.1080/09620214.2019.1619470

McNay, L. (2008) 'The trouble with recognition: Subjectivity, suffering, and agency', *Sociological Theory*, 26, 271–296. https://doi.org/10.1111/j.1467-9558.2008.00329.x

Medina, J. (2012) *The Epistemology of Resistance: Gender and Racial Oppression, Epistemic Injustice, and the Social Imagination.* Oxford, UK: Oxford University Press.

Mirza, H.S. (2015) 'Decolonizing higher education: Black feminism and the intersectionality of race and gender', *Journal of Feminist Scholarship*, 7(8), 1–12.

Mirza, H.S. (2018) 'Respecting difference: Researching the intersectionality of gender, race, faith and culture in higher education', in Burke, P.J., Hayton, A., and Stevenson, J. (Eds) *Evaluating Equity and Widening Participation in Higher Education.* London: UCL IOE Press.

Molla, T., and Gale, T. (2015) 'Inequality in Ethiopian higher education: Reframing the problem as capability deprivation', *Discourse-Studies in the Cultural Politics of Education*, 36(3), 383–397. https://doi.org/10.1080/01596306.2013.871447

Moreau, M.-P., and Robertson, M. (2019) '"You scratch my back and I'll scratch yours"? Support to academics who are carers in higher education', *Social Sciences*, 8(6), 164. https://doi.org/10.3390/socsci8060164

Msigwa, F. (2016) 'Widening participation in higher education: A social justice analysis of student loans in Tanzania', *Higher Education*, 72(4), 541–556. https://doi.org/10.1007/s10734-016-0037-5

Nichols, S., and Stahl, G. (2019) 'Intersectionality in higher education research: A systematic literature review', *Higher Education Research and Development*, 38(6), 1255–1268. https://doi.org/10.1080/07294360.2019.1638348

Olssen, M., and Peters, M.A. (2005) 'Neoliberalism, higher education and the knowledge economy: From the free market to knowledge capitalism', *Journal of Education Policy*, 20(3), 313–345. https://doi.org/10.1080/02680930500108718

Oyarzún, J.D.D., Perales Franco, C., and McCowan, T. (2017) 'Indigenous higher education in Mexico and Brazil: Between redistribution and recognition', *Compare – a Journal of Comparative and International Education*, 47(6), 852–871.

Slaughter, S., and Leslie, L.L. (1997) *Academic Capitalism: Politics, Policies and the Entrepreneurial University.* Baltimore: John Hopkins University Press.

Ward, K., and England, K. (2007) 'Introduction: Reading neoliberalization', in England, K., and Ward, K. (Eds) *Neoliberalization: States, Networks, Peoples.* Oxford: Blackwell Publishing. https://doi.org/10.1002/9780470712801.ch1

WCCES (World Congress of Comparative Education Societies) (2024) *Conference Theme: Fostering Inclusive Ecologies of Knowledge: Education for Equitable and Sustainable Futures.* www.wcces2024congress.org/congress-theme

Webb, S., Burke, P.J., Nichols, S., Roberts, S., Stahl, G., Threadgold, S., and Wilkinson, J. (2017) 'Thinking with and beyond Bourdieu in widening higher education participation', *Studies in Continuing Education*, 39(2), 138–160.

3
CONCEPTUAL TOOLS FOR CRITICAL SOCIAL JUSTICE PRAXIS

Introduction

This chapter returns to the call for critical, decolonial, feminist, post/structural, and sociological commitments from Chapter 1, to explore in more detail an ensemble of conceptual tools for critical social justice praxis. We offer this not as a ready-made solution-producing apparatus, and we resist a move to total explanations that bound thinking or solidify commitments around a new common sense. Our aim is not to provide the final word on social justice and higher education; a challenge we see as requiring endless attention, vigilance, and judicious advocacy. Our aim here instead is to offer tools that help to embolden those involved in higher education equity and social justice contexts to inhabit a confidently uncomfortable orientation to the education contexts in which we are all entangled. We assert the importance of this discomfort as an ethical responsibility when it comes to navigating the fraught and political territories of equity, social justice, and higher education. The conceptual ensemble introduced in this chapter will be familiar to some readers and unrecognisable to others, given our different histories and concerns. Indeed, given the space this text affords, we are able only to begin to introduce in a satisfactory manner the terms and concepts that might be new to some readers. In this way, the chapter is an entrée of sorts, a beginning point for continued pursuit in your own contexts of research, practice, and policymaking; and the bringing together of conceptual ensembles of your own.

We strongly assert the importance of attempts to make more explicit the conceptualisations underlying terminological technologies we all deploy daily – mostly implicitly – undergirding as they often do the most insidious aspects of entrenched inequality in our institutions. We see this as one way of

DOI: 10.4324/9781003257165-5

approaching the transformation of long-embedded inequitable structures and arrangements; a way that at least acknowledges the enormously complex set of power relations that circulate around processes, possibilities, and aspirations for *the making of difference*. We see this as an endless set of opportunities to approach ideas of 'progress' and change without easily supporting simplistic, linear, and/or reductive positions, instead challenging all those involved in equity in higher education to lean towards a permanent critical praxis of generative and ethical reflection/action.

The first section of this chapter articulates the role that we see explicit conceptualisation playing in relation to critical equity praxis. That section takes up an ongoing advocacy for rejecting atheoretical and/or uncritical approaches in equity and widening participation. It reinforces a case for destabilising norms to generate contexts for debate, contestation, and assertively tentative claims; to support the creation of diverse spaces in which agitation can survive; where an atmosphere of possibility is held, and whereby unstable orientations emerge that can take account of "the reciprocal recognition of our common vulnerability and finitude" (Mbembe, 2019: 3). The second section of this chapter offers a conversational history of why *this* conceptual ensemble is offered for the reader to interpret towards their own contexts. It is not common to know why certain conceptual or theoretical frameworks are adopted by authors or researchers. Again, as part of being explicit about projects of equity, we are attempting here to 'dig into' our own commitments as a reflexive process that can help the reader to make sense of this text and the different possibilities they might make from it. Moving on from this conversational form, in the final section of the chapter, we move to specifically unpack (albeit again only partially and framed as an invitation to the reader) the many terms adopted throughout the text, to make clearer the conceptualisations we are attempting to conduct through their use, all of which have important and diverse histories.

Conceiving concepts

The decision to devote this space to a focus on concepts is because we feel is important to articulate the role we see explicit conceptualisation playing in relation to critical equity praxis in higher education. We are leaning here into connotations that allow us to conceive of *concepts* and their role in social justice praxis as '*conception*' – that is, as formulation, as invention, as creation, as beginnings – rather than any crude attempt at an explanatory apparatus that is static and totalising. In a critical, feminist, decolonial, post/structural, and sociological formation of social justice praxis, we want to acknowledge the risk of over-reification here (i.e. making the abstract overly concrete) because we see an essential pedagogical aspect of our approach in writing this book being the emergence of relations and connections beyond our own conceptions, a *burgeoning* (Lumb and Ndagijimana, 2021) that we can only hope to promote carries with it forms of the anti-misogynist, anti-racist, anti-colonial, anti-capitalist, and pro-queer feminist commitments we have sought to bring into the text.

Following Haraway (2016), we acknowledge the importance of reparative scholarship to better build alliances and connect to social movements, resistances, and radical moments. Indeed, Haraway's *tentacular thinking* is helpful as a provocation in this context; a manner of thinking and doing that we see helping to resist certain conceptualisations of 'delivery' for example, that are so common in contemporary higher education. We take up perspectives throughout this text that turn away from the *project deliverable*, the *delivery of teaching or curriculum*, on *delivering outcomes*, and of *efficient delivery of things*. We reject these as holding connotations of transactional consumer relations and move instead to tentacular conceptualisations in which 'delivery' can relate to the conceiving of, the invention of, the birthing of: new spaces, encounters, attentions, sayings, not saids, doings, and not dones (Haraway, 2016). In this chapter, we sketch out a conceptual ensemble that has helped produce the book, and that we offer with the intention of making explicit, yet, of course, invitingly open to interpretation *with* the reader, how our positions have formed in relation to the way the problem of equity is commonly understood. We offer the ensemble also in the hope of providing tools for the reader to take up in the analysis of, and action within, their own contexts of policy, practice, research, and/or evaluation in higher education. As we have already stated, we do not offer this framework as a set of stable guidelines or solutions. Indeed, this chapter actively troubles some of the foundations we establish, by acknowledging and engaging with critiques of prominent theorists and conceptualisations. This we see as one way to 'stay with the trouble' (Haraway, 2016) that a social justice notion of equity in higher education brings; one way of not falling into naïve hope or pessimistic despair; one way to acknowledge the entrenched systems of inequality at play, that can be so overwhelming, whilst building imperfect formations of resistance and renewal that hold the possibility of emergent alternatives.

This text, formed as it is in the context of our collaborative work in the CEEHE, is an expression of what Fraser (2020) has called "critical social theorising with practical intent" (2020: xiii). Certainly, the ways in which these concepts conceive will be evident in different ways across the other chapters of the book (e.g. in relation to time, and/or pedagogy, and/or evaluation). In our commitment to it being *Time for Social Justice Praxis*, we offer this conceptual ensemble because we believe it is important to "think what we do" (Arendt, 1958) if we are to claim any form of ethical or moral grounding in projects of justice, including acknowledging and paying attention (Back, 2007) through processes of reflexive practice that can also account for our own complicity in complex distributed power relations (Burke, 2012) and the heterogenous networks of discursive and non-discursive formations of which we and our work both consist and constitute. Acknowledging entrenched systematic inequality, complex webs of power relations, and collusive complicity does not tend however, at least in our view, towards an understanding that transformation is not possible. As this text foregrounds – by adopting forms of critical hope (Bozalek et al, 2014) and anti-colonial hope (Zembylas, 2022) – it is the apprehension and engagement of these dynamics as an ethical practice that presents the possibility of (imperfect) alternatives. We believe that there are alternatives to our deeply inequitable status quo, and we seek the reimagining of arbitrary arrangements through collective struggle. To echo Mbembe, this will involve however the struggle of thinking and doing together in a globalised set of contexts in which "we must grapple with what it means to live on a planet with other living beings – caring, repairing and sharing" via connections in which we "free ourselves together from 'one way' visions of history and emancipate ourselves from the colonial temptation" (Mbembe, 2023).

It is in the next section that, we, in a conversational form, offer glimpses into the historical formation of a conceptual ensemble. In doing so, we intend to explore how the broad orientations and commitments on display within this text have solidified and become coherent in and over time, in the form of Penny's solo and collaborative work (e.g. Burke, 2002, 2017; Burke and Jackson, 2007) and then in our work together and with others (e.g. Burke and Lumb, 2018; Lumb and Burke, 2019). These broad orientations and commitments form something of a *milieu*; a set of contexts or surrounding conditions from which the ensemble emerges.

The auto/biography of conceptual ensembles

Writing this book, we did a lot of walking and talking. Mostly we moved through the streets, beaches, and suburbs of Newcastle in NSW, but we also travelled in airports, campuses, cars, phone lines, and videoconference rooms. Next is given an exchange we recorded one day following a long walk in which we reflected on the significance of context in the shaping of relations to different conceptualisations and theoretical perspectives. We offer this exchange to share how we too, in writing a book driven by our particular commitments, continue ourselves to try and make sense of higher education as an idea, project, discourse, institution. We share this less conventional form here with a view to creating new (dis)connections with differently positioned readers and writers in relation to the contexts of research, practice, policymaking, and personhood they bring to the possible meanings generated through our exchange and through different readings and interpretations at play.

Penny: I think it would be helpful to talk explicitly about our approach to writing this book. Writing processes are usually hidden, especially in academic contexts. As a reader, you get the finished product and it ends up looking fairly clean and well put together and it sort of conceals all of the struggle and thinking and messiness of writing as a process of meaning-making. Readers generally don't have access to the iterative processes of moulding and reshaping material that finally becomes a more polished version in the form of a book. It's quite special to have the opportunity to think about that in the context of co-authorship, and to think about writing as part of the process of theorising, to making sense of what we do and the actions we take.

Matt: Yeah, early on for me, I was reading different sociologies of education in a confused state around this equity and widening participation practice and research that I'd stumbled into, and wanting in that reading to lean into that cleanness that you talk about, wanting to be reassured that everything had this trueness to it, this rightness, a legitimacy. I was looking for answers I suppose. I'm embarrassed to admit it these days because, with access to different sorts of contexts like CEEHE and engaging with your work and continuing to read and develop, I'm mostly looking for those kinds of underlying commitments now. But you're right, it's not discussed.

Penny: Yeah. That's an important set of questions epistemologically that are often absent from the debate about the way that knowledge is generated and produced through what we read, have access to and eventually how that shapes what and how we write. This includes the examination of the contestations around claims to knowledge that are grounded in universalism. Critical theory enables, and insists on, a grappling with the politics of knowledge and knowing. Readers are often discouraged to look at texts in that questioning, reflexive way.

Matt: Something you've introduced with our centre is the 'autobiography of the question'. I'm always struck by the way in which something different for me personally comes out each time that I earnestly engage with that activity. I'd just be interested to discuss what theory and methodology offer in terms of getting to those underlying sort of troubling politics that are often part of those insidious dynamics that you talk about. The autobiography of the question, can you say a few words about how that relates to I guess the conceptual ensemble we're developing in this chapter? What are some of the ideas and assumptions that are built into Jane Miller's work and that activity, would you say?

Penny: I think first, to acknowledge Jane Miller and her work in grappling with processes of teaching at the master's level and engaging people who have quite a range of experiences to draw from, but come into an academic context in which their experiences are often discounted from view. She was attempting to provide a framework that enabled students to not only speak to their experiences but also critically reflect on those experiences by bringing them into dialogue with the questions that they are interested in exploring and then layering that in terms of the different readings that they're encountering. Jane was inviting her students to discover a more personal relationship with academic texts – often not encouraged in postgraduate studies. Indeed, students are often guided to read in dry ways that exclude their position, context and values from the process of making meaning of the text. So to bring the autobiography of the question to play with broader debates is quite a challenging thing to be inviting students to do. Jane's thinking about this was pedagogically rich and inclusive, underpinned by feminist efforts to bring the personal and the political together in conversation.

What's exciting about feminist and critical epistemological contributions is the acknowledgement that we're always in processes of change, including in relation to knowledge and knowing. This recognises the fluidity of both knowledge and identity, and our inevitable relation to lifelong learning, in the broadest sense. The process of learning and making sense of things is always an ongoing one, whether or not we are enrolled in formal education. So the autobiography of the question enables us to recognise that every time we come to question, there are different discourses, contexts, experiences, and ideas we might bring to our thinking always in relation to wider questions and debates more capacious than our own.

As you say, you can work with similar questions again and again and find new things every time. Engaging with the autobiography of the question is a way of exercising critical reflexivity. It helps us to examine what values we are bringing and where these have emerged from. It helps to consider the theoretical perspectives we bring to the questions we ask even when we assume theory is outside of the questioning process. Relating theory to our own questions helps to situate them in the social and cultural contexts that have inevitably shaped our own location.

Matt: That idea of the challenging character of that practice is fascinating and it's certainly something that feels so related to this book. This idea of – it might be discomfort, but also the challenging character of, well, 'safe' pedagogical spaces. This idea of how it is we can challenge ourselves through those sorts of reflexive practices but also create contexts for conversations about, more transformative possibility around equity in higher education. Challenge and discomfort but also support is an interesting interplay.

Penny: Yeah, it makes me think about the different theoretical perspectives I've encountered over the years and how and why those have spoken to me. Patti Lather's work, for example, has been so influential in the questions I have asked about equity and widening participation research, policy and practice. It was Lather's 1991 publication, *Getting Smart*, that really grabbed my imagination when I was doing my PhD around 1998. It was her questioning of what we know that really struck me, that there was something connecting with my experiences that was already compelling me to challenge ideas of certainty related to positivist-driven epistemologies. Lather's work was exciting to challenge who can know, what we know, and who makes claims to truth and to knowledge.

This has such resonance for exploring the autobiography of the question of access, equity and widening participation in higher education. It provides the space to challenge the hegemonic bodies of work and the way we think about valid references that students and writers are expected to bring in. Shouldn't that be contested? Who asserts what valid references are and why are those deemed to be valid? We need to ask how are those bodies of knowledge connected to colonial histories, patriarchal histories around equity or the development of higher education even.

By raising questions about knowledge and knowing, we are suddenly open to questions about participation and who participates in knowledge formation and in what ways. This questioning broadens the scope of how we think about equity.

Matt: It's fascinating to think about the history of the present in terms of your work and this book and the serendipity around these things. You talk about the way in which Patti Lather's work spoke to you and has become something you've drawn upon. Me finding your text *The Right to Higher Education* in our university library felt quite serendipitous. I was in quite a confused moment as a practitioner and student researcher. It really spoke to me because it was reassuring me by saying that doubt is there for a reason. In terms of sensing why certainty is a problem, for example, in the context of evaluation, which was where I was at the time. It's interesting thinking about knowledge and the way society draws on knowledge-producing institutions like universities. There seems to be so much serendipity around the social sciences that is not often discussable.

Penny: I totally agree. I think it is serendipity that brings us into contact with particular theories at particular moments, but there's also some form of draw – a sense that you're drawn towards particular ways of thinking. I was drawn towards critical and feminist theories because of my and other's experiences of social injustice, and feeling passionate to do something about that injustice. Education seemed central to this. So particular approaches within sociology deeply resonated with me whilst others felt really alienating. So that set up a kind of intuitive sense of what it was I really wanted to explore and how. When I started off on my higher education journey, I had no idea and I felt out of my depth, but I did have access to an incredible sociology teacher through my Access to Higher Education programme. Everybody was afraid of her. She was quite fierce. But I thought she was amazing in her fierceness because I could recognise the passion that she had for social transformation. Her influence provided a strong foundation. She was the reason that I ended up then deciding that I wanted to study sociology at university.

But it was only serendipity again that I happened to have access to a couple of inspiring sociology lecturers who opened up bodies of critical theory to me that I would spend loads of time in the library with, particularly Black feminist theory. Black feminist theory resonated because I felt deeply incensed about racial injustices but wanted to understand how these worked with gender. Part of the questioning, or perhaps the permission to question, came from those theorists and thinkers, such as Angela Davis and bell hooks, who were pushing back, and showing how resistances, refusals, and contestations are possible through praxis. Then again, serendipity is so interesting, that somebody who was a former mentor to me suggested that I do a master's in women's studies and education at the Institute of Education at the University of London. There I was introduced to the breadth and depth of feminist theories, and the many contestations within it, and I also had direct access to some influential and inspiring feminist sociologists of education; Debbie Epstein, Valerie Hey, Jane Miller, Elaine Unterhalter and the late Diana Leonard. Indeed, I was fortunate to access this programme in its final year in 1996, before it closed, an international trend [closing Women's Studies programmes] across higher education.

But it was through this incredible access that I discovered feminist post/structuralism and I remember thinking, "I don't understand a word of this, but I love it". There was something about it that resonated deeply with me and I just wanted to keep pushing and try to find my way in, even though I found some of the fundamental ideas very disturbing, like the idea that we don't pre-exist discourse. Eventually, these theories penetrated my thinking and shaped my research, writing, pedagogy, and praxis, but always through the lens of feminism. My position was that structure matters but that discourses are profound in shaping power/knowledge and subjectivity. However, getting to that "positioning" took time, thinking and discussion with my teachers, mentors, peers and the bodies of work that at times seemed impenetrable!

Matt: Yes. That challenge, that discomfort, that context of letting go of deeply held, stable beliefs. What discourse does, I suppose, is help hold in place a sense of ourselves and the world and what is true and the sort of solid foundations upon which we're able to act and react. I find it refreshing to be able to talk about not understanding something. How do we create those moments where people are able to sit with that long enough and lean into that when they might sense there's something important there, but it's confronting?

Penny: My own experience as a PhD student was quite lonely because I was looking after my two sons and my stepson whilst undertaking a full-time PhD under an ESRC studentship and working part-time too. During these foundational years, I often felt disconnected and a deep sense of not belonging. I began to understand these emotions through the lens of feminist post/structural theories and particularly Fraser's concept of misrecognition. These readings spoke to me, together with the feminist pedagogies that surrounded me, that enabled me to persist despite the challenging circumstances of my life. The feminist pedagogies I encountered shaped my commitment to reframing widening participation through praxis, which was outside of these spaces. This disconnection – of widening participation to feminist and critical praxis – frustrated me.

My research questions changed in relation to those ideas and commitments. I started to understand that post/structuralism is building on, and critiquing, the ideas of structuralism because a feminist politics recognises that power is fluid and shifting but also shaped by structures of inequality. Inequalities are materially and discursively formed. Having access to theory to make sense of inequality, and to continuously question assumptions, is incredibly generative for new ways of researching and thinking about what kinds of knowledge we want to produce.

Matt: It's interesting to think about what is concealed in our every day – what has become normalised – and at population scale, deeply in the political landscape, deeply imbued with these commitments but difficult to even discuss or apprehend or analyse. One of things over recent years I've come to appreciate about your work and CEEHE is this idea of acknowledging that there're always concepts in practice.

Penny: Yes. It's such an important point. Coming back to the autobiography of the question, Jane Miller is bringing attention to that very point – we are all theorists. That not only takes away the intimidating nature of theory which can seem so kind of distant and inaccessible but also brings to light that we are always theorising about what we do, even if this is implicit. The autobiography of the question is a tool for exercising deep reflexivity, as it helps make explicit those implicit values, assumptions and perspectives and our situatedness in complex power dynamics. This shows that practice is theoretical and theory is practical. So this distinction between theory and practice is problematic. Theorising is a practice and we are engaged in this practice as we make meaning of ourselves in the world. But the divisions between research, theory, and practice are embedded in unequal power relations deeply structured in universities and the subjective positions we occupy differently, and unequally, within them. Thus, questions of equity in higher education demand the problematisation of these hierarchical structures and divisions that are so often overlooked in the everyday discourses of equity policy and practice.

Matt: Yeah, so it's important for us to ask questions of ourselves, and to consider where our influences are coming to us from – maybe another take on 'the personal is the political'. Which people or experiences does that make you think about?

Penny: Widening participation as a field is largely atheoretical. I see this as a significant problem as there tends to be an absence of the very theoretical insights that might enable a deeper understanding of how inequality, exclusion, misrepresentation, marginalisation, and ongoing struggles to participate in higher education are produced and sustained. The absence of critical feminist theories that illuminate how the personal is the political greatly diminishes the possibilities of creating a more inclusive, participatory, and representative higher education system.

So in asking the question "How do we develop equity and widening participation in and through higher education?" my sense is we require an assembling of different theories to address what is a complex, multidimensional problem. As a PhD student, you're often encouraged to take more of a monodimensional approach or at least a single theoretical perspective that is your framework. I had the privilege of developing my PhD thesis and the first years of my research career at the Institute of Education where the critical sociology of education was housed. It was a theoretically rich environment and that liberated me to explore different theoretical perspectives and to bring those together. In particular, I have been drawn to the work of Foucault, to understand power/knowledge and subjectivity through feminist and decolonial lens, Freire to develop pedagogical methodologies that challenge hegemonic practice in higher education and Fraser who contributes a multidimensional social justice framework. However, through engagement with feminist and decolonial bodies of work, many other theorists are woven in and through this thinking.

Matt: Yeah. I like the way in this text how we're drawing on Donna Haraway and her idea of reparative scholarship. It feels related to what you're talking about there, these feel like times where alliance building – rather than totalising the explanations of inequality – are desperately needed, trying to recognise the contribution of scientific disciplines but also interrogating their historical and exclusion formation. It feels important that careful eclecticism you're talking about. We need to create new and anticipate different sort of futures rather than commit to only particular tools and only use them. I suppose that's part of our invitation of this chapter – this conceptual ensemble. They're not necessarily solution-making devices, they're provocations, carefully offered, and I find that quite a thrilling prospect but also slightly overwhelming.

Penny: Yes time to think is imperative in these processes. Time is needed to engage deeply and carefully with different theoretical perspectives so that we avoid a tokenistic, monodimensional approach. Building equity praxis in and through higher education demands making these ideas accessible without reducing them to an oversimplification that then distorts the meaning of complex theoretical frameworks. So our intention in this book is to communicate in an accessible way the meaning and significance of social justice theoretical frameworks without making it completely inaccessible to people who are working in other contexts. This is a challenge we have set out for ourselves as the authors of this book.

Weaving theories together and apart for equity praxis

In the previous section, we explained why we are drawing on particular fields of thought, and also why we believe doing so matters for equity and social justice in higher education. This effort we see as part of making sense of higher education, and its purpose, as an idea, project, discourse, and institution. It is also part of problematising power/knowledge in the way it works across moments, her/their/our/his/stories, and the everyday practices in higher education. In this section of the chapter, we delve further into some of the ideas, scholars and theorists mentioned in the exchange earlier, offering a deepening of detail around them, and showing how we see them being woven together and apart for equity and social justice throughout this book.

Our exchange shared above signals how the work of Paulo Freire is an important foil for us. Indeed, we adopt a feminist engagement with Freirean commitments throughout the book. Contemporary scholarship readily borders on disregard for the contribution to critical conceptualisation that Freire brought to education research and practice. Criticism of aspects of his body of work is important to acknowledge and address, yet it would be careless in our view to discard the insights Freire's work contributes to counter-hegemonic equity praxis. We contend that part of this dismissal relates to how Freirean approaches have been depoliticised in recent times through uncritical implementation and through a professionalisation of equity and inclusion. An example is the call to reject 'banking style education' while assuming a neo-liberalised 'student-led' approach will 'deliver' solutions to problems rooted in inequitable formal education systems. This is clearly a problem for educational theorists, as translations into contexts of practice distil and distort methodological and meta-theoretical conjecture into everyday practices, for a method-only imaginary risks losing the insights and challenges that Freire offers, conceptualising education as ongoing processes of critical praxis.

> For apart from inquiry, apart from the praxis, individuals cannot be truly human. Knowledge emerges only through invention and re-invention, through the restless, impatient, continuing, hopeful inquiry human beings pursue in the world, with the world, and with each other.
>
> *(Freire, 1970: 53)*

This call to communal restlessness within a critical praxis is key to Freire's contribution. It also echoes Foucault's 'restive dispositions' we cite at different points in this book. Freire's question was, and is, relevant to equity commitments. Crudely put: Can education, including formalised education, be a liberatory project? And, if so, how? Freire's was a utopian orientation not about a destination but about always anticipating the political aspects of educational projects (including domination/oppression) and finding pedagogies in which 'knowing critically' becomes the orientation. For Freire, the notion of utopia was about "an act of knowing critically. I cannot denounce an oppressing structure if I do not penetrate into it and know it" (Freire cited in Webb, 2013: 602).

A well-worn critique of Freire is described by Glass:

> if knowledge is tied to human interests (Habermas, 1971) and relations of power (Foucault, 1972, 1973) that embed ideological commitments, and if culture itself is permeated with ideology and structured by unanalyzable and prereflective patterns of action (Geertz, 1973), then explanations of oppression continually beg the question of their validity.
>
> *(Glass, 2001: 21)*

Freire's contribution however was about articulating that systems of oppression have real effects, and how this related to knowledge, and what the implications are for shifting arbitrary and deeply politicised systems such as formal education. Freire's humanism is also an easy target in 'post-human'/'more-than-human' times. Misiaszek and Torres (2019) remind us though that Freire's focus on humans can be interpreted as being about the responsibility humans hold to each other and to the damage we have done to human and more-than-human sets of relations. Whilst it is important to identify the blind-spots, silences, and social inequalities alive in any theorisation, it is possible to recognise scholarship as imperfect and important, in the spirit of reparative scholarship (Haraway, 2016), bringing in important contributions, not necessarily 'regard-less', but carefully. Indeed, it is part of the imperfection that invites an ongoing thinking-with. Further, insights of Freire's such as how "oppressors use their 'humanitarianism' to preserve a profitable situation" (1970: 54) are valuable when attempting to remind and hold accountable privileged actors (including ourselves) of the potential violence 'goodwill' can entail.

The challenge of modern neoliberal humanism in educational theory and practice, and the way it operates as a schema has been heavily critiqued. Biesta (2021) has recently pointed towards rejecting a humanism that is individualistic and striving instead for one that is collective and political. This is part of pointing out that formal education across the globe have become imbued with a 'duty to learn' agenda rather than exploratory, liberatory and/or democratic possibilities. We see this in higher education policy as an increasing drive towards an employability discourse in relation to rapidly shifting capital and labour markets. Biesta makes the point that these developments should not be understood in terms of different agendas for education, but rather signify an ongoing functionalisation and instrumentalisation of education (Biesta, 2021). Instead of crudely rejecting or working back towards a particular humanistic vision, Biesta argues that the goal should be the emancipation of formal education itself. Contemporary anti-colonial/post-colonial scholars such as Achille Mbembe navigate these challenges of modern neoliberal humanism through a thinking with epistemology and a call for a more capacious humanism

> to open new paths for a critique of atavistic nationalisms. Indirectly it also reflects on the possible foundations of a mutually shared genealogy and thus of a politics of the living beyond humanism.
>
> *(Mbembe, 2023: 2)*

Postcolonial theory and decolonial praxis can reconfigure equity and social justice in higher education, drawing on, and building beyond, post-colonial scholars including Fanon (1963) and Said (1993), who led theorisation and demonstration of the violences that forms of colonisation adopt. Mbembe (2019), for example, challenges us to consider how a refusal of ownership of knowledge might have profound implications for research and practice. In the context of intersecting and complex crises, Mbembe's work yearns for a future made through participatory and democratising relationships to and with knowledge-making as a collective project of transformation; a set of *participations* of equals, with a focus on knowledge co-production that takes in a breadth of epistemic diversities. Mbembe positions these forms of knowledge production as critical investments in a certain way of doing, thinking, and feeling that is important for decolonising and democratising knowledge.

Decolonial feminist thinking extends epistemological challenges, inviting us to think and become differently with. Donna Haraway (2016) offers the concept of *tentacular thinking* to contest a context in which "human exceptionalism and bounded individualism, those old saws of Western philosophy and political economics" (2016: 30) dominate. In our author exchange we mention Haraway's reparative scholarship and 'tentacular thinking' – a *building on* positioned not within the Anthropocene or even the Capitalocene but "the Chthulucene . . . made up of ongoing multispecies stories and practices of becoming-with" (Haraway, 2016: 55). The Chthulucene is described by Haraway as *feeling* and *trying* spaces, drawing inspiration from the Latin, tentare, meaning 'to feel' and 'to try' and tentaculum meaning 'feeler'. In the face of multispecies injustice, Haraway discourages dithering and encourages what we interpret as a form of anger that does not fall into a particular form of destructive tribalism; tending more towards a 'becoming with' that is counter-hegemonic. One point of departure is taking this as inspiration for careful contemporary eclecticism in term, concept, theory, and practice for equity and social justice. We share Haraway's concern to build *alliances* that can undo and redo within a care with and for. This type of alliance-building requires however the making of kin with whom alliances can be made, not by subtracting and discarding but by working through *addition*; not through decisiveness but through open-ness, by holding onto anger without creating hostilities, violences or enemies. In this, Haraway calls for an intersectionality as first signalled by legal Black scholarship; a decomposing and recomposing that interrogates and builds new attachments.

We draw inspiration from Haraway's call to 'stay with the trouble' in re/composing with a conceptual ensemble helping to imagine new approaches to equity research and practice. Across the text you will see calls for different *participations*, in the form of participatory approaches, methods, politics and ethics. What we want to bring to the term 'participation' here and across the text is not a simple nor generic functionality only of 'being involved' but an ongoing challenge to crude forms of inclusion often referred to by widening participation regimes. We want to imbue the term 'participation' instead with a restlessness, a *showing up* that Haraway describes as the essential condition of 'staying with the trouble'; a being-in-common that is not afraid to mourn, to recognise violence and loss, and, importantly, refuses a lazy melancholia or pessimism. Instead, we call for participation that includes mourning-with; participation that is about opening on plurally valuable terms, without denying the political possibility of wounding and death through opening to human and non-human. This form of unstable participation we see as an interrogative that accords with Penny's reflection in the author exchange provided earlier (in relation to Patti Lather's work) regarding who can know, what we can know, who makes claims to truth and to knowledge, and with what facts?

Lather's work spirals out in tentacular fashion across this text, as we see her contributions offering so much to the ongoing reconceptualisation of equity and inclusion in any context. The challenges that Lather brings in relation to power, uncertainty and productive-ness provide conceptual spaces to challenge hegemonic bodies of work and the way we think about which work needs to be used in reconceptualisation. Lather's texts *Getting Smart* (1991) and *Getting Lost* (2009) highlight the importance of acknowledging her/their/our/his/stories of contestation and how by raising questions about knowledge and knowing we might unfold further questions regarding *participation*, including who participates in knowledge formation and in what ways. Lather helps us imagine *participations* that involve subjectivities beyond the "intending, perceiving and commanding style of subjectivism of humanism" (Lather, 2015: 10), asking us:

> What would the "incalculable subject" look like that was toward something not containable, in excess of meaning, rather than rational or disciplined or socialized or interpellated? As a counter to neoliberal and Big Data efforts to count and parse, capture and model our every move, how might we think a subject outside the parameters of the algorithms?
>
> *(Lather, 2015: 9)*

A focus on subjectivities, recognition, performativity, and embodiment have been an enduring focus in the developing of a conceptual ensemble over decades of our critical scholarly praxis in higher education (Mayo, 1997; Skeggs, 1997; Thompson, 1997; Williams, 1997; Burke, 2001, 2002, 2012; Archer and Leathwood, 2003). Drawing on foundational feminist scholars such as Lather, Butler, Fraser, Haraway and McNay, this book continues a sustained argument for critical, feminist, post/structural, decolonial and sociological conceptualisations in higher education that shift the gaze from only the individual student, teacher, or researcher to a simultaneous account of the social. The notion of 'the subject' in this context helps to challenge discourses of the 'core self' that underpin statements such as 'untapped potential' which reinforce imaginaries of potential as essence rather than developed through our social location, access to opportunities, and the ways that others construct us. Feminist theorisation helps to examine how educational institutions, groups, and individuals are constituted (and gendered) within competing sets of discourses, unequal social relations, and complex sets of social practices, whilst simultaneously being represented as apolitical, neutral, objective, and decontextualised. *Subjectivity* then is not the opposite of *objectivity* but instead a way of understanding the ongoing production of identity through difference (and sameness). And this raises many important questions, including: how are subjects constituted through and against institutional cultures and practices? How are hegemonic cultures and practices subverted, resisted, and transformed?

How do subjects 'do' differently? And how are institutional contexts constituted through the different subjects within them who make (sense of) the space in particular ways? Conceptualising the subject shifts the focus away from a rational, contained set of individuals towards *subjects* as discursively constructed within specific social contexts and relations. This highlights the complexities of schools, colleges, and universities as negotiated, fluid, and discursive spaces where meanings are contested and shifting because institutions are gendered, as are practices.

> According to poststructuralist thought, the subject is constituted through discourse while the fully unified, completed secure and coherent identity is a fantasy. Instead, as the systems of meaning and cultural representation multiply, we are confronted by a bewildering, fleeting multiplicity of possible identities, any one of which we could identify with – at least temporarily.
> *(Hall, 1992: 227 cited in Burke, 2001: 154)*

Subjectivity then is a concept that helps us to understand that identity is always constituted through wider social relations and competing discourses and practices, fluid across time and space. Subjectivity is about our sense of self, our conscious and unconscious thoughts, feelings and emotions. Notions of self are always tied to notions of the Other, with Othering considered a key process in the formation of self, for example, masculinity as relationally constituted through difference from the Other (femininity). This begs the question then of how subjectivity is produced, constituted, and legitimated, that is, who can be a subject? Judith Butler draws attention to the performative nature of gender and how this is related to being recognised as a subject. Constituted through discourse and what Butler terms 'performativity', subjectivity disrupts hegemonic ideas of identity as fixed and stable. In this explanation, gender is something we 'do' rather than something we 'are'.

> Discursive performativity appears to produce that which it names, to enact its own referent, to name and to do, to name and to make . . . [g]enerally speaking, a performative functions to produce that which it declares.
> *(Butler, 1993: 107)*

Recognition is central to processes of subjective formation, achieved through the dual processes of submission and mastery. Subjectivity highlights the relational, discursive, and embodied processes of identity formations. This focuses on the ways people "are both 'made subject' by/within the social order and how they are agents/subjects within/against it" (Jones, 1993: 158). This is however challenging for projects of equity and social justice, contesting notions of empowerment and transformation that commonly underpin 'mainstream' common sense. *Embodied subjectivity* emphasises the idea of the workings of power and difference as they are marked and inscribed on the body. This fore-grounds the ways that different bodies are positioned, mobilised, and regulated in relation to complex inequalities across time and space. In education, this idea helps to interrogate how different bodies take up and use the different pedagogical spaces available, and how pedagogical spaces are constructed and re/shaped in relation to the different bodies that move through and are positioned within them. A feminist orientation helps to deconstruct how this is gendered and tied to questions of authority. For example, McNay (1992) draws from and critiques, pointing to

> the way Foucault tended to neglect the different ways in which bodies were disciplined. E.g. criticisms of the ways in which prisons were theorised by Foucault ignored the different treatment of men and women and how these were related to dominant constructions of masculinity and femininity.
>
> *(McNay, 1992: 32)*

McNay (1992) also acknowledges Foucault "as an important figure in feminism's own dynamic interrelation with its own theoretical context" (Ransom, 1994: 116), including an articulation of emancipatory potential for gender justice through recognising his later work as an effort to reinstate a form of agency within conceptions of practices of, and ethics of, the self. Nancy Fraser too has brought important critiques of Foucault's work, including the difficulty of drawing together a normative framework for social justice action (Fraser, 1981). For Oksala though, "Foucault's radical intervention in feminist theory, and more generally in the philosophy of the body, has been the crucial claim that any analysis of embodiment must recognise: how power relations are constitutive of the embodied subjects involved in them" (Oksala, 2011: 104). The question of a post/structural ethics and politics is explored in depth in the methodology chapter (Chapter 7) where we consider an approach that can navigate the fraught terrain of whose perspectives should govern *how things ought to be* in higher education. This is not about rejecting governance but rejecting forms of governance that include overly imposed control of bodies in time and space. We see this linked to a form of critique, a critical attitude akin to

> the art of not being governed or, better, the art of not being governed like that and at that cost . . . not wanting to accept these laws because they are unjust because . . . they hide a fundamental illegitimacy.
>
> *(Foucault, quoted in Butler, 2002: 30)*

Across the book, you will see us using a conceptualisation of power/knowledge that accords with the Foucauldian project of exposing epistemological horizons, apprehending for example the ways in which categories are themselves instituted and how fields of knowledge are arbitrarily ordered (Butler, 2002). Contemporary translations of Foucault's legacy into education and higher education, including by Ball (1990), Bacchi (2009), Burke (2012), and Bennett (2012), guide our use of *discourse* as a conceptual tool within this text. This follows from Penny's enduring elaborations (Burke, 2002, 2012, 2017) in which post/structural notions of subjection, subjectivation, discipline, and dividing practices adopt a Foucauldian analysis of the capillary microphysics of power/knowledge that constitute higher education institutions and practices. Even within Foucault's oeuvre though, there is not one stable 'definition' or orientation to power. In *The Subject and Power* (1982), Foucault described how he saw his work on power having developed over time, reflecting on the need for a new economy of power relations; more empirical, more to do with theory and practice. For example, in the discursive struggles for meaning in political landscape, that to identify what is meant by the term *equity*, we should look to the study of *inequity*. That is, "Rather than analysing power from the point of view of its internal rationality, it consists of analysing power relations through the antagonism of strategies" (Foucault, 1982: 780). In this work, Foucault spends considerable time investigating again what the nature of power is and expresses its close relation to shifting ideas of governance, governing, and government. Rehearsing the idea that power is productive and relational.

Reader, in our relationship too, in this moment with you, there is power. One might argue you have submitted, to some degree, to this text. Yet you are not totally beholden nor dominated. You might stop reading at any given moment, never giving this text another thought. There is power within this relation because you are *relatively speaking* 'free'. Indeed, the possibility for recalcitrance is what produces a relation:

> Power is exercised only over free subjects, and only insofar as they are free. Individuals or collective subjects who are faced with a field of possibilities in which several ways of behaving, several reactions and comportments, may be realized.
>
> *(Foucault, 1982: 790)*

This is indeed where the challenge of developing a normative yet transformative framework emerges. For, if we accept the claim that neoliberalism produces new kinds of subjects, what does this imply for equity in higher education? Any relations of power are constitutive of the subjects involved in them. We must acknowledge that subjects do not enter neutral arenas to participate. Their subjectivities are already traversed by the relations of power at play. For this reason, it is not enough to 'shift the numbers' within existing equity categories. Instead, as we argue across this text, it is a more complicated yet urgent project to understand how the categories, the foundations of identification, are constituted by the relations of power that a project of 'social justice' or equity might claim or seek to challenge and even dismantle. A question therefore we must grapple with using this conceptual ensemble is: Do we mean *equity* here by taking up descriptions and advocacy for the subjects presumed by economic liberalism? We mean something bigger. Something harder. Something more complicated and in which we ourselves are implicated.

Chapter 7 of this book draws on feminist, Freirean, and Foucauldian accounts of power as an ongoing articulation of praxis-based approaches to research, practice, policymaking, and evaluation. This effort is part of continuing to build the idea of PPoEMs as an approach to equity and social justice work in higher education, one that can bring in a politics of knowledge through Foucault's conceptualisation of knowledge and power as intricately intertwined, to account for how discourses shape our meaning making in relation to experiences, and in terms of the positions we take up, and the kinds of questions we can and do ask (Burke, 2012). For example, given that discourses shape our identities, positions, and sense of the worlds we inhabit, what it means in a particular context to be 'a woman' or 'a man' will sit in comfort or contestation with what it means to be accomplished (e.g. mechanically, studiously, physically in a sporting setting). In his PhD study, Matt (Lumb, 2020) explored some of the unintended consequences of university widening participation activity. This included analysing retrospectively 'role modelling' as being deeply gendered via polarising discourses that directly shaped the imagination of WP practitioners, university students, teachers, and school student participants. Indeed, part of the cautionary tale of Matt's study was how a different set of methodological commitments in programmatic practice would have produced different and arguably less hegemonic outcomes by drawing generatively on a

> critical scholarship on role-modelling offered by feminist, queer theorists such as Britzman (1993), and anti-racist theorists, such as Crichlow (1999), who draw attention to the political effects of such as disciplinary regime in terms of its capacity for enforcing normalization and rigid categorization.
> *(Martino and Rezai-Rashti, 2012: 5)*

In Chapter 6, we draw on Foucauldian and post-Foucauldian conceptualisations of neoliberalism to interrogate contemporary conventions of policy and programme evaluation. Bringing in a Foucauldian governmentality understanding of neoliberalism whereby we apprehend a specific mode of government rooted in economic discourses of competition (Foucault, 1978), we argue that dominant contemporary evaluation is both inhabited by neoliberal commitments and an ideal tool for ongoing neoliberalisation of institutions and practices. A feminist, post-Foucauldian approach views neoliberalism not only as an economic transformation but also primarily as a political project, as a set of governmental techniques and strategies that aim to extend economic evaluation and market rationality to all aspects of social life. Rather than offering a total explanation for neoliberalism, a governmentality approach offers an analysis of the techniques and configurations that appear differently across diverse contexts. Dominant imaginaries of contemporary policy and programme evaluation can operate as tools *par excellence*. Evaluation is a prominent way power relations have been increasingly governmentalised. What this means is that 'the state' has become not just one formation of the exercise of power but a specific situation of power to which other relations must then refer. Power is not derived from the state, yet power relations have become increasingly under the influence of 'the state' through this technology of referral. Education, for example, has become elaborated, rationalised, and centralised through state institutions.

A challenge that we acknowledge and respond to across this book is that a key process within these governing relations is the formation of new kinds of neoliberal subjects. This is a form of governance that seeks to organise populations through the management of their liberty. Individuals are constantly encouraged to operate as subjects of the market. Governance operates as a seeming 'lack of governance' because our subjectivities are already co-opted, and we are 'free' to choose within this new political rationality. We want however to push for an 'agonism' of incitation and struggle, something of a permanent generative provocation (Foucault, 1982). We see opportunities for resistance and oppositions *as* attention (Back, 2007). The neoliberal onslaught instrumentalises our best ideas, yet these are still socially constructed ideas and processes, and thus can be socially challenged. Arguably, we have openings to reclaim ideas through our attentiveness (Back, 2007: 226). Attention can readily be conceptualised through a sort of 'zombie positivism' (Lather, 2015) of 'taking notice' of real and immutable objects and activities. Instead, the connotation we want to pursue has more to do with ethics and relations of care (Tronto, 2015). This is an attention therefore that is part of methodology and a praxis of generative critique; an orientation that is about being attentive to power, *in relation* and *in response*.

Conclusion

This chapter returned to our call in Chapter 1 for critical, decolonial, feminist, post/structural, and sociological commitments. Firstly, we articulated the role that explicit conceptualisation plays in relation to critical social justice praxis. We reinforced a case for destabilising norms with a view to supporting the creation of new and diverse spaces in which restive and collective questioning can survive; an idea that we continue to develop in subsequent chapters that sustain a focus on methodologies capable of producing new forms of spatio-temporality in contexts of higher education. Secondly, this chapter offered insight into the personal formation of *this* conceptual ensemble, a 'digging into' our own commitments so that you as a reader might make sense of our work together and the different possibilities you might make from it. The final section of the chapter continued to unpack some of the terms and concepts this book makes sustained use of, to clarify our conceptualisations when using terms that have important and diverse histories.

When asked about a recently elected (Mitterrand) government in France in the early 1980s, and whether it will be possible for progressive forces to work with them, Foucault responded:

> We must escape from the dilemma of being either for or against. After all, it is possible to face up to a government and remain standing. To work with a government implies neither subjection nor total acceptance. One may work with it and yet be restive. I even believe that the two things go together.
>
> *(Foucault in 1981, published 1988: 154)*

We want to hold onto this notion of *restive* dispositions as we take this ensemble of conceptual tools into the remaining chapters, continuing to resist the binarised dilemma of being only 'for' or 'against', but to build spaces in which questions such as 'Why are we thinking about 'the problem' in this way?' can survive and thrive through critical praxis. In the next chapter, we bring this orientation into the context of pedagogical relations in higher education, examining how a 'peripherisation' of equity, and discourses of 'excellence', contributes to misframing equity. We consider how pedagogical relations significantly impact questions of the right to higher education in largely hidden ways.

References

Archer, L., and Leathwood, C. (2003) 'Identities, inequalities and higher education', in Archer, L., Hutchings, M., and Ross, A. (Eds) *Higher Education and Social Class: Issues of Exclusion and Inclusion.* London: Routledge Falmer, 171–191.

Arendt, H. (1958) *The Human Condition.* Chicago, IL: University of Chicago Press.

Bacchi, C. (2009) *Analysing Policy: What's the Problem Represented to Be?* Frenchs Forest, NSW: Pearson Education.

Back, L. (2007) *The Art of Listening.* Oxford: Berg Publishing.

Ball, S.J. (1990) *Foucault and Education: Disciplines and Knowledge.* London: Routledge.

Bennett, A. (2012) *The Power Paradox: A Toolkit for Analyzing Conflict and Extremism.* Lanham, MD: University Press of America.

Biesta, G. (2021) 'Reclaiming a future that has not yet been: The Faure report, UNESCO's humanism and the need for the emancipation of education', *International Review of Education,* 68, 655–672. https://doi.org/10.1007/s11159-021-09921-x

Bozalek, V., Leibowitz, B., Carolissen, R., and Boler, M. (2014) *Discerning Critical Hope in Educational Practices.* London: Routledge.

Burke, P.J. (2001) *Access/ing Education: A Feminist Post/Structuralist Ethnography of Widening Educational Participation.* London: Institute of Education, University of London.

Burke, P.J. (2002) *Accessing Education: Effectively Widening Participation.* London: Trentham.

Burke, P.J. (2012) *The Right to Higher Education: Beyond Widening Participation.* London and New York: Routledge.

Burke, P.J. (2017) 'Difference in higher education pedagogies: Gender, emotion and shame', *Gender and Education*, 29, 430–444.

Burke, P.J., and Jackson, S. (2007) *Reconceptualising Lifelong Learning: Feminist Interventions.* London: Taylor and Francis.

Burke, P.J., and Lumb, M. (2018) 'Researching and evaluating equity and widening participation: Praxis-based frameworks', in Burke, P.J., Hayton, A., and Stevenson, J. (Eds) *Evaluating Equity and Widening Participation in Higher Education.* London: Trentham Books Limited.

Butler, J. (1993) *Bodies That Matter: On the Discursive Limits of "Sex".* New York & London: Routledge.

Butler, J. (2002) 'What is critique? An essay on Foucault's virtue', in Ingram, D. (Ed) *The Political: Readings in Continental Philosophy.* London: Basil Blackwell. www.ias. edu/sites/default/files/sss/pdfs/Critique/butler-what-is-critique.pdf

Fanon, F. (1963) *The Wretched of the Earth.* New York: Grove Press.

Foucault, M. (1978/2001) 'Governmentality', in Faubion, J.D. (Ed) *Power: Essential Works of Foucault, 1954–1984.* London, UK: Penguin Random House.

Foucault, M. (1981/1988) 'Practicing criticism', in Kritzman, L.D. (Ed) *Michel Foucault: Politics, Philosophy, Culture – Interviews and Other Writings 1977–1984.* London: Routledge.

Foucault, M. (1982) 'The subject and power', *Critical Inquiry*, 8(4), 777–795. www. jstor.org/stable/1343197

Fraser, N. (1981) 'Foucault on modern power: Empirical insights and normative confusions', *PRAXIS International*, 3, 272–287.

Fraser, N. (2020) 'Preface', in Bozalek, V., Holscher, D., and Zembylas, M. (Eds) *Nancy Fraser and Participatory Parity: Reframing Social Justice in South African Higher Education.* London: Routledge.

Freire, P. (1970/1968) *Pedagogy of the Oppressed.* New York: Continuum.

Glass, R. (2001) 'On Paulo Freire's philosophy of praxis and the foundations of liberation education', *Educational Researcher*, 30(2), 15–25.

Haraway, D. (2016) *Staying with the Trouble: Making Kin in the Chthulucene.* Durham: Duke University Press.

Jones, A. (1993) 'Becoming a "girl": Post-structuralist suggestions for educational research', *Gender and Education*, 5(2), 157–165.

Lather, P. (1991) *Getting Smart: Feminist Research and Pedagogy with/in the Postmodern.* New York and London: Routledge.

Lather, P. (2009) 'Getting lost: Feminist efforts toward a double(d) science', *Frontiers: A Journal of Women Studies*, 30(1), 222–230. www.jstor.org/stable/40388724

Lather, P. (2015) *Against Proper Objects: Toward the Diversely Qualitative.* www.mmu. ac.uk/media/mmuacuk/content/documents/esri/events/siqr-2015/lather.pdf

Lumb, M. (2020) *Re/cognising the Fr/ames of University Equity Outreach: A Cautionary Tale of Unintended Consequences in Australian Equity and Widening Participation policy, Practice and Evaluation* (PhD thesis). Newcastle, NSW, Australia: University of Newcastle.

Lumb, M., and Burke, P.J. (2019) 'Re/cognising the discursive fr/ames of equity and widening participation in higher education', *International Studies in Sociology of Education*, 28(3–4), 215–236. https://doi.org/10.1080/09620214.2019.1619470

Lumb, M., and Ndagijimana, L. (2021) 'Writing the value(s) of colonised equity practices in higher education', *Access: Critical Explorations of Equity in Higher Education*, 9(1), 41–56.

Martino, W., and Rezai-Rashti, G. (2012) *Gender, Race, and the Politics of Role Modelling*. London: Routledge.

Mayo, M. (1997) *Imagining Tomorrow: Adult Education for Transformation*. Leicester: NIACE.

Mbembe, A. (2019) *Necropolitics*. Durham, NC: Duke University Press.

Mbembe, A. (2023) *Public Lecture to UNESCO Conference: Transforming Knowledge for Just and Sustainable Futures*. www.unesco.org/archives/multimedia/document-6002

McNay, L. (1992) *Foucault and Feminism: Power, Gender and the Self*. Cambridge: Polity Press.

Misiaszek, G., and Torres, C. (2019) 'Ecopedagogy: The missing chapter of pedagogy of the oppressed', in Torres, C. (Ed) *Wiley Handbook of Paulo Freire*. Hoboken, NJ: Wiley-Blackwell.

Oksala, J. (2011) 'The neoliberal subject of feminism', *Journal of the British Society for Phenomenology*, 42(1), 104–120. https://doi.org/10.1080/00071773.2011. 11006733

Ransom, J. (1994) 'Review of Foucault and feminism: power, gender and the self, by L. McNay', *Feminist Review*, 47, 115–116. https://doi.org/10.2307/1395267

Said, E. (1993/1978) *Orientalism*. New York: Pantheon Books.

Skeggs, B. (1997) *Formations of Class and Gender: Becoming Respectable*. London: Sage.

Thompson, A. (1997) 'Gatekeeping: inclusionary and exclusionary discourses and practices', in Williams, J. (Ed) *Negotiating Access to Higher Education: The Discourse of Selectivity and Equity*. Buckingham: The Society for Research into Higher Education & Open University Press.

Tronto, J. (2015) 'When we understand care, we'll need to redefine democracy', in *Who Cares? How to Reshape a Democratic Politics*. Ithaca, NY: Cornell Scholarship Online. https://doi.org/10.7591/cornell/9781501702747.003.0002

Webb, D. (2013) 'Critical pedagogy, utopia and political (dis)engagement', *Power and Education*, 5(3), 593–608. https://doi.org/10.2304/power.2013.5.3.280

Williams, J. (1997) 'Institutional rhetorics and realities', in Williams, J. (Ed) *Negotiating Access to Higher Education: The Discourse of Selectivity and Equity*. Buckingham: The Society for Research into Higher Education and Open University Press.

Zembylas, M. (2022) 'Affective and biopolitical dimensions of hope: From critical hope to anti-colonial hope in pedagogy', *Journal of Curriculum and Pedagogy*, 19(1), 28–48. https://doi.org/10.1080/15505170.2020.1832004

4

TOWARDS SOCIALLY JUST PEDAGOGICAL PRAXIS

Introduction

This book builds an urgent call for reconceptualising equity in higher education as transformative equity praxis. Equity tends to be located at the peripheries of higher education, external to core academic practices such as teaching and learning. It is often in tension with the contemporary preoccupation in higher education with 'excellence', driven by marketisation and commercialisation. Yet 'excellence' and 'equity' are structured as two distinctive and unrelated strategies despite the potential contradictions underpinning these entangled discursive schemas. While excellence is seen as central to teaching, equity is structurally positioned as outside of the core 'business' of higher education unless specific attention is being made to 'equity students'. This attention is usually paid by creating centralised systems of student support through an individual role or unit tasked with carrying out an institution's equity programmes. In the markets of higher education, increasingly this is outsourced through strategies seen to fix the problem, often using technicist tools such as learning analytics as a key institutional resource, and with little or no opportunity to interrogate what problem it is that is attempting to be resolved. This reinforces the assumption that 'equity' is a specialised concern, tied to dedicated professional intervention, outside of academic practice and located at the peripheries of the university. In this way, teaching tends to be treated as separated from what equity is constructed to be, although this is not to deny the commitment of many academics to developing inclusive forms of teaching and learning. However, it does raise questions about the institutional value placed on those efforts when equity is not judged as 'core business' in the neoliberal contexts that institutions are situated within. In systematic

DOI: 10.4324/9781003257165-6

and structural terms, equity is largely positioned as peripheral to pedagogical development in higher education, including pedagogical matters of curriculum and assessment. In a context increasingly regulated by mechanisms such as workload management, and constrained by tighter and tighter budgets, equity might be viewed by higher education managers as an ideal but not a priority.

This chapter troubles the peripheral position of equity as a major roadblock in progressing social justice praxis. We interrogate hegemonic equity structures by considering their relation, which is often tangential, to the pedagogical dimensions of higher education strategy, practice, and experience. We attend to this through our concept of the 'peripherisation of equity', which we argue significantly contributes to the *misframing* of equity in higher education. Misframing here refers to how 'the problem' of equity is re/presented in ways that are framed through hegemonic socio-political processes reproductive of dominant gendered, raced, and classed imaginaries. We will show that 'peripherisation' exacerbates the deficit imaginaries that focus on the remediation of 'equity students' who are regularly constructed through pathologising discourses that diagnose students as suffering from deficiency disorders. Lack of ability, confidence, motivation, and resilience are commonly re-cited as part of the repertoires of deficit imaginaries. This is problematic not only as it locates the problem of equity within the bodies of people and communities who face the full onslaught of entrenched injustices but also because it leads to pedagogical logics that fail to recognise how *practices* of teaching, curriculum development, and assessment contribute to perpetuating multidimensional inequalities in and through higher education. We argue that combined with the pathologising discourses of deficit imaginaries are the sanitising constructions that conceal the violent and oppressive practices that exclude bodies of people and knowledges through intersecting structural, material, and symbolic inequalities. We bring to light the equity repertoires, which circulate a comforting language yet minimise the capacity to challenge hegemonic relations of power. We argue this is part of an agenda to avoid the pedagogical discomfort of engaging with power and difference that continue to shape who is seen as having the right to higher education and on what terms. Indeed, this is often articulated by university leaders as recruiting the 'right' students, without analysis of the power dynamics underpinning judgements, assessment and the construction of potential and capability, tied to the politics of emotion. Elizabeth Ellsworth (1997) wrote of an 'ignore-ance' whereby through fear or hatred of one's own complicity in a particular unjust dynamic, an active negation is held onto which can even work "against the conscious intentions or desires of one who otherwise wants to learn" (1997: 57). When considering questions of pedagogy and equity in higher education, this dynamic of denial (whether conscious and/or unwitting) is important to consider if we are going to move beyond the comforting language of equity, towards a different social space to tackle entrenched inequalities "informed by historical conjunctures of power and social and cultural difference" (Ellsworth, 1997: 38).

In this chapter, we examine discourses of teaching in the context of the peripherisation of equity, while also reconceptualising pedagogies through social justice perspectives. We consider how pedagogical relations, inevitably shaped by power and difference, have a significant but largely hidden impact on questions of the right to higher education. Weaving together pedagogical insights from social justice theories, we aim to illuminate the relational, affective, and embodied formations of identity and knowledge, knowing and being known in and through the contemporary timescapes of higher education (e.g. Zembylas, 2013; Bozalek et al, 2014; Luckett, 2016). We offer this as part of a post-Freirean pedagogical praxis; that is, we invite our readers to continually reconceptualise with us and beyond this book as a commitment to staying with the trouble of pedagogical praxis, un-knowing and challenging the dangerous postures of certainty and universalism that frame teaching excellence discourses. We use the term 'post-Freirean' to signal a way of drawing on Freire that simultaneously recognises the vast influence of his work that created so many contexts of critical social justice-oriented educational possibility, and to also acknowledge and engage with critiques of his work.

Our position is that all bodies are entwined in shaping and reshaping the meanings we give to what it is to be in and of the world. Thus, everyone is a pedagogical subject, in relation. With this broad understanding of pedagogical be(com)ing, higher education is and should be a *timescape* (see Chapters 3 and 5) of continually forming knowledge-with, a necessarily social (rather than hyper-individual) process. Banking education, in Freirean terms, is the act of taking the authoritative position as a knower and depositing hegemonic knowledge structures into the minds of passive learners, thus sustaining oppressive relations through pedagogical practice. Moving towards critical pedagogical praxis requires an ethical reflexivity; a willingness to move beyond ignore-ance (Ellsworth, 1997); a deep commitment to continually questioning the values, assumptions, and practices that create the conditions of knowledge-making. We are inviting readers as participants in such an ethical-reflexive process of both developing pedagogical understanding and simultaneously recognising the need to keep open a questioning and un-knowing disposition to our pedagogical subjectivities as teachers/students in and of the world.

Reconceptualising pedagogies through social justice perspectives

Through the peripherisation of equity, and its pathologising and sanitising discourses, pedagogy is commonly framed in highly reductive terms as a set of teaching and learning styles, skills, techniques, or methods. Within this perspective, teachers simply 'personalise' their teaching as a way to address diversity. Simultaneously, teachers might add 'diverse material' with the aim to decolonise the curriculum and/or create systems of reasonable adjustment for assessment, as key methods to account for inclusion. Although none of these are examples of inappropriate methods, without examining the historical, material, ethical, political, and social dimensions of pedagogical relations of power, difference, and inequality, there is little possibility for social justice transformation. We are using the term 'transformation' here as part of our drawing on Nancy Fraser, to build our multidimensional social justice conceptualisation of equity (see Chapter 2), and in an advocacy for approaches and practices that can engage, disrupt, and shift deeply rooted systemic inequalities. This is difficult work, as it challenges commitments to efforts which are accepted as 'good things to do'. For example, Block (2018), in work on language and justice in education, draws on Fraser to ask whether affirmative action can ever really attack the roots of inequality and injustice in societies and to eliminate them:

> In Fraser's view, it cannot and does not, and she proposes instead that actions taken in favour of recognition and redistribution need to be "transformative", providing "remedies aimed at correcting inequitable outcomes precisely by restructuring the underlying generative framework".
>
> *(Fraser, 2008 cited in Block, 2018: 244)*

Our position is that relying on reductive ideas and practices such as teaching and learning styles, skills, techniques, or methods significantly limits the capacity to address underlying generative frameworks holding in place a deeply inequitable status quo in higher education. Instead, we advocate for engaging in ongoing collective processes of reconceptualising pedagogy through transformative equity praxis, where we might exercise a form of *ethical reflexivity*. We suggest that all our lived encounters within the world are pedagogical, whether these are attached to formal education institutions or are part of our everyday, taken-for-granted practices and relations. Pedagogy inevitably involves sense-making of ourselves and our inter-dependent connection to other beings in and of the world. Thus, to re-cognise the harmful dynamics of inequality and injustice that inevitably shape pedagogical relations, encounters, entanglements, and subjectivities, we need the tools of reflexivity within a deeply ethical framework of social justice pedagogical praxis. Ethical reflexivity pushes against the ongoing insistence of a white-masculinised, neocolonial, ableist reiteration of the independent and aspirational learner who adds value through their diversity in terms of neoliberal imperatives for economically oriented modes of success. Rather, engaging with multidimensional reframings that insist on working *with* rather than *against* difference demands that action and reflection are in continual conversation even while we are confronted by the contradictions and discomforts of our differences.

This requires an uncomfortable pedagogical process of considering our location in past and contemporary relations of oppression that are institutionalised in our taken-for-granted identities, methodologies, and practices. Binary and evidence-based logics lock us into static and limiting epistemologies, reducing complex inequalities to overly simplistic, technicist practices of 'teaching and learning'. The misframing of the problem means we focus on fixing *the Other* (Beauvoir, 1952; Fanon, 1963; Said, 1978, 1993) and thus protect the hegemonic and privileged positions of power that work only to reproduce inequality even while claiming to be about inclusion, belonging and diversity.

Indeed, discourses that are seen as largely unproblematic (e.g. 'inclusion', 'belonging' and 'diversity') often work as forms of symbolic violence, coercing those seen as 'excluded' to conform to hegemonic conventions, expectations, and values and to participate in a process of *individual* transformation into normalised personhoods. In the context of equity and higher education, we have written previously with others about a related dynamic facilitating exclusion through collusion

> involving 'those in on it constitute a collusive net and those the net operates against, the excolluded' (Goffman, 1974, p. 84). Social policy operates to frame as desirable and legitimate certain ways of being, knowing and doing. This framing across social fields is taken up by a policy 'collusio', with largely middle class backgrounds forming an "implicit collusion among all the agents who are products of similar conditions and conditionings" (Bourdieu, 2000, p. 145). When a policy collusio – guided by a privileged set of pre-dispositions creates the conditions for particular personhoods to not be value-able within the frame, these personhoods are mis-framed and experience a sort of 'political death'.
>
> *(Lumb, Burke and Bennett, 2021: 10)*

This largely hidden collusion-producing-exclusion dynamic includes for example students (and staff) in higher education becoming 'flexible' and 'adaptable' to volatile market conditions and thus being recognised as an appropriately 'resilient' participant. The discourses of 'resilience' however are also individualised, so that the social structures and cultural misrecognitions that undermine a person's recognition as 'resilient' are concealed from view. Thus, inclusion often perpetuates problematic deficit perspectives that place the responsibility on those individuals who are identified as at risk of exclusion through their 'lack' of aspiration, confidence, adaptability, or resilience. Inclusion might also be seen as a discursive space in which the politics of shame play out in ways that are experienced as a personal failure and simply not being the 'right' kind of person worthy enough for participation in higher education (Reed et al, 2007: 19).

Therefore, it is imperative to reconfigure 'inclusion' in higher education as a broader social justice project of transforming higher education, in all its deeply relational multidimensions. This involves the redistribution of resources and opportunities to access and participate in obstruse academic practices whilst simultaneously troubling those practices. This requires challenging engrained misrecognition of the experiences, histories, resources, values, and knowledges of those communities who have been systematically and persistently marginalised. This includes co-creating pedagogical timescapes for the representation of those marginalised experiences, histories, values, resources, and knowledges that unsettle the re/privileging of hegemonic subjectivities, ontologies, and epistemologies. Imperative to this is thinking-with differences and contestations *within* communities as well as across them. We argue that pedagogical transformation demands the reconceptualisation of the project of equity in higher education as transformative equity praxis rooted in social justice; to mobilise the power of collectively staying with the trouble with and for socially just pedagogical reorientations:

> Higher education has a key role to play in ensuring more socially just and thus peaceful and stable societies into the future. The power of higher education is immeasurable and profound but this power is often *reproductive* of, rather than *disruptive* to, social injustices and inequalities. The project of changing pedagogical spaces in higher education is necessarily long-term and challenging [and . . .] requires *enduring and sustained levels of commitment and attention to the insidious and subtle ways that inequalities and misrecognitions play out in and through pedagogical spaces.* Individual teachers and students must be part of such enduring and sustained levels of commitment but must also be fully supported by wider policy frameworks and their institutions to develop the theoretical, conceptual, structural and material resources necessary to effect change.
>
> *(Burke, Crozier and Misiaszek, 2017: 142)*

Socially just pedagogical reorientations matter in the context of the urgencies of our times; including the deepening of inequalities and societal divisions, conflict, violence and macro and micro instabilities, global pandemics, disease and viruses, climate change and environmental degradation, and ongoing imperatives to redress the harm of colonial histories and neocolonial dis/positions. In the context of these urgencies, and in the space of different professional and academic contexts, we offer a framework of transformative equity praxis in higher education to spark new pedagogical imaginations through collaborative, ethical and response-able frameworks, anticipating and generating new possibilities and practices.

Transformative equity praxis enables us to think beyond the technical, instrumental, to get beyond simplistic discourses of 'how to' teach or 'how to' learn. Indeed, it struggles against increasingly globalised forces operating through formal education systems such as PISA, which have narrowed ideas about 'quality' education "foregrounding standardisation, competition, an emphasis on core subjects that allow for the measurement of learning outcomes, corporate-style principles in education, and test-based accountability policies" (Sahlberg, 2016)" (Elfert, 2023: 407). Pedagogy is reconceptualised as a framework to support the rigorous development of teaching, curriculum and assessment related to social justice aims, philosophies, and principles. This disrupts the contemporary forms of 'banking education' that emphasise individual investment in higher education as a means for self-improvement, financial gain and neoliberal constructions of success that rely on competitive, individualised and market-based logics. By creating praxis-based spaces for reconceptualising pedagogy as an ongoing process of social justice transformation, we can bring to light often hidden dimensions of pedagogical experiences in and out of the formal classroom: the emotional, cultural, and symbolic dimensions of becoming differently with others. This we consider a reframing of research – not as the privilege of the sole academic but as a collective process of re-searching-with. It is through reorienting pedagogical practice as a form of re-search praxis that we can engage differently and generate new understanding and practices of what it is to learn and make meaning. We explore this idea in more detail throughout this book, offering a new framework of pedagogical methodology; PPoEMs. This requires attention to time-space in new pedagogical conceptualisations, which we explore later in this chapter. We first turn to Freirean and post-Freirean theoretical perspectives to progress our discussion of pedagogical praxis.

Social justice pedagogical praxis

Forming foundations for generating socially just pedagogical praxis is part of an extensive body of Freirean literature (1970, 1973, 2009) along with work drawing from, building on, and critiquing, his pioneering and influential contributions. At the heart of Freire's work is a foregrounding of how education is a political project and can be an institutional site of oppression and dehumanisation, produced through 'banking education'. His work sets out the potential of transforming pedagogical relations to create the conditions for more socially just and liberatory possibility. One of his important contributions was to recognise how "domination was not only economic and structural but also pedagogical, ideological, cultural, and intellectual and that matters of persuasion and belief were crucial weapons for creating engaged agents and critical subjects" (Giroux, 2021: 116). Freire draws on Hegelian notions of recognition to illuminate the interplay between self, social experience, and knowledge formation as crucial to challenging inequalities. His analysis of relations of inequality through education brings to light "a dialectic of mutually destructive dependency", arguing that "only the mutuality of recognition can challenge that dialectic of violence and abuse" (Nixon, 2015: 152).

Thus, a social justice conceptualisation of equity can only be approached through a mutual critical consciousness of the power relations that both make and constrain us. This relates to Freire's development of the concept of praxis, which demands an "orientation towards critical action that such consciousness provides" and makes possible forms of collective action that provide the possibilities for transformation to occur (ibid.: 152). Praxis in Freirean terms emphasises the need for dialogic processes, for educators and students to collaboratively challenge the structures embedded in unequal relations. This unequal form of (what Freire calls) 'banking education' is a powerful institutionalised structure that perpetuates multidimensional injustices, privileging the knowledge and culture of those occupying positions of (relative) power and excluding the knowledge and cultures of communities marginalised by educational (and other interrelated institutional and political) practices. Freire understood this in a range of diverse contexts and his praxis drew from the critical pedagogies he developed with the Indigenous communities he worked with in rural parts of Latin America. His critique of banking education included but also extended beyond formal and institutionalised teaching and learning. It is important to understand then that the dynamic 'banking education' can also operate through taken-for-granted practices such as outreach and student support programmes aiming to widen participation in contemporary higher education contexts.

Within this banking education framework, the educator's role is to deposit knowledge into the repository (the student) to fill the student with the narrative of the teacher (the knower), who occupies a powerful position in oppressive relations (Freire, 1970). In banking education, students from underrepresented communities are expected to internalise the values, cultures, and perspectives of the hegemonic order, reinforcing sensibilities of unworthiness, shame and inferiority (Burke, 2015, 2017). These power relations entrench deficit imaginaries in educational structures, cultures, and practices, framing research, evaluation, policy, and practice in taken-for-granted ways. This is what we mean by *insidious inequalities.*

Freirean pedagogy brings attention to the power of transforming pedagogical relations to dismantle dehumanising banking education, repositioning educators and students as partners in the re-creation of knowledge (resonant of Fraser's representative justice) for what become processes of generating hope and humanisation. This relationship places emphasis on the creative power of students to draw on their histories and experiences to generate understanding and meaning to then challenge relations of inequality, oppression, and exclusion. In drawing on Freire, and adopting notions of hope and humanisation, we take account of critiques of his work; for example, questions raised by feminist scholars about the possibility of empowerment, pointing to the dynamic and unpredictable nature of power in diverse pedagogical contexts (e.g. Hooks, 1994; Weiler, 1994; Ellsworth, 1997). Ellsworth (1997) has shown that putting Freirean methods into practice in the classroom can sometimes lead to situations worsening for those who were supposed to be 'empowered', in relation to sexist and phallocentric paradigms of liberation (Hooks, 1993) and patriarchal discourses (Brady, 1994). More recently, scholars have pointed out that Freirean theory and critical pedagogy are not always readily compatible with decolonial projects (e.g. Tuck and Yang, 2014; Zembylas, 2018).

We agree that post-Freirean thinking needs constant checking and development to avoid becoming co-opted to the status quo (Zembylas, 2018). Our analysis of possibility in this context aligns with contemporary conceptualisations of *critical hope* (Bozalek et al, 2014) and even *anti-colonial hope* (Zembylas, 2022) whereby a questioning: "How can educators theorize and cultivate hope's radical and transformative dynamism in ways that pay attention to the demands of anti-colonial praxis?" (Zembylas, 2022: 30). It is not a naive hope we argue for, that is, one that readily concurs with a neoliberalised language of individualised progress. We advocate for a *critical hope* that "recognises that we live within systems of inequality" (Boler, 2004: 128) and that allows for generative contestations to emerge across ethical, affective and political terrains, acknowledging suffering and injustice in the present, whilst emphasising different possibilities in time (Bozalek et al, 2014). We also recognise arguments that pedagogies of critical hope are 'not enough' for contemporary conditions, including the urgency of addressing manifold ongoing destructive colonialities

> because negative critiques of neoliberalism are limited to identifying what is wrong and needs to change; hope that takes into consideration coloniality must also be found in affirmative accounts, outside of the framework of critique, which is considered to be ultimately rooted in utopian accounts.
>
> *(Zembylas, 2022: 33)*

A good portion of critique has been to do with Freire's notion of 'banking education' being taken up as a method rather than a methodological provocation and concept, which has frustrated and arguably depoliticised the uptake of Freire's work. As Aronowitz (2015) has argued:

> The task of this revolutionary pedagogy is not to foster critical consciousness in order to improve cognitive learning, the student's self-esteem, or even to assist in his aspiration to fulfill his human "potential" . . . . It is to the liberation of the oppressed as historical subjects within the framework of revolutionary objectives that Freire's pedagogy is directed.
>
> *(Aronowitz, 2015: 116)*

Freire's contribution challenges perspectives that assume there are no alternative ways of doing education, emphasising instead the interplay between objectivity and subjectivity and permanence and change. He points out that people are in a continual process of becoming and remaking, which is what makes education 'an exclusively human manifestation'.

> The point of departure of the movement lies in the people themselves. But since people do not exist apart from the world, apart from reality, the movement must begin with the human-world relationship. Accordingly, the point of departure must always be with men and women in the "here and now", which constitutes the situation within which they are submerged, from which they emerge, and in which they intervene . . . . They must perceive their state not as fated and unalterable, but merely as limiting – and therefore challenging.
>
> *(Freire, 1970: 85)*

In generating pedagogies of hope, with an emphasis on the potential of education to humanise and transform unequal relations of power, Freire insists on the importance of dreaming, which he identifies as an integral part of the historico-social manner of being a person. For Freire, this was part of being human, which, within history, is in a permanent process of becoming: "There is no change without dream, as there is no dream without hope" (Freire, 2009: 77). In emphasising the capacity to dream in these ways, Freire opens possibilities for creating the conditions for more equitable forms of higher education, for holistic forms of parity of participation (in Fraserian terms) and for building hope, belonging, and wellbeing in communities who experienced the full force of social, political, and educational oppression, exclusion, and violence over generations. While it is important to stay with the trouble of the many critiques of Freire's work, we also recognise the significance of his body of work for offering alternatives to pursue rather than turning impatiently to the latest theoretical fad.

> Paulo Freire remains a shining example of philosophy made practical in educational reform. His early work as a teacher of adult literacy, working with desperately poor agricultural labourers in Brazil, shows how discussions about basic words – home, work, landowner, hunger, city – become processes of problematisation, including teasing out the threads of power that run through everyday habits and encounters.
>
> *(Wrigley, Thomson and Lingard, 2012: 106)*

Freire asserted the importance of exploring the world from the standpoint of marginalised communities, with the educator standing alongside the "dispossessed in a critical act of solidarity" (Nixon, 2015: 152). This emphasis on standpoint interrogates the projection of a deficit gaze that constructs a problem of lack as located in the body of the person or group who has experienced marginalisation, exclusion and/or oppression. Indeed, Freire resituates the gaze on those activating relations of oppression as not only oppressing others but also suffering from 'dehumanisation'. What Freire meant by dehumanisation was how people can be made objects of history and culture, denying their capability to engage in creating history and culture (Glass, 2001).

> Dehumanization, which marks not only those whose humanity has been stolen, but also (though in a different way) those who have stolen it, is a distortion of the vocation of becoming more fully human. This distortion occurs within history; but it is not an historical vocation. Indeed, to admit of dehumanization as an historical vocation would lead either to cynicism or total despair. The struggle for humanization, for the emancipation of labor, for the overcoming of alienation, for the affirmation of men and women as persons would be meaningless. This struggle is possible only because dehumanization, although a concrete historical fact, is not a given destiny but the result of an unjust order that engenders violence in the oppressors, which in turn dehumanizes the oppressed.
>
> *(Freire, 1970: 44)*

Freire's body of work compels us to reframe concepts of inclusion and belonging in contemporary higher education timescapes that rest on deficit imaginaries. This is a re-orientation that rejects remedial accounts of equity, which place the burden of inclusion on the individual student who must 'lose themselves', and their cultural history, to fit into the mainstream culture (Reay, 2001). Socially just inclusion becomes possible through dialogic processes of pedagogical praxis. This might involve: building diverse experiences and knowledges into research and evaluation processes through student-directed and community-based partnership (Cammarota, 2007; Cook-Sather, 2018); having inclusive curriculum development that recognises and draws from students' lived experiences and knowledges in the diverse contexts in which these unfold (Cammarota, 2007; Darling-Hammond and Friedlaender, 2008); and decolonising curriculum in ways that value and foreground Indigenous knowledges (Gyamera and Burke, 2018). Through such Freirean-inspired dialogic processes, education has the potential to contribute to processes that resist dehumanisation, but only through the difficult work of dismantling relations of inequality, injustice, and oppression (Arday and Mirza, 2018). Freirean pedagogical praxis draws from knowledges that have been institutionally marginalised to "produce healing, reflection, wisdom, transformation, and action in individual and collective ways" (Cervantes-Soon, 2017: 17).

Although hegemonic equity practices are often aimed at fostering a sense of belonging, an absence of analytical consideration of the affective and emotional layers of experience at play that produce social injustices of misrecognition often generates a sense of isolation and disconnection at the personal level

(Ahmed, 2004; Burke, Crozier and Misiaszek, 2017). Intentional social justice praxis can awaken attentiveness to the complex interrelationship between macro-level structures, institutional practices, and micro-level lived and embodied experiences of misrecognition, which perpetuate unequal relations deeply undermining commitments to build parity of participation (Fraser, 1997). Leathwood and Hey (2009) argue for the imperative of close attention to the emotional dimensions of experiences of inequality as a key part of equity strategies. In these contexts, through examining the intersections of power and emotion, students and teachers reframe care, belonging, inclusion and responsibility as deeply connected with practices of equity (Zembylas, 2013). Such pedagogical strategies "aim to transform students and teachers, as well as the schools and the communities that they serve, by identifying and challenging sentimentalist and moralistic discourses that often obscure inequality and injustice" (Zembylas, 2013: 506). Relatedly, Zembylas (2013) points out that surface-level claims of empathy and caring perpetuate 'privileged irresponsibility' and social inequalities. This requires that teachers and students find ways to deepen pedagogical practices through an ethics of care and through critical notions of empathy, compassion, and connection (Burke, 2012).

Themes of discomfort are examined through pedagogical praxis with the understanding that pedagogical encounters require learners "to frequent spaces where they are uncertain" (Lygo-Baker, 2017: 86). The explicit engagement of discomfort embraces a more "flexible sense of self" (Boler, 1999: 170), encouraging uncertainties and the capacity to stay with the trouble. Discomfort as an explicit pedagogical strategy, developed within an ethical framework of praxis, might then enable deep reflexivity, mobilising the "diversity of lives, experiences and identities shaped and refashioned within the classroom, a fractal of the wider world" (Mills and Spencer, 2011: 1 in Macdonald, 2013: 680). Discomfort in its capacity to facilitate emerging and unplanned insights that accompany attention to the politics of difference is also committed to building relations of trust in pedagogical timescapes as part of the recognition (rather than the 'ignor-ance' (Ellsworth, 1997)) of ambiguities and uncertainties (Barnett, 2011). In finding a sense of comfort in our discomfort, pedagogical oddkin (Haraway, 2016) might be co-situated to do the challenging work of collectively re-imagining ways of working with and through difference, rather than resisting, sanitising, or regulating it (Burke, 2017).

Working in and through differences via critical pedagogical praxis is challenging. We argue that this is necessary though to shift away from surface-level remedial approaches, which exemplify 'banking education' models, including within any form of teacher training. Rather, what is required is rich and rigorous forms of sustained pedagogical praxis to enable co-participants (students and teachers) to explore differences sensitively and ethically in classroom spaces (Burke, Crozier and Misiaszek, 2017). Later in the book, we propose more specific frameworks to support such processes including the development of communities of praxis within PPoEMS (see Chapter 7). These frameworks facilitate time, space, and conceptual and ethical tools to recognise and reduce the potential harm that might emerge from processes of re-examining identity and/or worldviews (Zembylas, 2015). In embracing discomfort as a necessary part of a process of transformation, teachers and students are encouraged to engage vulnerability, which is inevitably challenging and thus requires advanced pedagogical knowledge and understanding as related to histories of multiple forms of inequality affecting educational access and participation (Zembylas, 2015). Drawing from Butler's (2005) concept of 'ethical violence', Zembylas (2015) argues, however, that discomfort is a crucial dimension of social justice transformation and thus demands that teachers engage in a form of ethical violence guided by strong forms of pedagogic responsibility. This requires deep levels of pedagogical reflexivity in the continuous questioning of the contexts of discomfort being opened through an ethical framing of teaching and learning that minimises harm to all participants. This reinforces the need for rich forms of professional development in the context of the complexities raised by discomfort and difference, including attention to symbolic, cultural, and epistemic inequalities. These complexities include the effect of desires for research and teaching 'excellence', for preparing graduates for 'success' through employability agendas and for displaying innovation in relation to new technologies that appear to hold future promise.

The problem of 'excellence'

Excellence has gained hegemony as part of the rise of neoliberalism and is associated with discourses of 'quality', and neoliberal technologies of regulation, performativity, and subjectification. The form of quality foregrounded by the excellence agenda is imbued with a conceptualisation that is only 'reasonable' through the quantification of more tangible aspects of contexts, with more intangible aspects readily dismissed. We see here a sort of zombie positivism (Lather, 2015) guiding the epistemology at work, one that readily deems un/reason/able the affective, the symbolic, the ethical, the political – part of a "worldwide audit culture with its governmental demands for evidence-based practice and the consequent (re)privileging of scientist methods" (Lather, 2012: 2).

We link excellence to the economies of prestige that have ascended in higher education, related to league tables and global rankings (Blackmore and Kandiko, 2011; Rosinger et al, 2016; Kandiko Howson, Coate and de St. Croix, 2018). Prestige economies subject academics to the discourses of excellence through key performance indicators that claim to measure levels of productivity. Performativity is deeply connected to forms of subjectification; it is not only the external technologies of measurement that come to matter but also the ways these mechanisms shape sensibilities of self in the pedagogical contexts of higher education. In this way, university teaching is connected to the subjective construction of the responsible and enterprising self (Hatcher, 1998: 382 in Ball, 2012: 20), with powerful effects:

> The first order effect of performativity is to re-orient pedagogical and scholarly activities towards those which are likely to have a positive impact on measurable performance outcomes and are a deflection of attention away from aspects of social, emotional or moral development that have no immediate measurable performative value. Teachers' judgments about class or lecture room processes may thus be subverted and superseded by the demands of measurement or at the very least a new set of dilemmas is produced which set the tyranny of metrics over and against professional judgment. The second order effect of performativity is in the possibilities it creates to replace commitment with contract. That is to say, to the extent that HE practices – teaching, writing and research – can be rendered into calculabilities, they can also be re-written as contracts of performance that can, at some point, be put out to tender.
>
> *(Ball, 2012: 20)*

Teaching has thus been reframed through the neoliberal technologies of excellence, in which teachers are continually subjected to ranking and rating through the tyranny of metrics. Excellence is a core vehicle for neoliberal forces to progress the marketisation of higher education (Tomlinson, Enders and Naidoo, 2020; Gunn, 2018; Neary, 2016). Indeed, the Teaching Excellence Framework (TEF) emerged in the UK's market of higher education, as a mechanism to assist students to exercise 'consumer choice' about where to study in relation to institutional rankings (Ashwin, 2017). These moves have shifted higher education steadily towards becoming "a major business and revenue generator" (Hubble et al, 2016 quoted in Neary, 2016: 690). The UK Department for Business, Industry and Science (BIS) sets out the purpose of the TEF explicitly as informing student choice in a market economy system:

> The TEF will increase students' understanding of what they are getting for their money and improve the value they derive from their investment, protecting the interest of the taxpayer who supports the system through provision of student loans. It should also provide better signalling for employers as to which providers they can trust to produce highly skilled graduates.
>
> *(BIS, 2015: 12–13 quoted in Burke, Crozier and Misiaszek, 2017: 15)*

Roger Brown (2018) argues that the marketisation of higher education related to excellence discourses has been a key factor in growing inequalities and increased stratification in the UK (Brown, 2018), which is echoed in Mettler's (2014) analysis of how higher education is exacerbating inequalities in the US context (see Chapter 1). Drawing from Frank and Cook (2010), Brown considers higher education's role in 'winner-take-all markets', where "small differences in performance can lead to large differences in economic reward, together with a concentration of such rewards in the hands of a few top performers" (Brown, 2018: 38). He explores the relationship of such 'winner-take-all markets' to higher education, explaining:

> Competition for status – positional competition – becomes socially significant when it takes place in an economic context: when the market becomes the medium for such competition through variable tuition fees and student aid, institutional competition for both public and private funding, the introduction into the market of 'for-profit' providers, and officially sponsored (or condoned) performance indicators and rankings. The inevitable outcome of this process is increased stratification. This also reflects two seemingly immutable features of higher education, namely, (a) the seemingly insuperable difficulties in making valid and reliable comparisons of educational quality (Brown 2012) and (b) the market and political power wielded by the top-ranked institutions and the constituencies they serve (who of course include many in influential positions in politics, the professions and the media, often of course educated there). So the elite institutions seek to differentiate themselves as 'world-class'.
>
> *(Brown, 2018: 38)*

The excellence agenda has gathered such momentum in policy that it could be described as becoming a 'regime of truth'; a way of making sense of the world so embedded in the social imaginary that it is taken-for-granted (Foucault, 1977). Discourses of excellence "discipline (institutional and individual) practices and subjectivities, restricting conceptions of teaching, and limiting opportunities for critical pedagogies" (Stevenson, Whelan and Burke, 2017: 29). Brusoni et al (2014) explain that the excellence discourse signifies a breaking away from traditions of egalitarianism in Europe. They suggest that the excellence initiatives developed in Germany, Spain, and France are largely about processes of institutional competition; ensuring that only an exclusive group of institutions and centres are "capable of competing with the best Anglo-Saxon universities" mobilising competitive practices to increase funding and reputation (Brusoni et al, 2014: 16). This shift to the promotion of an increasingly competitive higher education market is motivated by the belief that this will lead to improved standards and quality (ibid.).

Excellence discourses have exacerbated deficit imaginaries with a persistent focus on recruiting the 'best' and 'brightest' without attention to the assumptions and shared values – that is, the intended and unintended collusions – that form assessments and judgements of who is seen as 'the best and the brightest' by whom, in recruitment and selection processes of teachers and learners in higher education. Policy discourses of equity and diversity in this drive towards excellence are largely in terms of the new 'consumer markets' they represent, rather than on equity and widening participation (Hunter, 2013).

An example is the steadfast assumption that if more students succeed in accessing higher education, especially when those students are from underrepresented communities and disadvantaged schools, then this indicates a form of social engineering in which standards have been lowered or inappropriate forms of 'grade inflation' have taken place. Rarely are the patterns of widening success of students identified as a positive outcome of sustained commitment to building equity, including the redistribution of access to high-quality educational resources and teaching. In Australia, prominent public commentary commonly positions progress on equity as akin to the lowering of standards, including at points in the recent past from Federal Ministers of the Higher Education portfolio. When Tony Abbott led the conservative federal Liberal National Party back to government in 2013, Christopher Pyne became education minister. He soon after announced a review into the growth of higher education student participation under the Labour reforms, focused on a particular notion of 'quality'

> to see if that is impacting on quality as some people believe that it has. It's a very important reputation to maintain and the poison that would undermine that reputation would be a diminution in quality.
> *(Pyne quoted in Hurst and Tovey, 2013: n.p.)*

This language is roughly representative of the public policy discourse in Australia under federal Education Ministers Pyne, Birmingham, Tehan, and Tudge who between 2013 and 2022 were content for 'the problem' (Bacchi, 2009) to be re/presented solely as the inadequacies of disadvantaged students. This rhetoric has been in existence for some time in the UK and continues to mirror these sorts of sentiments with prominent commentary such as that shared by 'leading economist' Roger Bootle in *The Telegraph* in 2022, "The waste of resources involved in sending about half of our youngsters to university, in many cases to collect worthless degrees, is appalling. That proportion should be drastically reduced" (Bootle, 2022: n.p.). The lack of attention around the responsibility involved and the importance of pedagogical expertise to widening educational access, participation, and success perpetuate the belief that ability reflects innate talent and deepens the myth of meritocracy (Young, 1958). This leaves the complex web of privilege, power, and inequality mostly invisible and means those dealing with the onslaught of multiple forms of inequality are vulnerable to further exclusion through meritocratic discourses and deficit imaginaries. As we have argued in Chapter 2, meritocratic discourses powerfully shape – and limit – our pedagogical imaginations about possibilities to challenge exclusion while blocking the capacity to collectively create strategies framed by social justice praxis.

Excellence agendas have produced various assessment and evaluation regimes and have arguably positioned teaching as a highly valued aspect of academic labour in relation to other aspects of higher education practice, such as research. As part of these agendas, a focus has evolved on developing *professional skills* and *techniques* to improve 'quality' and practice, rather than understanding teaching as a key dimension of *academic and disciplinary knowledge*. When combined with the low-status position of pedagogical research in the context of wider research excellence agendas, the prioritisation of developing instrumentalised professional competencies through innovative practice is reinforced. These instrumentalist approaches to teaching limit attention to the practical dimensions of teaching only, with pedagogical theories playing a lesser role in institutional approaches to teaching excellence. This arguably marginalises key theoretical insights of rigorous pedagogical research, as outlined earlier, that could better enable academics to grapple with the intersections of excellence and equity and interrogate the dynamic power relations and inequalities at play in pedagogical spaces, including processes of curriculum development.

Pedagogical praxis and the politics of knowledge and knowing

Pedagogical praxis stays with the trouble of what it means to know, what and whose knowledges are valued, and in what contexts. Those engaged in pedagogical praxis ask pertinent questions: What bodies, processes and methodologies are put to work to form knowledge? How is knowledge formed, valued, and legitimated unequally in relation to intersecting formations of difference and structures of inequality? What are the politics of knowing and knowledge across different geopolitical contexts and what are their social implications? How might contemporary assertions of 'post-truth', often associated with populisms, undermine critical commitments to equity and social justice? Critical questioning has the potential to shape curricular reframings and the pedagogical relations that underpin such processes. Staying with the trouble of knowledge-formation in and through higher education reveals the complexities that are otherwise hidden through the performativities, dis/positions and representations of research and teaching within and across professional and discipline-based contexts. Rather than further entrench knowledge in the universalisms and postures of certainty that characterise an anthropocentric (neo)colonialism, pedagogical praxis is "intent on the crucial refusal of self-certainty" and recognises that "the question of whom to think-with is immensely material" (Haraway, 2016: 434).

Pedagogical praxis recognises the imperative of social justice insights to curriculum reform but also the significant limitations of hegemonic strategies that set up to 'decolonise' or 'Indigenise' the curriculum. Additive approaches that seek to include 'diverse knowledge' have minimal capacity to grapple with the complexities of multidimensional injustices and intersecting inequalities embedded in curricular frameworks that reproduce epistemic injustice and symbolic violence. This includes the ways that histories of colonialism, racism, and patriarchy are interwoven in the knowledge systems and formations upon which academic, professional, and disciplinary foundations are based. Without interrogating the epistemological frameworks that have formed disciplinary knowledge over time, and the bodies (of people and knowledge) who are privileged and represented in such processes, simply stating that students' diverse knowledge is valued is not enough to transform the relations of power that author/ise knowing and knowledge practices within and across different professional and academic fields. Pedagogical praxis demands parity of participation in processes of curriculum transformation. The aim is to engage in ethical reflexivity with ontological and epistemological questions about being-with, knowing-with, and doing-with other bodies (of knowledge and living beings) as part of a decolonising process that interrogates engrained dis/positions to knowing and knowledge. Those dis/positions, ontologies and knowledges that are constructed as neutral, objective, or universal must instead be deconstructed and interrogated as a starting point for commitments to anti-colonialism, in struggles to dismantle multidimensional injustices in and through higher education.

We advocate here for forms of pedagogical praxis that follow the likes of Patti Lather (2015), in the tradition of "opening up our privileged spaces in the production of a politics of difference that recognises paradox, complicity and complexity" (Lather, 2015: 3). Being able to seriously ask questions such as, given our neoliberalised contemporary contexts:

> What would the "incalculable subject" look like that was toward something not containable, in excess of meaning, rather than rational or disciplined or socialized or interpellated? As a counter to neoliberal and Big Data efforts to count and parse, capture and model our every move, how might we think a subject outside the parameters of the algorithms? How does this map onto Deleuze's "becoming imperceptible" in the face of the ubiquity of new forms of calculation toward retailing the world?
>
> *(Lather, 2015: 9)*

This requires collective examination of the histories in which the knowledges of whole communities (whilst recognising heterogeneity and contestation within communities as well as across them) have been devalued through curricular frameworks that validate particular epistemological positions and then claim these as value-free (Harding, 1991, 2015; Quinn, 2003; Cammarota, 2007; Luckett, Morreira and Baijnath, 2019). An example is the neutralisation of scientific knowledge embedded in Western-centric, masculine-oriented and White-privileged ontologies. Instead, it is imperative to interrogate those positionalities that have largely been represented as neutral and/or unproblematic; whilst (largely pathologising) attention has been shone on Other positionalities associated with equity policy and practice. Mellor (2022) explains this in relation to Indigenous knowledges and peoples:

> In the university, Indigenous knowledges and peoples occupy a negative socio-epistemic space because the shared epistemic resources of patriarchal imperial Western knowledge and knowers subjugate the recognition, representation and production of knowledges produced by marginalised peoples.
> *(Mellor, 2022: 158)*

The politics of knowing and knowledge is often obscured in equity policy and practice in higher education despite efforts to decolonise the curriculum, further deepening the unjust timescapes in which the subjugation of marginalised knowledges peoples is sustained. This raises questions about the efficacy of the terms of reference used in higher education strategies, such as creating inclusive curriculum. The focus point on inclusion, particularly when inclusion is not problematised as a colonising device, tends to reiterate the institutional desire for marginalised knowledge to fit into and harmonise with the existing corpus of knowledge rather than challenging the underpinning epistemic structures that reproduce ontological subordination. The obsession of the corporatised university with key performance indicators as the predominant mechanism to guide action (that is in line with the corporate discourse) further entrenches a logic of change associated with patriarchal imperial Western dis/positions. We argue that this significantly limits the capacity to apprehend the long-term, complicated nature of challenging the epistemic and ontological violence inflicted on subjugated bodies of knowledge and people.

In the South African context, Luckett (2016) argues that it is an ethical imperative to "recreate curricula that will recuperate and build black student agency for integrated identity formation, deep learning and academic achievement" (2016: 424). This requires a process of dialogue and expanding and re-reading curriculum in new ways (Luckett, 2016), providing students with not only expanded content but also the critical tools to challenge and debate "inherited canons" (2016: 425). Shay and Peseta (2016) explore what an inclusive and socially just curriculum reform agenda might involve, bringing attention to the problems of policy instrumentalism that tend to gloss over complex epistemological tensions across disciplinary fields. They argue for the redistribution of 'powerful knowledge' and for broader attention to the effects of curriculum in reproducing the "conditions that alienate, demean, and ultimately reduce life opportunities for not only individuals but also the communities they come from and future generations" (Shay and Peseta, 2016: 361).

As Clegg explains: "Access is not just a question of entering higher education it also becomes an issue about what is being accessed in institutionally diverse higher education systems" (Clegg, 2016: 458). Inclusive and social justice approaches bring the social and epistemic together to enable critical examination of the curriculum "so that knowledge is judged by the extent to which it provides access to its objects, as well as the extent to which curriculum provides students with access to the structure of knowledge and systems of meaning" (Wheelahan, 2010: 47, quoted in Clegg, 2016: 468).

Pedagogical praxis requires engagement with postcolonial and decolonial theories that stimulate ongoing reimagining of knowing and knowledge (Fanon, 1963; Bhabha, 1994; Spivak, 1988; Said, 1993; Mama, 1995) to consider the relation of higher education curriculum to histories of colonialism and the racialised injustices that continue to profoundly oppress people of colour (Luckett, Morreira and Baijnath, 2019; Gyamera and Burke, 2018). This also requires attention to the intersecting forces of gender injustice that manifest in a continuum of GBV, whilst simultaneously maintaining the invisibility of knowing how GBV is lived and experienced in ways that undermine the contribution of women in knowledge-formation (Burke, Gyamera and the Ghanaian Feminist Collective, 2023; Burke et al, 2023; Coffey et al, 2023). Pedagogical praxis considers how we might engage in transforming our relationship to knowledge and knowing by opening our capacity to listen and learn from those who have been silenced, marginalised, or made invisible, moving towards a critical project of creating new knowledge structures (Lugones, 2010).

Attention to the politics of knowledge and knowing brings to the fore the urgencies of our time in relation to multidimensional injustices, including the planetary crises we are facing (Mbembe, 2023). It demands we think-with difference through praxis with attention to knowing as doing-with rather than knowledge as static depositories of data and information. Difference becomes a rich resource for the process of generating knowing; or 'knowledge commoning', in Mbembe's (2023: 13) terms, as part of a planetary project of social responsibility, developing a new 'ecology of meaning'. This requires digging into the 'world archives' of knowledge, generating new forms of knowing, and discarding knowledge that is devastating our capacity to live. This points to the im/possibilities of building new forms of knowing-with or creating the conditions for planetary consciousness to emerge (Mbembe, 2023). To generate decolonising knowing we must abandon ideas of mastery or conquest and instead attend to the processes by which we make meaning, focusing on our relationality in and of the world. We need to build transdisciplinary knowledge of what it means to share a planet with other beings and to consider how we learn to care for it and for others. How might pedagogical praxis place care at the centre of the project of knowing-with and provide emancipation from the "colonial temptation to build hierarchies between beings, cultures and things"

(Mbembe, 2023: 12). Resistance to 'authoritarian universalism' and generating dis/positions of reparation in relation to epistemic justice is crucial. This demands that knowledge is decolonised by fully challenging the commercialisation practices that higher education institutions are increasingly being compelled into through neoliberalised funding frameworks that privilege markets rather than living beings. Instead, pedagogical praxis is concerned with fostering participatory relationships in the co-formation of knowing and knowledge constituted through the "full breadth of epistemic diversity" to decolonise knowledge towards the more-than-human world (Mbembe, 2023: 31). Pedagogical timescapes that foreground counter-hegemonic, social justice praxis thus might foster epistemic responsibilities for students and staff engaged in making meaning, keeping to the fore the contestations, and competing claims over knowledge, truth and justice.

Conclusion

In this chapter, we have focused on how equity is commonly positioned as outside of the core work of higher education institutions, approached instead as a bolted-on project of attention paid towards remedying the deficiencies of individual 'equity students'. We have identified the challenge in which systems of support (outsourced using technicist tools) are increasingly being adopted with only a narrowed conception of what problem these systems are designed to resolve. The chapter has demonstrated how this process of peripherisation disconnects the methodologies, approaches, and practices of teaching – the pedagogies of higher education – from questions of equity, with deep implications for projects intending to transform universities towards more socially just systems and practices. We have advocated for shifting the ways in which pedagogical development is supported and practised in higher education; towards the redistribution of resources and opportunities to access and participate in academic practices whilst simultaneously examining those practices, troubling conventional approaches to 'inclusion' that do nothing to destabilise the exclusive and damaging engrained misrecognition of the experiences, histories, resources, values, and knowledges of those communities who have been systematically and persistently marginalised and subjugated.

We have then considered histories of critical approach that offer a way to engage these challenges, drawing on the influential work of Paulo Freire whilst acknowledging some of the critiques made and contradictions identified over time within Freire's oeuvre. Through this, we have identified the important methodological aspects of Freire's contribution that we contend offer important material for the project of confronting deeply engrained misrecognition of marginalised bodies (of people and knowledge) in higher education when it comes to questions of teaching and learning. Drawing on feminist engagements with Freire, we have called for caution around a common appetite to snap quickly to the method. We make this call because we see that one ready way in which aspects of methodology (such as sitting in a sustained manner with the complexity of the politics of knowledge) are dismissed in the thirst for method (i.e. What Works for teaching in universities) and how this can willingly depoliticise the project of generating inclusive pedagogical practices. We have drawn on feminist engagements with Freire to articulate how the careful development of contexts in which these more difficult-to-define aspects of historically exclusive institutions such as universities can help to develop pedagogical practices that make new participations possible. As part of this call, we have troubled the notion of excellence, noting it as a problematic conceptual technology within higher education that holds in place exclusive pedagogical practices, imbued as it is with only specific connotations and conceptualisations. We have discussed too a troubling *ignore-ance*; an idea that, through fear and negation, attention is unconsciously not paid to these dynamics as part of a broader system of distributed, networked power that holds in place a common sense of, for example, how student or staff or programme 'quality' is assessed in higher education.

Given the urgency of these issues, and the lack of attention commonly paid to them, we want in the next section to continue to consider how they might be addressed in the contemporary conditions of higher education. In this effort, we identify assumptions and taken-for-granted characteristics of higher education institutions and practices which hold in place these attentions and imaginaries (Burke, 2012). Key taken-for-granted aspects of social life are time and space; concepts reified so totally within Western imaginaries as to be considered almost un/reason/able to interrogate. Contemporary scholarship however on time and temporalities, and how these relate intimately with spatial considerations, has helped to identify crucial underlying generative dynamics that create the conditions in which the misrecognitions, maldistributions and misrepresentations play out, preventing the possibility of parity of participation. The spaces in which bodies of people, material, and knowledge are differently mobilised and situated clearly matter in pedagogical formations. The timeframes and spaces of teaching and learning are formed in relation to the different and contested embodied experiences of participants – the feeling in space, how selves and thoughts are reformed in and through those times and spaces, how mal/distributions, mis/recognitions and mis/representations evolve. How might differently situated bodies in timescapes (Adam, 1998, 2004) of higher education reconfigure pedagogies to stay with the trouble of multidimensional inequalities? If timescapes are discursively and materially constituted, are these open to processes of collaborative re/imagining? How might we find possibilities for articulating differences and different beings, doings and knowings across, and between pedagogical spaces and relations? Pedagogical praxis demands ethical reflexivity to examine the relations between spatiality and temporality. Questions can certainly be raised, such as: How is time structured within and across pedagogical spaces, and with what effects? What are the different embodied relationalities to time-space across structural, material, and symbolic inequalities? These are some of the questions to which we turn in Chapter 5.

References

Adam, B. (1998) *Timescapes of Modernity*. London: Routledge.

Adam, B. (2004) *Time*. Cambridge: Polity.

Ahmed, S. (2004) *The Cultural Politics of Emotion*. New York: Routledge.

Arday, J., and Mirza, H.S. (2018) *Dismantling Race in Higher Education: Racism, Whiteness and Decolonising the Academy*. London: Springer.

Aronowitz, S. (2015) *Against Orthodoxy: Social Theory and Its Discontents*. New York: Palgrave Macmillan. https://doi.org/10.1057/9781137387189

Ashwin, P. (2017) 'What is the teaching excellence framework in the United Kingdom, and will it work?', *International Higher Education*, 88, 10–11. https://doi.org/10.6017/ihe.2017.88.9683

Bacchi, C. (2009) *Analysing Policy: What's the Problem Represented to Be?* Frenchs Forest: Pearson Education.

Ball, S.J. (2012) 'Performativity, commodification and commitment: An I-Spy guide to the neo-liberal university', *British Journal of Educational Studies*, 60(1), 17–28.

Barnett, P. (2011) 'Discussions across difference: Addressing the affective dimensions of teaching diverse students about diversity', *Teaching in Higher Education*, 16(6), 669–679.

Beauvoir, S.D. (1952) *The Second Sex*. London: Jonathon Cape.

Bhabha, H.K. (1994) *The Location of Culture* (2nd ed.). London: Routledge. https://doi.org/10.4324/9780203820551

Blackmore, P., and Kandiko, C. (2011) 'Motivation in academic life: A prestige economy', *Research in Post-Compulsory Education*, 16(4), 399–411. https://doi.org/10.1080/13596748.2011.626971

Block, D. (2018) 'The political economy of language education research (or the lack thereof): Nancy Fraser and the case of translanguaging', *Critical Inquiry in Language Studies*, 15(4), 237–257. https://doi.org/10.1080/15427587.2018.1466300

Boler, M. (1999) *Feeling Power: Emotions and Education*. New York: Routledge.

Boler, M. (2004) 'Teaching for hope: The ethics of shattering world views', in Liston, D., and Garrison, J. (Eds) *Teaching, Learning and Loving. Reclaiming Passion in Educational Practice*. New York: Routledge Falmer, 117–131.

Bootle, R. (2022) 'Next PM must end the Blairite worship of worthless university degrees', *The Telegraph*, 10 July. www.telegraph.co.uk/business/2022/07/10/next-pm-must-end-blairite-worship-worthless-university-degrees/

Bozalek, V., Leibowitz, B., Carolissen, R., and Boler, M. (2014) *Discerning Critical Hope in Educational Practices*. London: Routledge.

Brady, J. (1994) 'Critical literacy, feminism, and a politics of representation', in McLaren, P.L., and Lankshear, C. (Eds) *Politics of Liberation*. London: Routledge.

Brown, R. (2018) 'Higher education and inequality', *Perspectives: Policy and Practice in Higher Education*, 22(2), 37–43. https://doi.org/10.1080/13603108.2017.1375442

Brusoni, M., Damian, R., Sauri, J., Jackson, S., Kömürcügil, H., Malmedy, M., Matveeva, O., Motova, G., Pisarz, S., Pol, P., Rostlund, A., Soboleva, E., Tavares, O., and Zobel, L. (2014) *The Concept of Excellence in Higher Education*. Brussels, Belgium: European Association for Quality Assurance in Higher Education.

Burke, P.J. (2012) *The Right to Higher Education: Beyond Widening Participation*. London and New York: Routledge.

Burke, P.J. (2015) 'Re/imagining higher education pedagogies: Gender, emotion and difference', *Teaching in Higher Education*, 20, 388–401.

Burke, P.J. (2017) 'Difference in higher education pedagogies: Gender, emotion and shame', *Gender and Education*, 29, 430–444.

Burke, P.J., Coffey, J., Parker, J., Hardacre, S., Cocuzzoli, F., Shaw, J., and Haro, A. (2023) ' "It's a lot of shame": Understanding the impact of gender-based violence on higher education access and participation', *Teaching in Higher Education*, 1–16. https://doi.org/10.1080/13562517.2023.2243449

Burke, P.J., Crozier, G., and Misiaszek, L.I. (2017) *Changing Pedagogical Spaces in Higher Education: Diversity, Inequalities and Misrecognition*. London: Routledge.

Burke, P.J., Gyamera, G.O., and the Ghanaian Feminist Collective (2023) 'Examining the gendered timescapes of higher education: Reflections through letter writing as feminist praxis', *Gender and Education*, 35(3), 267–281. https://doi.org/10.1080/09540253.2022.2151982

Butler, J. (2005) 'Giving an account of oneself', *Diacritics*, 31(4), 22–40.

Cammarota, J. (2007) 'A social justice approach to achievement: Guiding Latina/o students toward educational attainment with a challenging, socially relevant curriculum', *Equity and Excellence in Education*, 40(1), 87–96.

Cervantes-Soon, C.G. (2017) *Juarez Girls Rising: Transformative Education in Times of Dystopia*. Minneapolis and London: University of Minnesota Press.

Clegg, S. (2016) 'The necessity and possibility of powerful "regional" knowledge: Curriculum change and renewal', *Teaching in Higher Education*, 21(4), 457–470. https://doi.org/10.1080/13562517.2016.1157064

Coffey, J., Burke, P.J., Hardacre, S., Parker, J., Coccuzoli, F., and Shaw, J. (2023) 'Students as victim-survivors: The enduring impacts of gender-based violence for students in higher education', *Gender and Education*, 35(6–7), 623–637. https://doi.org/10.1080/09540253.2023.2242879

Cook-Sather, A. (2018) 'Listening to equity-seeking perspectives: How students' experiences of pedagogical partnership can inform wider discussions of student success', *Higher Education Research and Development*, 37(5), 923–936.

Darling-Hammond, L., and Friedlaender, D. (2008) 'Creating excellent and equitable schools', *Educational Leadership*, 65(8), 14–21.

Elfert, M. (2023) 'Humanism and democracy in comparative education', *Comparative Education*, 59(3), 398–415. https://doi.org/10.1080/03050068.2023.2185432

Ellsworth, E. (1997) *Teaching Positions: Difference, Pedagogy, and the Power of Address*. New York: Teachers College Press.

Fanon, F. (1963) *The Wretched of the Earth*. New York: Grove Press.

Foucault, M. (1977) *Discipline and Punish: The Birth of the Prison*, Sheridan, A. (Trans). New York: Pantheon Books.

Frank, R.H., and Cook, P.J. (2010) *The Winner-Take-All-Society: Why the Few at the Top Get so Much More Than the Rest of Us*. London: Virgin Books.

Fraser, N. (1997) *Justice Interruptus: Critical Reflections on the "Postsocialist" Condition*. London and New York: Routledge.

Freire, P. (1970/2005) *Pedagogy of the Oppressed*. New York: Continuum.

Freire, P. (1973) *Education for Critical Consciousness*. New York: Seabury Press.

Freire, P. (2009) *Pedagogy of Hope*. London: Continuum.

Giroux, H.A. (2021) 'Remembering Paulo Freire as a freedom fighter', *Policy and Practice: A Development Education Review*, 33, 114–118, Autumn.

Glass, R.D. (2001) On Paulo Freire's philosophy of praxis and the foundations of liberation education', *Educational Researcher*, 30(2), 15–25.

Gunn, A. (2018) 'Metrics and methodologies for measuring teaching quality in higher education: Developing the teaching excellence framework (TEF)', *Educational Review*, 70(2), 129–148. https://doi.org/10.1080/00131911.2017.1410106

Gyamera, G.O., and Burke, P.J. (2018) 'Neoliberalism and curriculum in higher education: A post-colonial analyses', *Teaching in Higher Education*, 23(4), 450–467. https://doi.org/10.1080/13562517.2017.1414782

Haraway, D. (2016) *Staying with the Trouble: Making Kin in the Chthulucene*. Durham, NC: Duke University Press.

Harding, S. (1991) *Whose Science? Whose Knowledge? Thinking from Women's Lives*. Ithaca: Cornell University Press.

Harding, S. (2015) *Objectivity and Diversity: Another Logic of Scientific Research*. Chicago: University of Chicago Press.

Hatcher, C. (1998) *Making the Enterprising Manager in Australia: A Genealogy* (PhD thesis). Brisbane: School of Cultural and Policy Studies, Faculty of Education, Queensland University of Technology.

Hooks, B. (1993). 'Speaking about Paulo Freire', in McLaren, P., and Leonard, P. (Eds) *Paulo Freire*. London: Routledge.

Hooks, B. (1994) *Teaching to Transgress: Education as the Practice of Freedom*. New York: Routledge.

Hunter, C.P. (2013) 'Shifting themes in OECD country reviews of higher education', *Higher Education*, 66, 707–723.

Hurst, D., and Tovey, J. (2013) 'Christopher Pyne reveals university shake-up', *The Sydney Morning Herald*. www.smh.com.au/federal-politics/politicalnews/christopher-pyne-reveals-university-shakeup-20130924-2ucag.html

Kandiko Howson, C.B., Coate, K., and de St. Croix, T. (2018) 'Mid-career academic women and the prestige economy', *Higher Education Research and Development*, 37(3), 1–16.

Lather, P. (2012) *Getting Lost: Feminist Efforts Toward a Double(d) Science*. New York: State University of New York Press.

Lather, P. (2015) *Against Proper Objects: Toward the Diversely Qualitative*. www.mmu.ac.uk/media/mmuacuk/content/documents/esri/events/siqr-2015/lather.pdf

Leathwood, C., and Hey, V. (2009) 'Gender/ed discourses and emotional sub-texts: Theorising emotion in UK higher education', *Teaching in Higher Education*, 14(4), 429–440.

Luckett, K. (2016) 'Curriculum contestation in a post-colonial context: A view from the South', *Teaching in Higher Education*, 21(4), 415–428. https://doi.org/10.1080/13562517.2016.1155547

Luckett, K., Morreira, S., and Baijnath, M. (2019) 'Decolonising the curriculum: Recontextualisation, identity and self-critique in a post-apartheid university', in Quinn, L. (Ed) *Re-Imagining Curriculum: Spaces for Disruption*. Stellenbosch: African Sun Media, Sun Press, 23–44. https://doi.org/10.18820/9781928480396

Lugones, M. (2010) 'Toward a decolonial feminism', *Hypatia*, 25(4), 742–759.

Lumb, M., Burke, P.J., and Bennett, A. (2021) 'Obscenity and fabrication in equity and widening participation methodologies', *British Educational Research Journal*, 47, 539–556. https://doi.org/10.1002/berj.3663

Lygo-Baker, S. (2017) 'The role of values in higher education: The fluctuations of pedagogic frailty', in Kinchin, I., and Winstone, N. (Eds) *Pedagogic Frailty and Resilience in Higher Education*. Rotterdam, The Netherlands: Sense Publishers.

Macdonald, H.M. (2013) 'Inviting discomfort: Foregrounding emotional labour in teaching anthropology in post-apartheid South Africa', *Teaching in Higher Education*, 18(6), 670–682.

Mama, A. (1995) *Beyond the Masks: Race, Gender and Subjectivity*. London and New York: Routledge.

Mbembe, A. (2023) *Transforming Knowledge for UNITWIN/UNESCO Chairs Programme 3–4 November 2022*. Paris, France: UNESCO Headquarters, UNESCO.

Mellor, K. (2022) *Decolonising higher education: (re)conceptualising knowing and knowledge in pedagogical spaces* (PhD thesis). Newcastle, NSW, Australia: University of Newcastle. http://hdl.handle.net/1959.13/1466068

Mettler, S. (2014) *Degrees of Inequality: How the Politics of Higher Education Sabotaged the American Dream*. New York: Basic Books.

Neary, M. (2016) 'Teaching excellence framework: A critical response and an alternative future', *Journal of Contemporary European Research*, 12(3).

Nixon, J., Misiaszek, L.I., and Burke, P.J. (2015) 'First Freire: Early writings in social justice education', *International Studies in Sociology of Education*, 25(2), 150–163. https://doi.org/10.1080/09620214.2015.1024403

Quinn, J. (2003) *Powerful Subjects: Are Women Really Taking Over the University?* Stoke-on-Trent: Trentham Books.

Raphael Reed, L., Croudace, C., Harrison, N., Baxter, A., and Last, K. (2007) *Young Participation in Higher Education: A Sociocultural Study of Educational Engagement in Bristol South Parliamentary Constituency. Research Summary*. A HEFCE-Funded Study. Bristol: University of the West of England.

Reay, D. (2001) 'Finding or losing yourself? Working-class relationships to education', *Journal of Education Policy*, 16(4), 333–346. https://doi.org/10.1080/02680930110054335

Rosinger, K.O., Taylor, B.J., Coco, L., and Slaughter, S. (2016) 'Organizational segmentation and the prestige economy: Deprofessionalization in high- and low-resource departments', *Journal of Higher Education*, 87(1), 27–54.

Sahlberg, P. (2016) 'The global educational reform movement and its impact on schooling', in Mundy, K., Green, A., Lingard, B., and Verger, A. (Eds) *Handbook of Global Education Policy*. Chichester, West Sussex: Wiley-Blackwell, 180–196.

Said, E. (1993/1978). *Orientalism*. New York: Pantheon.

Shay, S., and Peseta, T. (2016) 'A socially just curriculum reform agenda', *Teaching in Higher Education*, 21(4), 361–366. https://doi.org/10.1080/13562517.2016.1159057

Spivak, G.C. (1988) 'Can the subaltern speak?', in Nelson, C., and Grossberg, L. (Eds) *Marxism and the Interpretation of Culture*. London: Macmillan.

Stevenson, J., Whelan, P., and Burke, P.J. (2017) 'Teaching excellence in the context of frailty', in Kinchin, I., and Winstone, N. (Eds) *Pedagogic Frailty and Resilience in Higher Education*. Rotterdam, The Netherlands: Sense Publishers.

Tomlinson, M., Enders, J., and Naidoo, R. (2020) 'The teaching excellence framework: Symbolic violence and the measured market in higher education', *Critical Studies in Education*, 61(5), 627–642. https://doi.org/10.1080/17508487.2018.1553793

Tuck, E., and Yang, K.W. (2014) 'Unbecoming claims: Pedagogies of refusal in qualitative research', *Qualitative Inquiry*, 20(6), 811–818. https://doi.org/10.1177/1077800414530265

Weiler, K. (1994) 'Freire and a feminist pedagogy of difference', in McLaren, P., and Lankshear, C. (Eds) *Politics of Liberation*. London: Routledge.

Wrigley, T., Thomson, P., and Lingard, B. (2012) *Changing Schools: Alternative Ways to Make a World of Difference*. London: Taylor and Francis.

Young, M. (1958) *The Rise of the Meritocracy 1870–2033: An Essay on Education and Society*. London: Thames and Hudson.

Zembylas, M. (2013) 'Critical pedagogy and emotion: Working through "troubled knowledge" in posttraumatic contexts', *Critical Studies in Education*, 54(2), 176–189. https://doi.org/10.1080/17508487.2012.743468

Zembylas, M. (2015) ' "Pedagogy of discomfort" and its ethical implications: The tensions of ethical violence in social justice education', *Ethics and Education*, 10(2), 163–174. https://doi.org/10.1080/17449642.2015.1039274

Zembylas, M. (2018) 'Decolonial possibilities in South African higher education: Reconfiguring humanising pedagogies as/with decolonising pedagogies', *South African Journal of Education*, 38(4), 1–11.

Zembylas, M. (2022) 'Affective and biopolitical dimensions of hope: From critical hope to anti-colonial hope in pedagogy', *Journal of Curriculum and Pedagogy*, 19(1), 28–48. https://doi.org/10.1080/15505170.2020.1832004

PART TWO

Methodologies for transformative equity praxis

Part Two argues for the importance of care-full and response-able methodological consideration in recontextualising, reimagining, and reframing higher education for equity. Methodology matters for equity research, but just as importantly for programmatic development, for evaluation design, and for policymaking. Conceptualising methodology as an ethical-political-epistemological-ontological complex, we consider how methodology animates method in space-time. Yet methodological concerns are often overlooked, with attention immediately on method in the pursuit of evidence-based policy and practice. In Part Two, we consider how knowledge and values are produced through methodological framings that, when ignored, can become complicit in the perpetuation of deficit imaginaries that hide power and inequality from view. This accords with a preoccupation with measurable and observable data, privileging decontextualised and metric-centred methods. This conceals the preference for methodologies that erase power from view and hide the interpretive processes necessarily involved in the construction of equity policy and practice. To trouble this blind spot in equity formation, we introduce a new methodological framework embedded in a social justice ethical-political-epistemological-ontological complex, which we call PPoEMs. Our aim is to open sPace; the time, space, and critical resources needed to participate in communities of praxis, in which co-participants engage in collective interrogation and build response-abilities with Others, and act with an ethics of care.

In this part of the book, we pay close attention to time, as a significant yet taken-for-granted dimension of collective and contested (re)imagining(s) of contemporary higher education. We explore how hegemonic discourses such as 'time management' ignore unequal relations to time, in which the

DOI: 10.4324/9781003257165-7

conditions of precarity are unequally distributed. We consider the contemporary 'timescapes' (Adam, 1998) in which increasing numbers of staff are on temporary, casual and/or fixed-term contracts, and temporal inequalities are further exacerbated by the diminished funding of higher education. Time is an intersecting form of social difference, and we explore how spatio-temporal relations re/produce inequalities in subtle ways through taken-for-granted structures, discourses, and practices, drawing on Sharma's 'power-chronographies' (2014) to attend to this relational focus. Our analysis shows the need for an ethics that can build participation across different differences to apprehend and resist 'mis/time/framing'.

In relation to these spatio-temporal questions of methodology, we point to evaluation, which has become central to equity policymaking and programmatic development. We consider how evaluation has become an effective form of modern governance practice that constructs the problem of equity through the perspectives of those in positions of relative authority. This dynamic requires interrogation if the value systems of those authorised to frame evaluation are not aligned with the spatio-temporalities and diverse values of underrepresented people and communities, who are most impacted by equity evaluation. The sustained analysis offered in Part Two demonstrates how evaluation methodologies, when concealed or ignored, become effective mechanisms for re-embedding neoliberal commitments and rationalities, helping to remake higher education in ways that are arguably anathema to notions of fairness and justice. There are important distinctions to be made between the *accountabilities* that these methodologies facilitate and different approaches we would advocate for that resonate with reciprocal *responsibility* to one an/Other. Ultimately, we demonstrate that evaluation is about values and valuing and argue for resisting a fixation on metric-centred methodologies that characterise hegemonic equity policy and programme evaluation.

In keeping with these concerns, PPoEMs is offered as a methodological framework to 'stay with the trouble' (Haraway, 2016) of equity in higher education, which is a powerful social institution that produces, legitimates, and disseminates knowledge. PPoEMs responds to the questions generated through collaborative praxis and is framed by social justice insights, including the need to keep thinking-with Others. A key aim is to bring together feminist, decolonial, post/structural, and sociological insights for communities of praxis, opening sPace for solidarity, compassion, response-ability, and a deep ethic of care.

References

Adam, B. (1998) *Timescapes of Modernity*. London: Routledge.
Haraway, D. (2016) *Staying with the Trouble: Making Kin in the Chthulucene*. Durham: Duke University Press.
Sharma, S. (2014) *In the Meantime*. Durham: Duke University Press.

5

TIME FOR EQUITY PRAXIS

Introduction

Interrogating the notion of time and its relation to equity praxis is a complex undertaking. Time is a powerful example of what this book consistently points to; those aspects of our social existence that we take most for granted, almost necessarily so if we are to continue to interact with each other, and yet these are aspects deeply implicated in making durable the multidimensional social inequalities which deny parity of participation. Each of us constructs, inhabits, relates to, and experiences time in ways shaped by our diverse cultural contexts. In many Western settings, it is common to adopt spatial metaphors to make sense of our taken-for-granted relations with/in time, for example, daily rhythms feeling 'circular', and discussing pasts, presents, and futures in mostly linear terms. Dominant imaginaries in these settings also tend to accept what has been demonstrated for a long time by anthropologists, that time is a social construction, and yet our bodies grow and change in ways that show an inescapable materiality rejecting our control. Time inhabits power relations with ourselves and each other in subtle ways, with endless consequences. Indeed, the final word in the previous sentence (con/sequence) is an example of the ways in which the formation 'cause and effect' is embedded deeply in our language and power-knowledge relations. Our belief in the con of sequence ('if x then y') is so entrenched that more uncertain and plural conceptualisations of 'impact' built on relational frameworks of the social are readily dismissed. Policy and programme evaluation is one example where the notion of cause and effect runs rampant as the 'proper' rationality for understanding whether an initiative demonstrates value through observed effects of an intervention.

DOI: 10.4324/9781003257165-8

A growing body of higher education literature considers the complexities of 'university time', including different conceptualisations and experiences of the temporal, and how this relates to projects of equity. It has become common to acknowledge the 'speed' of higher education, as part of a broader account of contemporary living. This chapter sets out an analytical lens for equity praxis which focuses more on the politics of time. Drawing on the scholarship of Adam (1998) and Sharma (2014), we foreground how time is an intersecting form of social difference that matters in higher education. With Adam's (1998) notion of 'timescapes', we show how intricately interwoven spatio-temporal relations re/produce inequalities in subtle ways through taken-for-granted structures, discourses, and practices. Sharma's 'power-chronographies' (2014) reinforce a balanced space-time approach to understanding differential and relational temporalities as power relations. These conceptual tools help bring new dimensions to the project of foregrounding how struggles over meaning and reconstitutions of the purpose of higher education are riven by contemporary (ir)rationalities of capitalism.

Time has become a significant but also taken-for-granted discourse in our collective and contested (re)imagining(s) of contemporary higher education and its future. Readers may recognise – and may have drawn on – the discourses of 'time management' as increasingly hegemonic in higher education through various iterations, systems, and technologies. These discourses play out in contexts often characterised by uncertainty and precarity, with increasing numbers of staff on temporary, casual, and/or fixed-term contracts, with continual uncertainties around the funding of higher education, with greater moves towards marketised constructions of the purpose of higher education, with corporate notions reshaping pedagogical orientations. These include 'teaching smart' (a code for spending less time with our students) and 'being productive' (a code for being published in high impact, peer-reviewed highly ranked journals) and 'being successful' (a code for demonstrating success through narrowly framed measurable outputs judged through the lens of performativity rather than process-oriented pedagogical and deeply relational commitments valued through the lens of social justice). These discourses also help to stabilise a valorisation of conquering time, drawing on a worrying modernist, neocolonial conceptualisation of progress equated with human capacity to control worlds.

These examples, together with numerous other time-related pressures, shape expectations in and of higher education and of ourselves and of student bodies, discursively re-cited through the continual references to words such as 'delivery', 'excellence', and 'success'. These discursive re-citations are entangled with temporal relationalities, in which deadlines, short, stackable delivery of programmes, juggling multiple projects and responsibilities effectively and 'in time', together with regulatory mechanisms such as key performance indicators, construct time in ways that often feel like *there is no alternative*. This is framed by the perceived need and desire to be future-oriented, often discursively constructed, and with thorough reference to 'aspiration', 'employability', and 'productivity'. The expectations of and pressures on students are echoed through the expectations of and pressures on staff, whilst simultaneously a discursive distancing is created through time and space – including who is seen to have time for students and how that time is institutionally valued – or not – and what spaces are constructed to create connection or hierarchical distancing from and with students. Students are not equitably positioned in these discourses with assumptions often made that 'equity students' are support intensive and thus drain valuable time and resources (e.g. Devlin et al, 2023). This assumption reverberates with the politics of access and admissions and who is seen as having the right to higher education (Burke, 2012). To resist these expectations is to be *trouble*. Whilst this book clearly values 'staying with the trouble', we are keenly aware of the risks that come with how 'troubling' (as in critiquing) readily gets constructed as being a troublesome person, commonly in gendered ways (Ahmed, 2006a; Butler, 1999). Trouble is seen to collide with efficiency and therefore in dominant neoliberal imaginaries that demand speed at the behest of restless capital, it can be seen as unreasonable for processes of the troubling to be taken seriously.

In the next sections, we argue that the timescapes in which bodies of people, material, and knowledge are differently mobilised and situated matter in pedagogical formations. The spaces, rhythms, and temporalities of teaching and learning are formed in relation to the different and contested embodied experiences of participants: the feeling in space and time, how selves and thoughts are reformed in and through these, and how mal/distributions, mis/recognitions and mis/representations play out. How might differently situated bodies reconfigure higher education pedagogies to stay with the trouble of multidimensional inequalities? If timescapes are discursively and materially constituted, are these open to processes of collaborative re/imagining? How might we find possibilities for articulating differences and different beings, doings and knowings across and between pedagogical timescapes and relations? Pedagogical praxis demands ethical reflexivity to examine the relations between spatiality and temporality. Questions might be raised such as how is time structured within and across pedagogical spaces? What are the different embodied relationalities to time-space across structural, material, and symbolic inequalities?

Pedagogical timescapes

Material space in higher education tends to be a common focus for research, practice, and policymaking. In relation to disability for example – a legislated area of responsibility for universities in many contexts – the configuration of material spaces is an important accessibility consideration. Research has certainly uncovered that many students find the physical spaces of colleges and universities intimidating, alienating, and marginalising (Burke, 2002, 2012) and that belonging and inclusion are closely related to spatial relations and structures (Bennett, 2006). Space has been identified in higher education research as structuring student experience (Souter et al, 2011; Radcliffe et al, 2008; Neary et al, 2010; Ahlefeld, 2009), with consideration to the ways spatiality impacts participation and transformation (Jamieson et al, 2000; JISC, 2006; Temple, 2008; Powell, 2014). Yet, some of this work has been critiqued as reproducing a homogenising construction of student bodies, whereby the capacity to access, engage, and transform the flexible potentialities of pedagogical spaces is represented as neutral (Ahlefeld, 2009; Neary et al, 2010; Scholl, 2012). The temporalities surrounding equity constructions in higher education require similar interrogation.

Liveley and Wardrop (2020) examine the notion in UK widening participation policy that the future might be imagined simply as a minimal departure from the present. Importantly, they argue that this "constrains the utopian potential of widening participation to always already repeat the status quo" and advocate for "rigorous imagining" as a methodological framework for interrogating the ways we make sense of the present, pointing to the "inherently fictive qualities of futures thinking and policymaking" (Beckert, 2013, in Liveley and Wardrop, 2020: 684). Indeed, research suggests that personal aspiration is not static but is contextually formed in relation to time and space; for example, the forms of aspiration seen to be appropriate and/or available are situated in classed, gendered and racialised inequalities that are historically and spatially dynamic (Burke, 2006). Furthermore, the aspirations of equity policy and practice are temporally framed by the constructions of what is seen as possible or not at a historical moment. Arguably this is exacerbated by the short-term nature of specialised equity funding, which disrupts efforts to create and hold time, space, and connection for meaningful forms of continuous professional learning, which could then support sustainable development for pedagogical praxis across the sector.

There are a range of changes we are compelled to manage *in time* – examples might include the continual restructuring of higher education institutions and/or of the sector and the different roles and responsibilities we must adapt to, connected to the call for higher education participants to be flexible and resilient in the context of change. Datafication has led to 'just in time' measures, in which decisions are made in response to the immediate availability of data through new technologies (Selwyn, 2020). University teachers are coaxed into thinking they can 'know' who their students are through reductive, homogenising, narrowly framed and monodimensional datafication processes (see also Chapter 7). In these misframings, it is assumed that with access to data, technologies, and the latest teaching techniques, EDI can be identified and addressed in a straightforward manner. Yet, drawing from the insights of social justice research, we assert that students cannot fully be known, nor do they want to be, through reductive, class/ifying, datafication processes. For this denies the possibility of instead being seen and recognised as complex beings-with Others.

It is common in the contemporary university to hear discussions of different forms of 'time poverty'. We believe this idea needs to be approached with great care when it comes to equity. Often taken up to advocate for more technical teaching and learning approaches in higher education, the understanding operating here is that if teachers are 'time poor', then we need not to 'burden' them with ongoing contexts of professional growth and development, and that instead more instrumental frameworks and training will be the key. This is a problem we argue because it again dehumanises (i.e. objectivises) people and projects of contexts of education and it undermines possibilities for prolonged and sustained engagement with critical theory/action (praxis). The idea of time poverty, sometimes used by those seeking to support 'the time poor', often runs down a technicist line of training and skill development, rather than advocating for longer-term, richer, more complex pedagogical professional learning spaces that we argue for in this book. The risk is a dehumanisation that turns people into objects within a particular problem construction rather than raising awareness of the politics of time and temporalities that is at play, always in relation to the politics of space and spatiality. It also tends to obliterate the broader consideration around experiences of time, different cultural and social orientations to time and different ways to conceive of and experience this concept that we take up with such common sense in terms of everyday clock time of society.

Students are expected to demonstrate their capability to manage learning *in time* – making sense of the pedagogical contexts in which they find themselves, negotiating transitions to the next stages of their university study, moving from course to course in a modularised system, change of teachers, change of peers – all of this complexity heightened for those navigating multidimensional inequalities. Bunn, Bennett and Burke (2019) consider the challenges to students in which *anytime* is study time and students are increasingly responsible for managing their time despite differential and unequal relations to time. In this way, time management hides from view temporal inequalities, as Streamas (2023) demonstrates powerfully in the context of the USA and in examining how time is racialised but constructed as neutral. He shows how unequal time structures can be challenged through negotiated contracts with students that recognise and value their different temporal positions. He argues that such practices are vital if higher education institutions aim to value and recognise the diverse temporal practices of different communities in which students are situated. Discourses of time management regulate difference through processes of homogenisation and assimilation, in which students are expected to appropriately manage time, and conceal and control the inequalities they experience.

In arguing for recognising and making visible the struggles of students who care for children while studying, Dent (2020) builds on work in the field (Moreau, 2016; Moreau and Kerner, 2015; Hook, 2018) to disrupt the problematic universalistic, individualising and deficit discourses of meeting the needs of 'all' students to illustrate the importance of context in the lived experiences of students who encounter time structures in higher education differently. The struggles of student parents have been analysed in the Australian context by Hook (2018), who explores the experiences of postgraduate students who largely work to hide their status as sole parents for fear of the potential pathologising effects of being exposed as caring for children while studying.

Anticipation is projected onto institutional and personal desires, hopes, fears, and the risks and possibilities that higher education promises in relation to present and future commitments. However, the inequalities, emotions, and lived experiences that underpin different future-oriented investments in higher education are often made invisible by the logic of making the 'right' (calculated and rational) choices and 'effectively' managing time in the present (this plays out differently in different contexts). The dearth of research on higher education that foregrounds questions of time tends in itself to assist in the taken-for-granted 'business-as-usual', reproducing particular spatio-temporal structures, practices, embodiments and investments. We require new conceptions of time for social justice pedagogies and praxis. We have drawn with our colleagues (e.g. Bennett and Burke, 2018; Bunn, Bennett and Burke, 2019; Burke and Manathunga, 2020) on the concept of 'timescapes' to bring to light the spatio-temporal relationalities that profoundly shape our subjectivities (e.g. as students, teachers, academics, practitioners and leaders), discourses (e.g. equity, aspiration, and choice), and practices (e.g. of teaching, learning, assessors, course developers, research, and leadership). Conceptualising higher education 'timescapes' vividly captures embodied sensibilities of self in time and space, to analyse the complex structures and relations of inequality and power that produce temporal and ontological dis/positions and propel us towards particular future aspirations and orientations. Timescapes point to the cultural and symbolic nature of time and space, as both material *and* discursive.

We also *feel* timescapes – our experiences of the timescapes of higher education are moulded by the politics of emotion and this forms aspirations, hopes, and imagined possibilities in complex ways. This brings into relief how cumulative experiences of misrecognition over time generate sensibilities of shame, alienation, and not belonging through the ongoing symbolic violence of status subordination through the residues of life histories of subjection to deficit imaginaries. Aspirational formations are tied in with residual and cumulative effects of misrecognition and project a sense of future possibility – or impossibility. This is tied to both collective and personal sensibilities, dis/positions, and aspirations, as well as the pressures that come with the accelerated pace in which we are expected to display our propensity towards 'success' through the outcomes or outputs we produce and then by which we are assessed and judged.

Dis/positionality is central to understanding that timescapes are experienced as relational, tied to our social positioning and embodied, dynamic being-with, our subjectivities, experienced through everyday and institutionalised routines, habits, and practices. That is, different relations to timescapes generate im/possibilities and im/mobilities across and between different institutional structures, rhythms, contexts, and pressures. Timescapes are not neutral or linear. Time and space are not something that we 'have' or 'manage' in any straightforward sense. Yet temporal and spatial resources are vital to parity of participation in higher education (in a Fraserian multidimensional sense) – the resources that enable pedagogical, ontological, and epistemic access and participation (Burke et al, 2017).

Spatio-temporal dis/positions are formed through the competing social relationalities to, with and against dynamics of time within different spaces. In this sense, dis/position, in challenging neoliberal discourses of choice and aspiration, considers the role of the embodiment of hegemonic systems in ways that are often enacted pre-consciously. These conceptual insights illuminate that structural, cultural, and symbolic inequalities are not erased through entry into higher education as in much of the fantasy discourse of widening participation (Burke, 2012).

Contradictory policy concerns shape subjectivities, discourses, and practices across diverse timescapes in complex ways. These include the need to address diversity, and relatedly to create more inclusive assessment, curricula, and pedagogies. These policy concerns operate against and within other discursive framings of the timescapes of higher education, articulated through the lens of 'the market', and the imperative to compete for rank and position in global prestige cultures that channel our energies across a range of competing spatio-temporal domains and desires. These include aspirations for research and teaching 'excellence', for preparing graduates for 'success' through employability agendas and for displaying innovation in relation to new technologies that appear to hold future promise.

The politics of mis/time/framing and change

The presence of the new prevailing discourse of EDI in and beyond higher education implies that processes, or access, or distributions of opportunity need to change. In this way, EDI engages with a temporal politics that is future-oriented but also often places itself outside of history. We argue that it is important to acknowledge a perennial problem for initiatives that seek change; that we need to ask on whose terms, on whose time, and on what values should 'transitions' towards new arrangements 'form', and why? And, if

we are to foreground power and acknowledge that temporality is the experience of power relations in time, we argue equity praxis must centre a politics
of time/frame. We advocate for critical frameworks of action/reflection, not
to point out if and how exactly something is 'correct' or not, but because we
argue it is important to continue to learn with and about each Other, across
our differences, including how it is we have come to think about an issue in
certain ways.

As Ahmed reminds us (2006b), it is never enough to say that we are not
equitable, diverse, or inclusive. By admitting this, we are positioning ourselves
in a way that can actually alleviate the pressure on ourselves, even when being
critical. "The language we think of as critical can easily lend itself to the very
techniques of governance we critique" (Ahmed, 2006b: 108). Whilst acknowledging this trap, we argue that to make facile gestures more difficult in the face
of ready convention, we need critical interrogative action-reflection in higher
education that can take "into account how our lives are mediated by systems
of inequity such as classism, racism, and sexism" (Lather, 1992: 223). These
forms of critical praxis can make more difficult the sorts of gestures Ahmed
helps us to think about as 'non-performative' (Ahmed, 2006b), in that they
provide *only* the perception of change, with their successful action being to
hold convention in place with little or no change at all. The nonperformative
"does not "fail to act" because of conditions that are external to the speech
act: rather, it "works" because it fails to bring about what it names" (2006b:
105). The proliferation of EDI in higher education can tend in this direction,
mostly unable to disrupt practices of exclusion that ensure institutions continue to benefit the most privileged in our societies and often gathered around
what the next 'positive' initiative should be rather than approaching anything
akin to attempts at structural transformation. Earlier in this book we drew on
Fraser's notion of 'mis/framing' (a deep dimension of misrepresentation to do
with setting the boundaries of the political in a particular context).

> Here the injustice arises when the community's boundaries are drawn in
> such a way as to wrongly exclude some people from the chance to partici-
> pate at all in its authorized contests over justice. In such cases, misrepresen-
> tation takes a deeper form, which I shall call misframing.
>
> *(Fraser, 2013: 197)*

Processes productive of nonperformative equity rely on conditions resembling
non-parity of participation. These are conditions that quietly set boundaries of
exclusion for subjugated knowledges, im/mobilities, temporalities, and ways
of being – all prior to the first step of 'consultation'. Misframing is underway
before the setting of committee terms of reference. Misframing occurs prior to
the commissioning of the evaluation. Misframing precedes the development
of the research question. We argue it is important to consider a politics of

time/frame in the context of equity in higher education, as hegemonic neoliberal imaginaries, subjectivities, and relationalities of contemporary globalised higher education produce time/frames for misframing, resulting in endless silent 'political death' (Fraser, 2013). In doing so though, we want to resist a move to a sociology of speed in which time compression within advanced capitalism becomes the dominant analysis. Our own critical praxis in higher education has demonstrated to us that authoritative structures do not necessarily ensure there is 'no time' for debate or change. Often, it is just as likely that 'it is not the time' for discussing or debating equity. This might seem like a trivial distinction, yet it shows an example of how social justice-oriented projects are up against more than a 'making time' challenge under heavy workloads. It is also about on whose authority higher education timescapes, and staff/students experience of these, are made. As we have already acknowledged, time is a difficult notion. What the concept 'timescapes' does is to help dislodge our sense of linear time as a common-sense orientation, helping us to think in more complex ways about relation, experience, affect, and politics.

Sarah Sharma describes 'power chronographies' (Sharma, 2013), providing further footing for thinking through how the speed up/slow down discourse is a part of the biopolitics of contemporary governmentality, and that our experiences in and of time are dependent upon others' experience in and of time. Sharma's work complements Adam's 'timescapes' to reinforce the importance of a balanced political space-time conceptualisation and helps to foreground 'time' as a deeply assumed and ingrained form of social difference.

> In terms of a political economy of time it provides insight into the processes where bodies are differently valued temporally and made productive for capital. By inhabiting the world with a critical eye towards the differential ways in which time is structured and experienced, the aim of power chronography is to provide a politicization of time that dispels individualistic accounts of time and allows the social and relational contours of power in its temporal forms to emerge.
>
> *(Sharma, 2013: 317)*

Power chronography seeks to identify the challenges with and in time that not only cause problems but also create the inability to identify problems at all. The *always-already* character of the way hegemonic timescapes construct time mean that it is difficult to remember the framing of time as an artefact of cultural hegemony. We have previously used a spatial metaphor of the Ames Room (Lumb and Burke, 2019) to explain how the arbitrary fabrications of our social institutions and practices become naturalised through a constrained sense-making orientation to a context, and the difficulty, at times indeed the impossibility, of re/membering the social constructions, the power/knowledge relations at play. The temporal dimensions of this metaphor seem even more difficult with which to grapple. Timescapes as a conceptual tool helps to do this work, providing an imaginative canvas for the fluid, networked, capillary power-relations of temporality, including that every person's experience in and of time is dependent on one another's experience in and of time. Later in the chapter, we explore in more depth the importance of thinking about time as always in-relation. Not only in the sense of interpersonal relationships (e.g. on who do we rely on for 'our' time) but also given that any social justice praxis engaging with a politics of time needs to consider relations with social characteristics, including how

> differential access to space and time are inextricably gendered; that control over time and space, or at least the ability to be able to freely choose how to use one's time and space, are for women substantially influenced by the interlocking of the public and private spheres and by women's structural position in these spheres.
>
> *(Davies, 2003: 135)*

The making of new timescapes through social justice praxis in higher education is then arguably about queering time. It is a praxis to do with refusing and countering hegemonic timescapes upon which our institutions and practices are constantly reformulated. This refusal must accept however that countering hegemony is always partial and must navigate the ethical dilemmas of installing new hegemonies via inclusions that exclude; that build new 'common senses' carrying our prejudices, blind spots, and agendas – in the name of equity. The social justice praxis we call for here however is more to do with interrogating the ways in which, for example, policy language and discourse adopting 'aspiration' places an intense gaze on community members positioned as 'future students'. Or about reminding ourselves of the connotations of the language of 'deadline' that holds on to its history emerging as it did as a term in the American Civil War in which 'the dead line' was a spatial boundary beyond which prisoners of war were shot dead. This is a praxis to do with resisting the perceived moral authority of 'employability' as it sweeps aside the idea of higher education as an institution that can facilitate new personhoods, ideally on people's own terms, through processes of cultural formation guided by discipline-based knowledge. It is a praxis about bringing forward a daily analysis that pays attention to how the casualisation of staff in higher education introduces new, highly gendered precarities for those commonly required to provide care for students in higher education (e.g. Read, 2023). This is a praxis that can turn its gaze in almost any 'direction' to interrogate taken-for-granted practices in higher education and the ways in which these subtly make social inequalities durable.

Consider for a moment the role of *minutes* and *minutia* in relation to equity in higher education. By 'minute' we might of course be referring to a variety of subjects and objects. For example, by minute, we can refer to '60 seconds' as a way of thinking about units of linear clock time. We might also refer to units of spatial measurement in geometry relating to the 'degrees of a circle'. For some of us, when we hear/read *minutes* in this context, our thoughts turn to the process of documenting discussions and decisions in meetings. These possible conceptualisations stem from a history of the term being used to refer to the *small*, the *chopped*, the *limited*, the *precise*, even the *petty*. And we would argue this can be where much mis/framing operates – in the 'minutia' of institutional practice. The political deaths which make social inequality durable happen within the mundane always-already conventions quietly guiding practices of exclusion. They live within the subtle prejudices that inhabit us, and our sense of ourselves, and our shared sense of what is legitimate and reason-able higher education. This is one way to think about capillary power in higher education, in that it is within the conduct at the extremities rather than any 'seat of power' which ultimately shape our relations to and within higher education. Structures and policies are of course important, and equity work requires many forms of accountability. Yet the minutia matters intensely, and it is the minutia that temporalises too, binding us and our embodied experiences in our sense of time. The term 'minutia' helps us also to think together time and space, and to consider what counter-hegemonic timescapes might resemble that take up social justice praxis. This challenges us to rethink equity practice, including who the equity practitioners are. Consider the role of meeting minutes, in the sense introduced earlier as a process of documenting statements, recitations, commitments, agendas, and policies. This responsibility of what becomes documented in higher education matters deeply for equity. The matter of how minutes are authored, who re-authorises these under processes of review, and under whose authority they are distributed are all opportunities for different timescapes of higher education to emerge that counter hegemonic convention holding in place a deeply inequitable status quo. Minutes, and their potential for consolidating the political death of mis/framing, are an endless opportunity for a praxis that refuses mis/framing.

Calling for equity praxis produces perhaps a precarious position given it connotes a need for change and risks being (mis)understood as calling for a modernist, neocolonial controlling project of progress. However, in calling for refusal, resistance, counter-hegemony, or even change, we don't want to already be boxing ourselves (excuse the overly spatial metaphor) into a future-oriented linguistic trap. We argue instead that refusal as part of equity praxis can be about a staying with the trouble that does not demand only certain progress/ions but instead commits to an endless queering together of time-space as critical, feminist, decolonial, post-structural, sociological methodological work in higher education.

Relational, political time

Sarah Sharma (2013) shows how 'our' time relies on Others and their labours. Drawing on and analysing the accounts of the likes of taxi drivers, business travellers, and yoga instructors, Sharma asks questions such as 'Whose time is spent in order to maintain the mobility and recalibration of others?' and 'How are bodies differently valued temporally, and what temporal processes are employed to make people productive for capital?' Acknowledging work in time geography, Sharma however "seeks to move beyond the spatiality of paths, itineraries and routes, and how bodies are orchestrated in space in order to delve further into distinctive temporal forms of power" (Sharma, 2013: 11). Against taken-for-granted views of temporal experience, Sharma provides a specific understanding of temporality as the awareness of and attention to power relations as they play out through time. What Sharma helps us to focus on is the relations that are multiple and interdependent and require a methodology that can apprehend how power is maintained and enforced through temporal structures, relations, and politics in the subtlest, most capillary forms. This focus on political (power/knowledge) relations in time is how we bring Sharma's work into our methodological use of timescapes as a conceptual tool.

This relational focus also speaks to the need for a sensitive ethics that can respectfully build participation across different differences to apprehend and resist the mis/time/framing we referred to earlier in the chapter; whereby dominant understandings of time-space operate only as a taken-for-granted aspect of our lives and realities, ensuring collusion by and for the relatively more privileged in a given context. The *ethic of care* can be a framework sensitive to both relations and differences. It is an approach to ethics that brings in questions and concerns to do with what 'good' relations across differences might mean. As we have mentioned earlier, EDI initiatives imply a need for change, and this raises the question of on whose terms the change is made. An emphasis on (or responsibility to) Other performs a guide of sorts on how to think about this change and even how it might be pursued. 'The Other' is an important idea to the study of personal and social identity, social inclusion, and exclusion. We live in worlds with other people and our sense of ourselves as subjects is determined by relating *to* and *with*. 'Other' relates to how social groupings are made durable as a 'We' through arbitrary sets of similarities. This sense of a 'We' is formed through comparison to those who do not readily share these similarities, becoming 'Other' to a primary group or norm. This is about how identifying occurs with (e.g. We) and differentiates from (e.g. Others) within these social dynamics. We must consider the importance of relation, partly because every identification is made through not identifying with or as someone or something. For example, identifying as White positions one as being in a different racial group than, for example, Asian. There are always relations at play.

'Other'-ness is about difference. A question then is: how do we relate to difference? The ideas we are exploring here are often associated with membership and belonging, often understood as only positive things. Unfortunately, history is full of examples where membership and belonging have led to demonisation, exclusion, bullying, even genocide, using an equivalence between difference and danger. When there is a norm, being abnormal can be readily and tragically weaponised. This can be more or less explicit, more or less intentional, more or less easily apprehended. Throughout this book, we have been pointing towards the challenge of categorisation and representation, and we have tried to consider the difficulty of how to recognise identification with a social group on people's own terms, without collapsing all differences within a group towards a worrying homogenisation. In the context of higher education:

> To be recognisable as a subject of (higher education) policy, the person must be subjected to the discourses of disadvantage, re/positioning the (Widening Participation) subject as the different and 'Other' (Said, 1977).
> *(Burke, 2012: 57)*

These considerations do go to the heart of EDI efforts, particularly as we consider what types of timescapes can prevent mis/time/framing in higher education. These are considerations that challenge us to consider questions such as: How do we work across relations and experiences of time when we rely on these differences for our personal and social identities? How can equity be achieved without the worst kinds of inclusion prevailing? (e.g. assimilatory approaches that tend to mis/frame Others). And is it possible to avoid the demand of those constructed as Other by a dominant social group that they find ways to become recognisable and includable within hegemonic timescapes?

A key contribution that feminist and care ethics makes is to move away from universal or total moral claims, towards a positive regard for difference and, one might argue, where empathy is built into the fabric of frameworks. Joan Tronto (1993, 2003, 2020) has for many decades drawn upon and built beyond feminist work by scholars such as Carol Gilligan, whilst working with Berenice Fisher and others to develop care ethics in new directions. Within any field, there is important distinctions and disagreements. For example, there are fundamental ways in which Tronto would respectfully locate her work as different to other influential care ethicists such as Nel Noddings. A key aspect of Tronto's which distinguishes it from overly psychologised interpretations of care ethics is an elaboration of power that is influenced by post/structural thinkers. This is therefore an elaboration of power that can work in with 'power chronographies' as we seek to identify the challenges with and in time that not only cause problems but also create the inability to identify temporal political problems at all. The next chapter of this book outlines PPoEMs in detail. In the final section of this chapter, we begin to sketch out a methodological argument for bringing time 'in' to research, practice, and policymaking contexts through the making of new timescapes of higher education.

sPace for new timescapes

A question some might hold is whether 'spending' time theorising/reflecting/acting on time in higher education in relation to equity is the most urgent priority given the level of misogyny, sexism, racism, classism, ableism, heteronormativity, and ongoing colonisation that abounds. We see it however as crucial that we engage with a politics of time in our responses to the scourges listed earlier, by engaging with (albeit always with/in) the power relations that produce spatio-temporalities in contemporary higher education. In calling for new timescapes in higher education, we don't imagine contexts that facilitate singular, totalising future-oriented visions, yet we also don't refer to 'purposeless' contexts. We draw on feminist, Freirean, and even Foucauldian perspectives in our call for new timescapes that are utopic in that they anticipate different sPaces, not in that they imagine some future-oriented destination where equity has 'happened'. They draw on histories of utopian work to anticipate different spatio-temporalities acquired through an endless attention to the complex classed, gendered, and racialised politics of time. These efforts are guided by a form of anti-colonial and critical hope that holds Freirean ideas to do with education as a political and cultural project of *becoming* on one's own terms, and that take inspiration from Foucauldian notions such as 'heterotopias' (e.g. the notion of contexts that can 'stand apart' from everyday social space and facilitate the possibility of contrast). These influences guide us towards the co-creation of contexts in which generative, critical, and restive dispositions can thrive.

'sPace' is a concept we are introducing to describe aspects of what we see as urgently needed new timescapes in higher education, developed by methodologies that pay attention to politics of space-time. These are contexts facilitating participations that resist and refuse the 'political death' of mis/framing in the Fraserian sense through being counter-hegemonic moments in that they are characterised by spatio-temporalities: that is, reflexive efforts to generate awareness of power relations that are both producing, and playing out within, space, and time. The 'counter' moment being a refusal of the hegemonic ir/rationalities guiding conduct in material and social space, and 'Pace' being about the care-full refusal of the flow of power relations in time through different rhythms of practice, whether that be a collective, ethically oriented 'speeding up' or 'slowing down' as the case may be. Countering here is not about 'controlling' space and time but practising together with an ethics that places dialogic relations, with each other, with material and pedagogical space, and with time, at the heart of social justice praxis.

We do not pretend that co-producing sPace in contemporary higher education is an easy prospect. The project is fraught with the possibility of adopting only a neoliberal democratic perspective on time that doesn't consider whose experience of time – and ideas such as 'patience' – can be performed. In arguing for contexts that produce reflexivity, we are cognisant too of the point that "reflexivity in the late modern age requires time – or a 'pause' – for self-reflection and for women this may well be difficult due to the nature of women's work and by the ways in which timespace is gendered" (Davies, 2003: 133). In Chapter 7, we explore examples from programmatic practice that take up methodologies in which participants 'with no time' were supported to co-produce new temporal publics in higher education – sPaces – in which they worked across differences to develop new relations (with students, colleagues, selves, and professional subjectivities) which were valued by participants.

sPace involves 'circulations' of care, returnings to and response-abilities (as capabilities) with each Other that refuse the patronising interactions of pastoral power (Foucault, 1982) and make possible more dialogic relations characterised by urgent patience.

> Because without patience, without waiting for the materials of the world to speak, interact and change, there can be nothing but a too quick compulsion to change, to fix, to smooth out, to end up the hero.
>
> *(Tronto, 2020: 158)*

Navigating spatio-temporalities of equity in contemporary times involves recognition of endless dilemmas of the sort we have canvassed previously in this book. Dilemmas tied to how reform of higher education for equity challenges us to consider the preservation of systems of power and the simultaneous preservation of knowledge that can erode these systems of power. How might we best, for example, continue to interrogate unequal burdens of caring labour and processes of casualisation whilst deconstructing the forms of masculinised leadership practice that help to reproduce toxic cultures in higher education? Engaging these dilemmas demands methodologies in which we pay attention to how power is maintained and enforced through spatio-temporal structures and politics in the subtlest, capillary forms. It is to the question of methodologies of research, practice, and policymaking that make time for social justice praxis that we now turn.

References

Adam, B. (1998) *Timescapes of Modernity*. London: Routledge.

Ahlefeld, H. (2009) *Evaluating Quality in Educational Spaces: OECD/CELE Pilot Project*. OECD. www.oecd.org/education/innovation-education/centreforeffectivelearningenvironmentscele/43904538.pdf

Ahmed, S. (2006a) 'Interview with Judith Butler', *Sexualities*, 19(4), 482–492. https://doi.org/10.1177/1363460716629607

Ahmed, S. (2006b) 'The nonperformativity of antiracism', *Meridians*, 7(1), 104–126. www.jstor.org/stable/40338719

Bennett, S. (2006). 'First questions for designing higher education learning spaces', *The Journal of Academic Librarianship*, 33(1), 14–26.

Bennett, A., and Burke, P.J. (2018) 'Re/conceptualising time and temporality: An exploration of time in higher education', *Discourse: Studies in the Cultural Politics of Education*, 39(6), 913–925. https://doi.org/10.1080/01596306.2017.1312285

Bunn, M., Bennett, A., and Burke, P.J. (2019) 'In the anytime: Flexible time structures, student experience and temporal equity in higher education', *Time and Society*, 28, 1409–1428.

Burke, P.J. (2002) *Accessing Education: Effectively Widening Participation*. London: Trentham.

Burke, P.J. (2006) 'Men accessing education: Gendered aspirations', *British Educational Research Journal*, 32, 719–733. https://doi.org/10.1080/01411920600895759

Burke, P.J. (2012) *The Right to Higher Education: Beyond Widening Participation*. London and New York: Routledge.

Burke, P.J., Bennett, A., Bunn, M., Stevenson, J., and Clegg, S. (2017) *It's About Time: Working Towards More Equitable Understandings of the Impact of Time for Students in Higher Education*. Newcastle, NSW: University of Newcastle.

Burke, P.J., and Manathunga, C. (2020) 'The timescapes of teaching in higher education', *Teaching in Higher Education*, 25(6), 663–668. https://doi.org/10.1080/13562517.2020.1784618

Butler, J. (1999) *Gender Trouble: Feminism and the Subversion of Identity*. London: Routledge.

Davies, K. (2003) 'Responsibility and daily life: Reflections over timespace', in May, J., and Thrift, N. (Eds) *Timespace: Geographies of Temporality*. London and New York: Routledge.

Dent, S. (2020) *Recognising Students Who Care for Children While Studying*. Bingley, UK: Emerald Publishing Limited.

Devlin, M., Zhang, L.-C., Edwards, D., Withers, G., McMillan, J., Vernon, L., and Trinidad, S. (2023) 'The costs of and economies of scale in supporting students from low socioeconomic status backgrounds in Australian higher education', *Higher Education Research and Development*, 42(2), 290–305. https://10.1080/07294360.2022.2057450

Foucault, M. (1982) 'The subject and power', *Critical Inquiry*, 8(4), 777–795. www.jstor.org/stable/1343197

Fraser, N. (2013) *Fortunes of Feminism: From State-Managed Capitalism to Neoliberal Crisis*. New York: Verso Books.

Hook, G. (2018) 'Starting with mother: Contesting the gendered binaries of care operating in higher education', in Henderson, E., and Nicolazzo, Z. (Eds) *Starting with Gender in International Higher Education Research*. New York: Routledge.

Jamieson, P., Fisher, K., Gilding, T., Taylor, P., and Trevitt, A. (2000) 'Place and space in the design of new learning environments', *Higher Education Research and Development*, 19(2), 221–236. https://doi.org/10.1080/072943600445664

JISC – Joint Information Systems Committee (2006) *Designing Spaces for Effective Learning: A Guide to 21st Century Learning Space Design*. Bristol, UK: JISC Development Group.

Lather, P. (1992) 'Critical frames in educational research: Feminist and post-structural perspectives', *Theory into Practice*, 31(2), 87–99. https://doi.org/10.1080/00405849209543529

Liveley, G., and Wardrop, A. (2020) 'Challenging chronocentrism: New approaches to futures thinking in the policy and praxis of widening participation in higher education', *Teaching in Higher Education*, 25(6), 683–697.

Lumb, M., and Burke, P.J. (2019) 'Re/cognising the discursive fr/ames of equity and widening participation in higher education', *International Studies in Sociology of Education*, 28(3–4), 215–236. https://doi.org/10.1080/09620214.2019.1619470

Moreau, M.-P. (2016) 'Regulating the student body/ies: University policies and student parents', *British Educational Research Journal*, 42, 906–925. https://doi.org/10.1002/berj.3234

Moreau, M.-P., and Kerner, C. (2015) 'Care in academia: An exploration of student parents' experiences', *British Journal of Sociology of Education*, 36(2), 215–233. https://doi.org/10.1080/01425692.2013.814533

Neary, M., Harrison, A., Crellin, G., Parkeh, N., Saunders, G., Duggan, F., Williams, S., and Austin, S. (2010) *Learning Landscapes in Higher Education*. http://learninglandscapes.blogs.lincoln.ac.uk/files/2010/04/FinalReport.pdf

Powell, G. (2014) 'In search of relevant learning spaces', in Fitzgerald, T. (Ed) *Advancing Knowledge in Higher Education: Universities in Turbulent Times*. Hershey: Information Science Reference.

Radcliffe, D., Wilson, H., Powell, D., and Tibbetts, B. (2008) *Designing Next Generation Spaces of Learning: Collaboration at the Pedagogy-Space-Technology Nexus*. The University of Queensland, Australian Learning and Teaching Council Report. http://documents.skgproject.com/skg-final-report.pdf

Read, B. (2023). 'The university as heterotopia? Space, time and precarity in the academy', *Access: Critical Explorations of Equity in Higher Education*, 11(1), 1–11.

Scholl, B. (2012) *Higher Education in Spatial Planning: Positions and Reflections*. Zurich: Die Deutsche Nationalbibliothek.

Selwyn, N., and Gašević, D. (2020) 'The datafication of higher education: Discussing the promises and problems', *Teaching in Higher Education*, 25(4), 527–540. https://doi.org/10.1080/13562517.2019.1689388

Sharma, S. (2013) 'Critical time', *Communication and Critical/Cultural Studies*, 10(2–3), 312–318. https://doi.org/10.1080/14791420.2013.812600

Sharma, S. (2014) *In the Meantime: Temporality and Cultural Politics*. Durham, NC: Duke University Press.

Souter, K., Riddle, M., Sellers, W., and Keppell, M. (2011) *Spaces for Knowledge Generation*. ALTC Final Report. www.olt.gov.au/resource-spacesknowledge-generation-framework-designing-studentlearning-environments-future-2011

Streamas, J. (2023) 'The war between "school time" and "colored people's time"', in Burke, P.J., and Manathunga, C. (Eds) *The Timescapes of Teaching in Higher Education*. London and New York: Routledge, 47–59.

Temple, P. (2008) 'Learning spaces in higher education: An under-researched topic', *London Review of Education*, 6(3), 229–241.

Tronto, J. (1993) *Moral Boundaries: A Political Argument for an Ethic of Care* (1st ed.). London: Routledge. https://doi.org/10.4324/9781003070672

Tronto, J. (2003) 'Time's place', *Feminist Theory*, 4(2), 119–138. https://doi.org/10.1177/14647001030042002

Tronto, J. (2020) 'Response-ability and responsibility: Using feminist new materialisms and care ethics to cope with impatience in higher education', in Tronto, J., Zembylas, M., and Bozalek, V. (Eds) *Posthuman and Political Care Ethics for Reconfiguring Higher Education Pedagogies*. London: Routledge.

6

HEGEMONIC EVALUATION AS A GOVERNING GAZE

Introduction

Adjudicating the merit, worth, quality, or impact of initiatives designed to build equity into contexts of higher education is a fraught project. The values and interests that end up mattering the most in the processes of policy or programme evaluation do not always align with what matters to underrepresented communities and individuals. These processes can therefore become key sites for the derogation and subjugation of ways of knowing, being and doing that are different to the prevailing cultural hegemony. Much evaluation in the field of equity and widening participation is tied to methodological frameworks underpinned by and reproductive of deficit imaginaries. As many nation-states increasingly invest significantly in 'equity-oriented' programmes, they are also reforming funding and evaluation regimes in ways that can undermine aspects of their stated equity agenda. One of the arguments we develop in this chapter is not only that policy and programme evaluation has increasingly been itself 'neoliberalised' but also that hegemonic policy and programme evaluation continue to be incredibly effective projects that embed neoliberal capitalism in contexts and institutions of higher education.

Our focus in this chapter is explicitly on programme and policy evaluation rather than other countless contexts in higher education we could explore using the lens of value and valuation – that is, student assessment, staff performance review and development, research excellence adjudication – all with arguably important considerations for equity. This more focused view will keep us more than occupied though because formal policy and programme evaluation, in its variety of time/frames (e.g. 'formative', 'summative', 'developmental', 'processual'), have become an *essential condition* of policy and programme

DOI: 10.4324/9781003257165-9

development. This omnipresence of policy and programme evaluation is still relatively recent and can be linked to histories in the USA whereby efforts to create an 'experimenting society' through evaluation were embedded in the bureaucratic imagination (Schwandt and Gates, 2021). Ongoing debates within the fields of policy and programme evaluation draw from larger disagreements in the social sciences to do with notions of objectivity and independence, the character of knowledge and/or realities, and the most appropriate ways to create knowledge in each context. In this chapter, we reinforce how evaluation is about valuing; about what is it we pay attention to. Commonly, we see attention paid to 'What Works' rather than to consideration of what might be valued, by whom, in what context, over what duration, and why? (Burke and Lumb, 2018). All too often, this is a 'What Works' constructed by only those in positions of authority, and this is a problem if forms of in/justice are our interest, due to an urgent need to co-create sPace for debate over what 'working' might look and feel like.

We begin this chapter by drawing on work from Critical Policy Sociology to show how evaluation can be an effective form of modern governance practice that readily takes up problem constructions developed largely by those in positions of relative privilege. We then move to the next section to argue that hegemonic approaches to evaluation can work to constantly re-embed neoliberal commitments and rationalities. Indeed, during the rise of neoliberalism, evaluation of policies and programmes has been a key driver in remaking institutions such as Universities into the neoliberal forms of modern governance that they are today. We do this work because if evaluation is such an important site of reworking values and processes of valuing, it is important to develop new practices of evaluation that can not only include but also celebrate and centre the values and value-systems of marginalised groups. A question we struggle with throughout this chapter is how evaluation as an idea and a set of contexts and practices operates so effectively as a tool of modern governance, constantly re-embedding neoliberal commitments and rationalities.

The chapter then surveys a range of prevailing work to think about some of the specific challenges associated with approaches to evaluation in the context of equity in higher education in Australia, the UK, and the USA. A key consideration in this section is how the proliferation of measurement authors 'truths' through market logics and economic calculus to undergird political machinery that is the broader issue. This review of hegemonic evaluation efforts also helps to see the conditions of audit cultures in action, whereby contexts of higher education become increasingly colonised by corporate accounting practices and the calculation, quantification, and metricisation of what it is to be a human subject. In closing the chapter, we briefly 'step back' from the field of higher education to acknowledge the diversity of approaches forging paths for evaluation practice, drawing on histories of thought to do with taking seriously notions of participation and justice. This moment foreshadows elements of the book yet to come, (see Chapter 8), in which we articulate some examples of counter-hegemonic evaluation (Gordon et al, 2022) of which we have personally been a part.

Evaluation as advanced neoliberal governance

> There is no need for arms, physical violence, material constraints. Just a gaze. An inspecting gaze, a gaze which each individual under its weight will end up interiorising to the point that he is his own overseer, each individual thus exercising surveillance over, and against himself.
>
> (Foucault, 1980: 155)

In this section, we develop the argument that formal projects designed to evaluate equity-related policies and programmes in different contexts of higher education tend to exemplify modern governance practice whereby parts of a population are made visible to bureaucracy through their construction as a problem demanding a solution. Through these practices, bodies within populations are rendered legible in ways that enhance their alignment with contemporary governance arrangements. The relations of power we want to interrogate here are complex, messy, and highly context-specific. In paying attention to these dynamics though, we aim to consider how framings of policy problems "stigmatise some, exonerate others . . . keeping change within limits" (Bacchi, 2009: 42). In this section, we also discuss how evaluation approaches and practices have increasingly been shaped by neoliberal commitments but, perhaps more importantly, that hegemonic forms of policy and programme evaluation function as highly effective projects of embedding neoliberal capitalism as 'common sense' in contexts and institutions of higher education. Indeed, it is our contention that hegemonic forms of policy and programme evaluation function as key sites for neoliberalisation, embedding a particular set of rules of law using market logics to exert distributed, de-centred and permanent forms of vigilance; a process that continues to refunction states to facilitate new forms of social power, in the interest of capital.

Governmentality is a concept that we work with to consider how the art of governing is practiced in the modern era by advanced liberal states. Scholars have used the concept differently (e.g. Foucault, 1991; Rose and Miller, 1992; Rabinow and Rose, 2003) to explain aspects of how modern state governance involves the representation of a population as citizens who need assistance to experience a particular legitimated form of productive and enjoyable life, and how, in a justification of 'the state', policymaking is understood as working to facilitate this outcome. Yet to do this policymaking, new forms of knowing the population become necessary. Commonly, statistical indicators become essential in the construction of the citizenry, making the population 'legible'

in ways now available via these forms of statistical visibility previously una-
vailable. Arbitrary boundaries are constructed which help to categorise and
represent. Difference is then made across arbitrary lines as new identities enter
discourse to become naturalised. Statistical representations are brought into a
process of understanding the problems of the population and bodies are constructed in particular ways by the bureaucratic gaze. This form of surveillance
helps to render the population 'docile', and 'productive' in Foucault's explanation (Foucault, 1991), in that to be legible to the state, people are guided
towards conducting themselves in ways that are readable by the bureaucracy.
While Foucault was interested in manifold processes of governing (e.g. that
of the self, that of others, and that by the state), we draw here specifically on
governmentality as a way of understanding the connections between advanced
neoliberal state governance practices and how this relates to the orientations
to social problems taken up by members of a population that come under the
gaze of the state.

This form of modern disciplinary power was famously expressed via the
metaphor of the *panopticon*, a conceptual model for a prison designed by
architect Jeremy Bentham to solve the challenge of efficient surveillance of
prisoners and taken up by Foucault in his studies of the treatment of devi-
ance in capitalist societies. Almost three decades ago, Shore and Roberts
(1993) argued that one way to gain insight into the epistemologies by which
higher education was increasingly being governed was through the lens of a
panopticism. The conceptual model of the panopticon consisted of a tower
at the centre of a courtyard surrounded by buildings divided into cells on
numerous levels. The window in each cell fell under the direct gaze of the
tower only. Importantly, this helps to construct people primarily as individuals and reinforce their individuation as important to modern society.
For our purposes in terms of working with the concept of governmentality,
the panopticon metaphor helps to explain a mode of modern-era governance whereby 'control at a distance' produces self-surveillance and how this
can be achieved in an efficient, depersonalised, depoliticised manner. As this
explanation of modern power goes, our bodies need not be disciplined if
we have taken on the correct governable *mentalities*. We henceforth govern
ourselves effectively via the imaginaries we carry forward and to which we
have become disposed.

As Oksala explains, "The factual, empirical account of the rise of neoliberal
hegemony is fairly uncontested" (2013: 53) yet there is an immediate challenge offered too in terms of considering how this empirical account does not
necessarily engage with how:

> On the level of historical ontology – the level conditioning our thought and
> experience of the world – the spectacular rise of neoliberalism is harder to
> understand and to account for. Rather than being the achievement of a few

key actors, it was rooted in much deeper structural and systemic changes in our conception of the political and the practices of governing.

(Oksala, 2013: 53)

We drew earlier in this book on Fraser's analysis of how the multiple dimensions of injustice that second-wave feminism helped to foreground (economic, cultural, and political) became separated from one another and from a sustained critique of capitalism, and how this separation arguably dove-tailed neatly with the rise of neoliberalism as the rationality of contemporary capitalism. We see too how equity policy and practice have developed in close concert with neoliberal agendas for globalised, corporatised, and marketised systems of higher education. Hegemonic approaches to evaluation accord neatly with the rise of discursive modernising practices of New Public Management (NPM) to accelerate processes of state transformation that (re)produce advanced social governance arrangements as new forms of capillary power over and through human populations.

Lumino, Gambardella and Grimaldi (2017) draw on governmentality studies in the Italian higher education context to describe the impacts of NPM policy ideas and technologies. In this, the authors analyse a new evaluative 'techne' (technologies, techniques and procedures) which they see as part of a calculative and instrumental turn towards damaging contractualisation, de-politicisation, and fabrication. This echoes work looking across nation-state contexts regarding how discourses of NPM have produced important shifts in the way institutions of higher education have defined and justified their institutional existence (Olssen and Peters, 2005). Specifically, Lumino, Gambardella and Grimaldi (2017) lament the establishment across Italian higher education of regimes where "fabrication, commodification and bureaucratisation are the paradoxical results of a process of modernisation inspired by the holy principles of NPM" (2017: 89). In this work, they draw on Neave (e.g. 2012) who has articulated *The Evaluative State* to describe a phenomenon in which nation states increasingly oversee higher education for markets rather than as a guardian of learning (Neave, 2012), and whereby evaluation is one of the primary tools by which this shift is achieved. Giannone (2016) builds on this conceptualisation to describe two overlapping processes: an 'evaluated state' whereby evaluation operates as a tool of global governance, acting "normatively to homogenize states and consistently with some neoliberal values, such as competitiveness and economic efficiency" (Giannone, 2016: 497); and an 'evaluative state' whereby states "constantly monitor and assess public action and policies, as well as the conduct of individuals and organization, for the purpose of introducing market rationality in non-economic domains, such as education, health system, justice and public services" (2016, p. 497). In these contexts, the social and arguably moral aspects of higher education that are not measurable are placed under threat.

As Rezai-Rashti, Segeren and Martino (2017) have shown, new systems of accountability foregrounding numerical measurement have been key in re-defining equity in the context of education.

> This shift in re-defining equity has been made possible by the development of new performative systems of accountability within the field of education involving measurement and the strategy of numbers and facticity (Ball, 2001, 2003; Keddie, 2013; O'Leary, 2013; Rizvi and Lingard, 2011; Thompson, 2013). The use of numbers and data in the form of standardised testing regimes is used to redefine the very conception of equity.
> *(Rezai-Rashti, Segeren and Martino, 2017: 160–161)*

Many would argue that "the problem is not measurement, but *excessive* measurement and *inappropriate* measurement – not metrics, but metric fixation" (Muller, 2018: 4, emphasis added), yet the role of conventional technologies of evaluation in lubricating new, globalised systems of accountability, including techniques such as rankings, ratings, audits, and indicators, is of concern for questions of equity within education systems. For, within such systems, we are convinced to make ourselves not 'memorable' but 'calculable' (Ball, 2012), for as Ball explains, in "regimes of performativity, experience is nothing, productivity is everything" (2012: 136). Processes that depersonalise, depoliticise, commodify, and metricise have been shown to create the conditions for misrecognition, misrepresentation, and misdistribution (Burke, 2012), undermining and foreclosing certain possibilities of higher education constructed on more socially 'just' terms. In a seductively non-confrontational manner, the evaluated and evaluative state – via claims to rationality, rigour, and impartiality – create the conditions for control at a distance that adheres to a hegemony deeply imbued with structural inequalities including intersecting concerns of class, race, and gender. This might appear at first a paradoxical claim that institutions could be afforded further 'freedoms' to pursue bespoke conventional initiatives yet the result being a tightening of order and control. As Ball (2010) argues however, "these techniques which rest upon the granting of greater autonomy to institutions and processes of deconcentration within education systems also provide the state with new modes of governing society and the economy and shaping and reshaping individuals and individual conduct" (Ball, 2010: 125). We see this point as crucial to understanding how evaluation *of* equity is a problem *for* equity if educational evaluation continues to reflect only a spirit of capitalism in which "gender, race and social class are often seen as background variables, rather than constructs embedded within evaluation processes and politics themselves" (Borrelli et al, 2019: 26).

'Audit culture' is a term coined to describe "not so much a type of society, place or people so much as a condition" (Shore, 2008: 279) shaped by techniques of financial audit yet situations significantly distant from actual financial accountancy. It is a phenomenon "closely linked to what sociological theorists have termed 'risk society' (Beck et al, 1994) and the 'political economy of insecurity' (Beck, 2000: 2)" (Shore, 2008: 280) and has become particularly entrenched in the UK and Australia with the extension of the process of NPM reforms that began during the 1980s.

> while these audit systems may have been designed to restore public confidence, they provide virtually no room for citizens' voices to be heard in any meaningful sense . . . the rise of audit culture in academia and elsewhere merits attention; it increasingly shapes our lives, our relationships, our professional identities and the manner in which we conduct ourselves.
>
> *(Shore, 2008: 280–281)*

Educational datafication (including crude learning analytics and decontextualised reporting templates) increasingly makes us more calculable subjects – "diminished, individualised, psychologised, essentialised, de-contextualised and malleable" (Ball and Grimaldi, 2022: 292). A fetish for quantitative methods runs rampant through policy and programme evaluation, the problem being that

> quantification distorts the character of what it claims to measure. What these statistics demonstrate is merely the extent to which 'targets' have been met. In short, statistics and league tables are the instruments through which a new regime of management is being imposed, one that extends audit technologies into the art of government itself.
>
> *(Shore, 2008: 287)*

And we would extend the argument, to say that for something to be quantified, it must first be rendered recognisable, usually within a particular existing categorisation. To be counted, qualities must first be rendered concrete. Qualitative work (recognition and misrecognition) pre-empts quantitative work. Whilst 'mixed method' work is often seen as a pragmatic resolution to paradigm wars, we would agree with the likes of Biesta (2010a) and Lather (2012) who lament such positions, given how the common sense of some mixed methods research and practice, or 'stats and stories' as it often expressed, can be a subtle conservative agenda de-politicising research and practice.

Made to measure: hegemonic evaluation as 'ruler'

The term 'ruler' in English can refer to a physical length-measurement device found in most school classrooms and offices. 'Ruler' is also often used to refer to a person exercising government, dominion, or control. These connotations are interesting provocations to think with as we consider how the measurements that we make of ourselves and each Other really matter. In the below section of this chapter, we survey the prevailing approaches to the evaluation of equity in higher education in Australia, the UK, and the USA. We do so to provide a foundation for moving beyond, towards approaches that can destabilise aspects of hegemonic evaluation practices around which we carry concern.

In reviewing the literature on equity policy and programme evaluation, it is immediately evident that implicit commitments embedded within approaches to evaluative research fundamentally shape (and limit) what can be known because of these processes. And, that in many contexts, particular approaches to evaluation have been constructed as more legitimate ways of knowing about interventions, despite the literature on equity in higher education demonstrating a diversity of available approaches being implemented in different contexts. In this section, as we review approaches and projects, we specifically identify ways in which processes of evaluation can unwittingly become sites of deficit framing, social pathologising, and individualisation of structural problems. We also see that evaluative research of equity in higher education can exemplify the types of descriptive and a-theoretical level of analysis which at times cited key theories (e.g. Bourdieu) as resources for analysis but then failed to fully engage these with worrying consequences for the credibility of the knowledge created. There is a large volume of literature making evaluative claims about the presence and/or absence of the impact, success, worth, and value of equity-related efforts in higher education; from small-scale one-off initiatives up to large-scale nation-wide programmes operating across multiple decades. At times, there is a blurring in this literature between what might be defined as monitoring, evaluation, and research, and also between attribution (activity caused outcome) and contribution (activity is related to outcome).

Equity in higher education is a complex and contested set of ideas and practices. This presents challenges relating to how evaluating the success of policy and funding can be readily achieved without carefully articulated characterisations of 'equity' and appropriate frameworks for constructing knowledge that are themselves imbued with these characterisations. Demonstrating the contested nature of the field, a systematic review of the evidence of the effectiveness of interventions and strategies for widening participation in higher education (Younger et al, 2019) found that there have been no robust evaluations of UK-based interventions. This work, however, takes up a definition of 'robustness' that adheres closely to a positivist 'evidence-based' decision-making set of commitments. And, as the American critical quantitative higher education researcher Stage (2007) has explained:

> A positivistic researcher seeks models that nearly completely explain phenomena of interest, aiming for confirmation and verification to explain universal human behavior. But because much of positivistic research is based

on previously developed models, the outcomes tend to replicate the status quo and verify meritocratic fairness.

(Stage, 2007: 10)

These debates regarding the construction of rigorous credible evidence are an important consideration for higher education policymaking. These are deliberations with direct implications for evaluative claims and are rooted in often implicit philosophical perspectives about the nature of reality and commitments regarding what constitutes knowledge and how it is created (Christie and Fleischer, 2009).

In Chapter 1 of this book, we drew on Suzanne Mettler's analysis of the US higher education crisis in which deficit assumptions relating to individual lack of ability or motivation to succeed in higher education guide the prevailing view of what 'the problem' is represented to be. In that US higher education context, large-scale evaluative research has been drawn into the project of building evidence regarding the effectiveness of interventions, helping to embed and naturalise this representation of a particular 'problem', making it difficult for new or challenging questions to emerge regarding the historical formation of social inequalities and higher education's role in exacerbating these formations. A situation therefore arises whereby even though it is claimed that quality education is a sacred value in American culture (Zaloom, 2021: 190), the hegemonic approaches to determining forms of value at play are so thoroughly ill-equipped to understand what is happening for people that a crude and conservative agenda is all but guaranteed.

There are many studies in equity evaluation literature in which experimental designs have been privileged in the USA attempting to measure the effectiveness of large programmes designed around the concept of *readiness* for college. These studies included assessments of elements of the multi-decade, multi-trillion-dollar TRIO programmes (comprising Upward Bound, Educational Talent Search (ETS), and Student Support Services). It was found that the educational attainment of minority students was successfully supported, yet that these have largely operated on the peripheries of educational systems issues plagued as they are by challenges of targeting and timing (Ward, 2006) combined with a limited ability to address the numerous issues that impact student achievement. Brewer and Landers (2005) investigated an 'ETS' TRIO programme targeting first-generation and low-income students using a causal-comparative design with a control group. Looking at 10,000 students who had participated in ETS between 1980 and 1989, they used systematic sampling with 100 students from each year drawn into their analysis, yet even this valiant longitudinal effort was thwarted by various limitations and returned inconclusive results. This certainly signals some of the risks regarding large-scale efforts to construct evidence bases around practice.

GEAR UP, developed in 1998, differed from TRIO in that it targeted entire cohorts, schools, or districts rather than individual students or specified 'at-risk' groups in recognition that short-term, discontinuous, and narrowly focused programmes are not as effective as more long-term, integrated, broadly focused ones (Schaefle, 2018). The establishment of GEAR UP (being long-term, cohort-based) appears however to have led to a methodological dominance that only produces particular forms of knowledge, and, as Swail and Perna (2002) have identified, "Billions of federal, state, and private dollars have been spent to close the enrolment and degree attainment gaps" (2002: 15) with quite a narrow ongoing focus on what might shift these gaps. Bausmith and France (2012) used a quasi-experimental design to show that, overall, a GEAR UP programme demonstrated positive evidence of improving college readiness outcomes for low-income students in 173 schools using a variety of college readiness measures. A Bettinger et al (2012) study looked at the effect of immediate assistance and streamlining of application processes for low-income individuals with participants also provided with aid estimates, finding "empirical support for policymakers choosing to continue investment in college access programmes generally, although further analysis of different programme structures and comparisons between whole school interventions versus targeting individual students is a promising area for further research" (2012: 597). Also, a Bettinger and Evans (2019) study deployed a TRIO and GEARUP school-level Randomised Control Trial using 'near-peer' model with no significant result on college enrolments but a subgroup analysis finding positive results among targeted Hispanic and low-income students. This seems to suggest that large-scale efforts to monitor progress can (albeit deploying normative success frames) signal 'where to look' in relation to more nuanced and context-driven evaluation. The construction of these indicators for system monitoring is however a factor requiring further consideration.

Efforts to understand the patterns of participation associated with these large-scale initiatives are laudable efforts at a form of accountability. If our review of these efforts holds a pejorative undertone, it is more to do with the methodological commitments that prefigure these projects of evaluation *of* equity. In these contexts, measurement itself is not necessarily the problem. We would instead argue that it is the proliferation, and reification through measurement (making concrete the abstract), that produces 'truth' by adopting logics of the market to support policymaking.

In a systematic review of evidence on the effectiveness of interventions and strategies for widening participation in higher education, Younger et al (2019) found (whilst recognising methodological issues including bias) some effectiveness of 'black box' WP programmes and financial incentives in the USA. This is a study that also claims there have been no 'robust' evaluations of UK-based interventions, with a conceptualisation of robustness that adheres closely to positivist 'evidence-based' decision-making and experimental designs in particular that many (e.g. Gale, 2018; Reay, 2020) have argued are not suited to educational contexts. The RCT certainly enjoys strong ongoing support (Bickman and Reich, 2009) with 'What Works Clearinghouses' promoting studies on social interventions commonly positioning RCT methodologies as the 'gold standard' for producing credible evidence. The US Department of Education standard for "strong evidence of effectiveness" requires a "well-designed and implemented" RCT; no observational study can earn such a label (Deaton and Cartwright, 2017: 2). These studies do not tend, however, to provide insight into why there are or are not effects, rendering their use to policymakers and practitioners somewhat limited. They also do not provide insight into the experiences of those involved. A risk to consider in adopting experimental designs in social contexts such as equity and widening participation is that they produce evidence that is simply not credible. The RCT gained dominance in the medical spheres in action towards the end of intensive scientific work that had explored the mechanisms of causality in the laboratory over long periods of time (Pawson, 2006). The risk therefore is great that, by not doing the necessary close-up research, policymakers and practitioners remain unaware of what works, for whom, over what duration, how, and in what context (Morrison, 2001). A more profound threat of experimental designs is the ignore-ance of social context, and the capacity for misrepresentation of the values of those who directly experience inequities.

Deficit framings remain a persistent underlying issue that curtails policy and institutional initiatives in many international contexts. Evaluation can be a particularly acute in which the approaches taken up to adjudicate success (of an individual or initiative) readily re-embed problematic deficit framings, construct pathologies, and individualise structural issues. The concept of 'readiness', so prevalent in the literature emanating from the USA, is deeply infused with a deficit discourse that requires 'treatment' (a troubling creation of a social pathology). Much higher education scholarship shows that 'the problem' for underrepresented groups in higher education is the historically formed and highly exclusive aspects of higher education institutions and practices. Yet the solution to this problem is commonly framed in terms of making underrepresented students 'ready' to participate within these highly inequitable arrangements (e.g. Brewer and Landers, 2005). Methodologies developed in the context of health and medicine carry with them connotations and commitments that are designed to pathologise. Bettinger and Baker (2014) in the US context found that students who were randomly assigned to a coach were more likely to persist during the 'treatment' period (2014: 14) and were more likely to be 'persisting' at university one year after the coaching. This again places the burden of responsibility on the student with the term 'persistence' working in tandem with a discourse of 'readiness', re-embedding the neutrality of higher education institutional aspects and ignoring structural concerns, seeing them as barriers to be overcome.

D'Souza et al (2018) similarly explored predictions of persistence and success, with the burden of persistence located at the individual level as a determinant of success. Here we can see what Harrison and Waller (2018) identify as a problematic epistemology for assessing the success for projects of equity and widening participation in higher education. In their view, practitioners commonly find themselves in 'a bind' that coerces them towards a What Works agenda rather than developing an "appropriate epistemology that allows for robust evaluations (of various types) in complex social fields" (2018: 157). These misalignments can embed unintended consequences of equity initiatives – an important consideration for policymakers at all levels. An example is Furquim and Glasener (2017), who identified a 'Quest Bridge' initiative impact to build the distinction of colleges through boosted enrolments rather than having a desired result on access, participation or success. These efforts are sustained by the idea that practices such as education should be based upon 'evidence', ignoring much 'evidence' that the 'what works' approach simply doesn't work (Biesta, 2007; 2010b). What Biesta raises, drawing on Otto, Polutta and Ziegler (2009), is that "the important question, therefore, is not whether or not there should be a role for evidence in processional action, but what kind of role it should play" (Biesta, 2010b: 492). Work by Bourke et al (2019) in the Canadian context challenges the 'readiness' language and discourse by drawing on Pollock to recognise that higher education institutions aren't simply a collection of buildings and policies and are of course "social and cultural processes that individuals from low-income communities find difficult to engage with" (2019: 161).

The imperative to evaluate policymaking efforts and/or the programmes that sit within them has grown and a field of 'evaluation theory' has emerged alongside this desire. In the Australian context, there have been multiple moves towards constructing a national evaluation framework of the Higher Education Participation and Partnership Program (HEPPP), and then IRL-SAF (Indigenous, Regional and Low-SES Attainment Fund). An Acil Allen evaluation of HEPPP, wedded as it was to an evidence hierarchy privileging experimental methodologies, inserted an imperative for the establishment of 'counterfactual' or 'control groups' with 'trial-registries', adopting the sort of medical language that reveals the origins of the RCT. This form of recommendation does not engage with literature that directly challenges the epistemological, ontological, and methodological claims upon which this evidence hierarchy operates, including the problems associated with adopting RCTs in social fields of investigation (Morrison, 2001; Clegg, 2005; Cowen, Virk and Mascarenhas-Keyes, 2017; Gale, 2018).

Following the Bradley Review of Australian higher education, a 'Design and Evaluation Matrix for Outreach' or DEMO (Gale et al, 2010) was established to assist with this specific dimension of equity work (outreach) in higher education. There has since been a growing body of relatively diverse work demonstrating different impacts of HEPPP (Bennett et al, 2015; O'Shea et al, 2016; Zacharias, 2017). There is also a growing interest in a nationally coordinated and contextualised approach to evaluation given the deployment of significant HEPPP funding and the complexity of the field of interests at play (Haintz et al, 2018). There are resources and perspectives available to support those tasked in the Australian context with the responsibility of understanding the value of EWP initiatives (e.g. Naylor, 2013). Some advocate systematic and objective approaches (e.g. Wilkins and de Vries, 2014) while others focus on the ethics and politics of evaluating what matters and to whom in processes of evaluation within EWP (Bennett, 2018; Burke and Lumb, 2018; Gordon et al, 2021; Smith, 2018). It has also been argued (Downing, 2017) that there is a need for further large-scale, objective, independent, outcome-driven evidence-production processes such as the Bridges to Higher Education programme evaluation conducted by KPMG (2015). Governments continue to develop efforts towards national approaches (the most recent iteration in the Australian context being the SEHEEF (Student Evaluation in Higher Education Evaluation Framework).

Reports associated with these types of attempted national frameworks (e.g. SEHEEF in Australia) do often acknowledge the importance of challenging deficit models of equity; developing evaluation methods that can engage with the context of the communities involved and the initiatives developed in those contexts; the value of evaluation frameworks that enable representation of key stakeholders, including representatives of marginalised communities. Yet these are frameworks rooted methodologically in a worrying set of commitments and assumptions; for example, the notion that experimental designs produce credible results in social settings prior to even understanding whether or how a particular initiative might operate in a given context. Indeed, there are multiple concerns one might raise with these types of frameworks. The diversity of equity practices and programmes is commonly not fully engaged with, leaving significant gaps across the range of life stages (pre-access, access, participation, attainment, and transition out) as well as overlooking key communities. Not including a focus on non-school leavers is common in these contexts. The frameworks are highly focused on 'impact' which leaves out many different possible contributions that evaluation can make. And the resourcing and implementation challenges for these types of frameworks are enormous.

'Axiologically bereft' accountability

In the UK, evaluation of equity and widening participation interventions at different scales and across the student lifecycle have for many years produced a heavily contested debate. Stevenson and Leconte (2009) and Burke and Hayton (2011) advocated some time ago for consideration of the ethically fraught and value-laden character of the field in question when adjudicating the impact, worth or success of policies and practices. Evaluation of equity in higher education is still consistently built through a mono-dimensional logic though, as we have argued throughout the book. Large amounts of funding are deployed within systems to understand if equity initiatives are 'working', but the logics of experimentation and metrification used often fail to identify, or simply overlook, fundamental dimensions of social inequality, let alone more insidious inequalities at play. The evaluation of policies and programmes within and across higher education institutions in Australia and the UK is a field of applied research increasingly guided by toolkits, frameworks, organisations, and government policies and statements designed to support increased evaluation practice. As Lumb and Gordon (2023) have recently shown, this constellation of forces typically presents tools of evaluation – for example, 'credible evidence', 'rigour', 'expertise', 'accountability' – as only technical, uncontested, 'value-free' terms with a clear meaning and purpose. This ignores important work done in the realm of evaluation literature to reclaim these tools of evaluation practice as 'value-full', politically charged and requiring debate and decisions on how to deploy them (Schwandt and Gates, 2021). In recent times, the notion of ethical conduct has appeared more prominently in these frameworks and policies. The Australian Federal Labor government has recently invested $10 million to establish an Australian Centre for Evaluation to "improve the volume, quality, and impact of evaluations across the Australian Public Service" (Australian Government Treasury, 2023, np) which will shape federally developed frameworks including with higher education (e.g. Australian Department of Education, 2021: np). The evaluation toolkit associated with this announcement calls for evaluation that is 'robust, ethical and culturally appropriate" (Australian Centre for Evaluation, 2023, np). In another context, the UK federal government has established a What Works Network that guides the sorts of approaches taken up by What Works Centres such as the Transforming Access and Student Outcomes hub. This group also states the importance of ethical considerations, with a view to delivering "best practice in research/evaluation while respecting the rights of participants and minimising potential harm" (TASO, 2023, np). There is no doubt the need for foregrounding ethical considerations in evaluation practice in higher education is long overdue, yet, in a similar way to the deployment of other evaluation tools, ethical conduct is often presented with little depth, nuance, or the need for debate on how it might be deployed in an evaluation context.

Our concern here is an ongoing drift (under the claims of ethical conduct) towards what Michael Fielding (2001) described as an 'axiologically bereft' form of accountability. Analysing the UK's OFSTED (the Office for Standards in Education, Children's Services and Skills) practices at that time, Fielding criticised efforts designed to ensure effectiveness as "at best manipulative and at worst totalitarian" (2001: 702). In this work, Fielding made an important distinction between the forms of *accountability* that the managerialism of neoliberal economic frameworks facilitates, versus approaches that resonate with reciprocal *responsibility* to one an/Other. Fielding argues that holding each other to account can tend to rely on and embed existing imbalanced power relations, whilst holding each other responsible can reach different relations of reciprocal engagement. These distinctions should not be written off as wordplay. We agree with Fielding in that the language we use reverberates with power, guiding the concept in practice towards some relations whilst circumscribing others. Thinking about the language we adopt in equity work is an important part of social justice praxis. As Fielding offered over 20 years ago, "New hope needs new language to name new realities" (2001: 701).

The problem of evaluation in contexts of equity and widening participation has been described in the UK as 'complex' and 'vexed' by Harrison and Waller (2018); the authors noting that enduring pressure to produce evidence of impact can undermine effective efforts by encouraging managers and practitioners to narrow the focus of their activity to that which is most easily evaluated. They also point to the emergence of 'partnerships of least resistance' where activities are tolerated not because they are innovative or effective but because they fit existing (e.g. schooling) structures and are easier to evaluate. The authors offer a clear warning that there are critical challenges in the emerging calls for RCTs and instead point to the importance of longitudinal studies, the fostering of multiple approaches, and the need for ongoing efforts to understand 'why' initiatives produce claimed effects. Also taking up the importance of coming to grips with 'why' initiatives work, Younger and Warrington (2009) in the UK context articulate the problem that a lack of clarity had within both practice and evaluation (in the specific example, a mentoring program) regarding why particular projects might be thought to work, under what circumstances, and for whom.

Evaluation is an imperative increasingly attached to all policies and programmes. We have spent most of this chapter showing it to be an effective tool for advanced neoliberal governance and the remaking of higher education institutions. We believe however that this dynamic can be shifted in diverse directions, not as a solution necessarily in overwhelming times, but as an active refusal that generates different possibilities.

'New' possibilities of e-valu-ation

This chapter has offered at times a bleak perspective on policy and programme evaluation. In Chapter 8 of this book, we articulate sPaces that we argue build towards notions of counter-hegemonic evaluation (Gordon et al, 2021). These are contexts we contend can help to destabilise some of the worst effects articulated earlier (i.e. how evaluation can help to reproduce dominant value frameworks and facilitate the ongoing 'neoliberalisation' of higher education). It is important to acknowledge though that there are equity in higher education examples in the literature of efforts that move in these counter-hegemonic directions. Work by Anderson and Larson (2009) investigating an 'Upward Bound' programme in the US context (one of the 'TRIO' programmes that has operated in that context for over 45 years) explored how the programme attempts to increase educational opportunity for urban youth and how this approach plays out in the lived experiences of young men who participate in the programme. This chapter raises important concerns regarding the assumptions guiding much research and policymaking. Their findings suggested for example an urgent need for coordinating support programmes with other social, economic, and human service agencies serving communities if there is to be a move towards equality of opportunity for underrepresented youth. This resonates with Rallis' (2009) view regarding just how important it is to consider how processes of evaluation, as a matter of rigour and integrity, can develop essential insights by attending to "the means and context more than the outcome of a programme. The latter approach commonly asks, 'What does the experience mean to the individual?'" (Rallis, 2009: 281). There is work in South Africa (Essack and Quayle, 2007) using qualitative methods to evaluate a higher education 'bridging' programme, that brings the subjective experiences of students into the programme evaluation and emphasises the importance of student perceptions of access programmes being important. In a different geographic context, Cammarota (2007) demonstrates a particular form of accountability to communities served in work that uses quantitative methods imbued with social justice commitments to demonstrate that "if universities hope to consummate their missions of diversity, then working to expand a social justice approach in K-12 institutions holds significant potential" (Cammarota, 2007: 95).

Broadly though, there remains an acute need even within these impressive cases to continue to shift from a narrow focus on method in evaluative research to more generative discussion regarding methodology. One way we contend the field might better work through this complicated terrain is via carefully constructed evaluation policy-theory-practice nexus. There is growing interest in how dedicated *evaluation policies* might guide evaluation practice. Evaluation policies can act as guiding mechanisms, signalling clearly what types of evaluations could and should be done, organising the construction and accumulation of knowledge in ways that allow for generative contestation and debate. As Trochim (2009) observes, "Many recent and current controversies or conflicts in the field of evaluation can be viewed, at least in part, as a struggle around evaluation policy" (2009: 14). Evaluation policy can serve as an important "connector between the collective body of knowledge in our field and the ever-evolving challenges" (Christie and Lemire, 2019: 494). The obsession with method will no doubt remain a challenge though (as we discuss in more detail in Chapter 7). As leading evaluation scholars in the USA Mark, Cooksy and Trochim (2009) have argued, "When evaluators are asked to think about evaluation policy, many of them may tend to think first of policies that guide the methods for carrying out an evaluation" and that "debates about the place of randomized controlled trials (RCTs) reflect one example in which the focus of evaluation policy is on methods" (2009: 6).

There is a diversity of evaluation approaches available to those trying to understand the intended and unintended consequences of equity-oriented initiatives across contexts and scales. Indeed, the breadth of possibility for e-valu-ation for transformative equity and social justice praxis is vast, making it something of a tragedy, in our view, to see a myopic dedication in many contexts to impoverished evidence hierarchies privileging methods and adopting only experimental designs that objectify whilst seeking decontextualised generalisations regarding 'best practice' that is 'scalable'. The cases we share in Chapter 8 of this book draw on the PPoEMs methodology to show that it is possible to sensitively navigate contested valuations of equity and widening participation work, including what is developed, who participates in such processes, and in what ways. There are alternatives to the hegemonic evaluation approaches currently ruling equity.

References

Anderson, N.S., and Larson, C.L. (2009) 'Sinking, like quicksand: Expanding educational opportunity for young men of color', *Educational Administration Quarterly*, 45(1), 71–114. https://doi.org/10.1177/0013161X08327556

Australian Centre for Evaluation (2023) *What is Evaluation.* Australian Government Treasury Portfolio. Canberra. https://evaluation.treasury.gov.au/toolkit/what-evaluation#:~:text=Robust%2C%20ethical%20and%20culturally%20appropriate,programs%20and%20evaluations%20on%20stakeholders

Australian Department of Education (2021) *The Student Equity in Higher Education Evaluation Framework.* http://www.education.gov.au/heppp/resources/student-equity-higher-education-evaluation-framework-seheef-final-report

Australian Government Treasury (2023) *Australian Centre for Evaluation to Measure What Works.* Australian Government Treasury Portfolio. Canberra. https://ministers.treasury.gov.au/ministers/andrew-leigh-2022/media-releases/australian-centre-evaluation-measure-what-works

Bacchi, C. (2009) *Analysing Policy: What's the Problem Represented to Be?* Frenchs Forest: Pearson Education.

Ball, S.J. (2010) 'New voices, new knowledges and the new politics of education research: The gathering of a perfect storm?', *European Educational Research Journal*, 9(2), 124–137. https://doi.org/10.2304/eerj.2010.9.2.124

Ball, S.J. (2012) 'Performativity, commodification and commitment: An I-spy guide to the neoliberal university', *British Journal of Educational Studies*, 60(1), 17–28. https://doi.org/10.1080/00071005.2011.650940

Ball, S.J., and Grimaldi, E. (2022) 'Neoliberal education and the neoliberal digital classroom', *Learning, Media and Technology*, 47(2), 288–302. https://doi.org/10.1080/17439884.2021.1963980

Bausmith, J.M., and France, M. (2012) 'The impact of GEAR UP on college readiness for students in low income schools', *Journal of Education for Students Placed at Risk*, 17(4), 234–246.

Bennett, A. (2018) 'Access and equity programme provision-evaluation in Australian higher education: A what matters approach', *Educational Research and Evaluation*, 24(8), 523–537. https://doi.org/10.1080/13803611.2019.1643740

Bennett, A., Naylor, R., Mellor, K., Brett, M., Gore, J., Harvey, A., James, R., Munn, B., Smith, M., and Whitty, G. (2015) *Equity Initiatives in Australian Higher Education: A Review of Evidence of Impact*. Report prepared for the Department of Education and Training National Priority Pool.

Bettinger, E.P., and Baker, R.B. (2014) 'The effects of student coaching: An evaluation of a randomized experiment in student advising', *Educational Evaluation and Policy Analysis*, 36(1), 3–19. https://doi.org/10.3102/0162373713500523

Bettinger, E.P., and Evans, B.J. (2019) 'College guidance for all: A randomized experiment in pre-college advising', *Journal of Policy Analysis and Management*, 38(3), 579–599.

Bettinger, E. P., Long, B.T., Oreopoulos, P., and Sanbonmatsu, L. (2012) 'The role of application assistance and information in college decisions: Results from the H&R Block FAFSA experiment', *The Quarterly Journal of Economics*, 127(3), 1205.

Bickman, L., and Reich, S.M. (2009) 'Randomized controlled trials: A gold standard with feet of clay?', in Donaldson, S.I., Christie, C., and Mark, M.M. (Eds) *What Counts as Credible Evidence in Applied Research and Evaluation Practice?* Thousand Oaks, CA: Sage Publications, 51–77.

Biesta, G. (2007) 'Why "what works" won't work: Evidence-based practice and the democratic deficit in educational research', *Educational Theory*, 57(1), 1–22. https://doi.org/10.1111/j.1741-5446.2006.00241.x

Biesta, G. (2010a) 'Pragmatism and the philosophical foundations of mixed methods research', in Tashakkori, A., and Teddlie, C. (Eds) *Sage Handbook of Mixed Methods in Social and Behavioral Research*. Thousand Oaks, CA: Sage, 95–118.

Biesta, G. (2010b) 'Why "what works" still won't work: From evidence-based education to value-based education', *Studies in the Philosophy of Education*, 29, 491–503. https://doi.org/10.1007/s11217-010-9191-x

Borrelli, D., Gavrila, M., Spanò, E., and Stazio, M. (2019) 'Another university is possible: Towards an idea of meridian university', *Italian Journal of Sociology of Education*, 11(3), 16–39.

Bourke, A., Vanderveken, J., Ecker, E., Shearer, N., and Atkinson, J. (2019) 'Bringing college classrooms to the community: Promoting post-secondary access for low-income adults through neighbourhood-based college courses', *The Canadian Journal of Higher Education*, 49(1), 159–175.

Brewer, E.W., and Landers, J.M. (2005) 'A longitudinal study of the talent search program', *Journal of Career Development*, 31(3), 195–208.

Burke, P.J. (2012) *The Right to Higher Education: Beyond Widening Participation*. London and New York: Routledge.

Burke, P.J., and Hayton, A. (2011) 'Is widening participation still ethical?', *Widening Participation and Lifelong Learning*, 13(1), 8–26.

Burke, P.J., and Lumb, M. (2018) 'Researching and evaluating equity and widening participation: Praxis-based frameworks', in Burke, P.J., Hayton, A., and Stevenson, J. (Eds) *Evaluating Equity and Widening Participation in Higher Education*. London: Trentham Books Limited, 11–32.

Cammarota, J. (2007) 'A social justice approach to achievement: Guiding Latina/o students toward educational attainment with a challenging, socially relevant curriculum', *Equity and Excellence in Education*, 40(1), 87–96.

Christie, C.A., and Fleischer, D. (2009) 'Social inquiry paradigms as a frame for the debate on credible evidence', in Donaldson, S., Christie, C., and Mark, M. (Eds) *What Counts as Credible Evidence in Applied Research and Evaluation Practice?* Thousand Oaks, CA: Sage Publications.

Christie, C.A., and Lemire, S.T. (2019) 'Why evaluation theory should be used to inform evaluation policy', *American Journal of Evaluation*, 40(4), 490–508. https://doi.org/10.1177/1098214018824045

Clegg, S. (2005) 'Evidence-based practice in educational research: A critical realist critique of systematic review', *British Journal of Sociology of Education*, 26(3), 415–428.

Cowen, N., Virk, B., and Mascarenhas-Keyes, S. (2017) 'Randomized controlled trials: How can we know "what works"?', *Critical Review*, 29(3), 265–292.

Deaton, A., and Cartwright, N. (2017) 'Understanding and misunderstanding randomized controlled trials', *Social Science & Medicine*, 210, 2–21.

Downing, L. (2017) 'The emerging equity evaluation landscape in higher education', *Evaluation Journal of Australasia*, 17(1), 19–29. https://doi.org/10.1177/1035719X1701700104

D'Souza, M.J.P., Shuman, K., Wentzien, D., and Roeske, K. (2018) 'Working with the Wesley college cannon scholar program: Improving retention, persistence, and success', *Journal of STEM Education: Innovations and Research*, 19(1), 31–40.

Essack, Z., and Quayle, M. (2007) 'Students' perceptions of a university access (bridging) programme for social science, commerce and humanities', *Perspectives in Education*, 25(1), 71–84.

Fielding, M. (2001) 'OFSTED, inspection and the betrayal of democracy', *Journal of Philosophy of Education*, 35(4), 695–709, November. https://doi.org/10.1111/1467-9752.00254

Foucault, M. (1980) *Power/Knowledge*, Gordon, C. (Ed). New York: Vintage.

Foucault, M. (1991) 'Governmentality', in Burchell, G., Gordon, C., and Miller, P. (Eds) *The Foucault Effect: Studies in Governmentality*. London: Harvester Wheatsheaf, 87–104.

Furquim, F., and Glasener, K.M. (2017) 'A quest for equity? Measuring the effect of questbridge on economic diversity at selective institutions', *Research in Higher Education*, 58(6), 646–671.

Gale, T. (2018) 'What's not to like about RCTs in education?', in Childs, A., and Menter, I. (Eds) *Mobilising Teacher Researchers: Challenging Educational Inequality*. London: Routledge, 207–223.

Gale, T., Hattam, R., Comber, B., Tranter, D., Bills, D., Sellar, S., and Parker, S. (2010) *Interventions Early in School as a Means to Improve Higher Education Outcomes for Disadvantaged Students*. National Centre for Student Equity in Higher Education. http://dro.deakin.edu.au/view/DU:30064931

Giannone, D. (2016) 'Neoliberalization by evaluation: Explaining the making of neoliberal evaluative state', *Open Journal of Socio-political Studies*, 9(2), 495–516. https://doi.org/10.1285/i20356609v9i2p495

Gordon, R.B., Lumb, M., Bunn, M., and Burke, P.J. (2022) 'Evaluation for equity: Reclaiming evaluation by striving towards counter-hegemonic democratic practices', *Journal of Educational Administration and History*, 54(3), 277–290. https://doi.org/10.1080/00220620.2021.1931059

Haintz, G.L., Goldingay, S., Heckman, R., Ward, T., Afrouz, R., and George, K. (2018) 'Evaluating equity initiatives in higher education: Processes and challenges from one Australian university', *International Studies in Widening Participation*, 5(1), 92–105.

Harrison, N., and Waller, R. (2018) 'Challenging discourses of aspiration: The role of expectations and attainment in access to higher education', *British Educational Research Journal*, 44(5), 914–938.

KPMG (2015) *Evaluation of Bridges to Higher Education – Final Report*. www.uws.edu.au/data/assets/pdf_file/0007/898504/04302015Bridges_to_Higher_Education_Final_Report.pdf

Lather, P. (2012) *Getting Lost: Feminist Efforts Toward a Double(d) Science*. New York: State University of New York Press.

Lumb, M., and Gordon, R. (2023) 'Care-full evaluation: Navigating ethical challenges in evaluation with an ethics of care', *2023 SRHE International Research Conference Higher Education Research, Practice, and Policy: Connections & Complexities*, Birmingham, December. http://hdl.handle.net/1959.13/1495923

Lumino, R., Gambardella, D., and Grimaldi, E. (2017) 'The evaluation turn in the higher education system: Lessons from Italy', *Journal of Educational Administration and History*, 49(2), 87–107. https://doi.org/10.1080/00220620.2017.1284767

Mark, M., Cooksy, L.J., and Trochim, W. (2009) 'Evaluation policy: An introduction and overview', *New Directions for Evaluation*, 123, 3–11.

Morrison, K. (2001) 'Randomised controlled trials for evidence-based education: Some problems in judging "what works"', *Evaluation and Research in Education*, 15(2), 69–83.

Muller, J. (2018) *The Tyranny of Metrics*. Princeton, NJ: Princeton University Press. www.jstor.org/stable/j.ctvc77h85.4

Naylor, R., Baik, C., and James, R. (2013) *A Critical Interventions Framework for Advancing Equity in Australian Higher Education*. Report prepared for the Department of Industry, Innovation, Climate Change, Science, Research and Tertiary Education.

Neave, G. (2012) 'The evaluative state: A formative concept and an overview', in *The Evaluative State, Institutional Autonomy and Re-Engineering HE in Western Europe*. Issues in HE. London: Palgrave Macmillan. https://doi.org/10.1057/9780230370227_3

Oksala, J. (2013) 'Neoliberalism and biopolitical governmentality', in Nilsson, J., and Wallenstein, S.O. (Eds) *Foucault, Biopolitics and Governmentality*. Huddinge: Södertörn Philosophical Studies.

Olssen, M., and Peters, M.A. (2005) 'Neoliberalism, higher education and the knowledge economy: From the free market to knowledge capitalism', *Journal of Education Policy*, 20(3), 313–345. https://doi.org/10.1080/02680930500108718

O'Shea, S., Harwood, V., Howard, S., Cliff, K., and Delahunty, J. (2016) *Final Report: Investigating the Effectiveness of the In2Uni Year 12 University Preparation Program (UPP)*. Wollongong, NSW: University of Wollongong.

Otto, H.-U., Polutta, A., and Ziegler, H. (2009) 'A second generation of evidence-based practice: Reflexive professionalism and causal impact in social work', in Otto, H.-U., Polutta, A., and Ziegler, H. (Eds) *Evidence-Based Practice: Modernising the Knowledge-Base of Social Work*. Opladen: Barbara Budrich, 245–252.

Pawson, R. (2006) *Evidence-Based Policy: A Realist Perspective*. London: Sage.

Rabinow, P., and Rose, N. (2003) 'Foucault today', in Rabinow, P., and Rose, N. (Eds) *The Essential Foucault: Selections from the Essential Works Of Foucault 1954–1984*. New York: New Press.

Rallis, S.F. (2009) 'Reasoning with rigor and probity: Ethical premises for credible evidence', in Donaldson, S., Christie, C., and Mark, M. (Eds) *What Counts as Credible Evidence in Applied Research and Evaluation Practice?* Thousand Oaks: Sage Publications.

Reay, D. (2020) 'Sociology of education: A personal reflection on politics, power and pragmatism', *British Journal of Sociology of Education*, 41(6), 817–829. https://doi.org/10.1080/01425692.2020.1755228

Rezai-Rashti, G., Segeren, A., and Martino, W. (2017) 'The new articulation of equity education in neoliberal times: The changing conception of social justice in Ontario', *Globalisation, Societies and Education*, 15(2), 160–174. https://doi.org/10.1080/14767724.2016.1169514

Rose, N., and Miller, P. (1992) 'Political power beyond the state: Problematics of government', *The British Journal of Sociology*, 43(2), 173–205. https://doi.org/10.2307/591464

Schaefle, S. (2018) 'The relationship between GEAR UP program involvement and Latina/o students' performance on high-stakes tests', *Journal of Latinos and Education*, 17(3), 201–214.

Schwandt, T., and Gates, E. (2021) *Evaluating and Valuing in Social Research*. New York: Guilford Publications.

Shore, C. (2008) 'Audit culture and Illiberal governance: Universities and the politics of accountability', *Anthropological Theory*, 8(3), 278–298. https://doi.org/10.1177/1463499608093815

Shore, C., and Roberts, S. (1993) 'Higher education and the panopticon paradigm: Quality assessment as "disciplinary technology"', *Proceedings of the Society for Research into Higher Education Conference*, Brighton, 14–16 December. https://files.eric.ed.gov/fulltext/ED368243.pdf

Smith, J.A. (2018) *Strengthening Evaluation in Indigenous Higher Education Contexts in Australia*. Report for the Australian Government, Office for Learning and Teaching, Department of Education and Training. National Centre for Student Equity in Higher Education, Curtin University, Perth, WA.

Stage, F.K. (2007) 'Answering critical questions using quantitative data', *New Directions for Institutional Research*, 133, 5–16.

Stevenson, J., and Leconte, M.-O. (2009) '"Whose ethical university is it anyway?": Widening participation, student diversity and the "ethical" higher education institution', *International Journal of Diversity in Organisations, Communities and Nations*, 9(3), 103–114.

Swail, W.S., and Perna, L. (2002) 'Pre-college outreach programs: A national perspective', in Tierney, W.G., and Hagedorn, L.S. (Eds) *Increasing Access to College: Extending Possibilities for All Students*. New York: State University of New York Press, 15–34.

TASO (Transforming Access and Student Outcomes in Higher Education) (2023) *Research Ethics Guidance*. https://taso.org.uk/evidence/research-ethics-guidance

Trochim, W.M.K. (2009) 'Evaluation policy and evaluation practice', *New Directions for Evaluation*, 123, 13–32. https://doi.org/10.1002/ev.303

Ward, N.L. (2006) 'Improving equity and access for low-income and minority youth into institutions of higher education', *Urban Education*, 41(1), 50–70. https://doi.org/10.1177/0042085905282253

Wilkins, P., and de Vries, J. (2014) *Monitoring and Evaluation of Higher Education Equity Initiatives*. Perth, WA: The National Centre for Student Equity in Higher Education, Curtain University.

Younger, K., Gascoine, L., Menzies, V., and Torgerson, C. (2019) 'A systematic review of evidence on the effectiveness of interventions and strategies for widening participation in higher education', *Journal of Further and Higher Education*, 43(6), 742–773. https://doi.org/10.1080/0309877X.2017.1404558

Younger, M., and Warrington, M. (2009) 'Mentoring and target-setting in a secondary school in England: An evaluation of aims and benefits', *Oxford Review of Education*, 35(2), 169–185. https://doi.org/10.1080/03054980802666737

Zacharias, N. (2017) *The Australian Student Equity Program and Institutional Change: Paradigm Shift or Business as Usual?* The National Centre for Student Equity in Higher Education (NCSEHE). Perth: Curtin University.

Zaloom, C. (2021) *Indebted: How Families Make College Work at Any Cost*. Princeton: Princeton University Press.

7

EXPLORING POSSIBILITIES FOR PRAXIS

Introduction

In this chapter, we introduce PPoEMs as a way to 'stay with the trouble' (Haraway, 2016) within a social institution that holds a unique and powerful position in the production, legitimation, and dissemination of knowledge. In the machinery of higher education, as we negotiate new twenty-first-century forms of the production of knowledge, whilst apprehending and situating past bodies of knowledge, how might we open sPace to create the temporalities, spatialities, and relationalities for transformative possibilities? What role might higher education play in generating decolonial, social justice praxis to address the urgent issues of our times; the human and more-than-human crises that knowing differently and collectively could enable us to act in the world response-ably? An aim of this chapter is to reclaim the significance of methodological considerations, resisting the urge to jump directly to method, as has arguably become part of the institutional machinery of producing evidence. We will explain how PPoEMs draws from the theoretical perspectives outlined so far in this book, bringing together feminist, decolonial, post/structural, critical, and sociological insights for communities of praxis, opening sPace for solidarity, compassion, response-ability, and a particular ethic of care.

As we have argued in previous chapters, hegemonic imaginaries of the purpose of higher education over-emphasise economic, market-oriented, utilitarian, and commercialised imperatives to the detriment of equity, social justice, and planetary flourishing. We understand this hegemonic framing as deeply irresponsible, given the multidimensional, multi-scale socio-ecological crises facing our more-than-human communities across the globe. Yet this hegemonic framing has saturated ways of thinking, being, and doing in relation to all

DOI: 10.4324/9781003257165-10

domains of higher education policy and practice, including its funding, budgets and financing, leadership and management systems, research and teaching, graduate futures, *and* its always related equity practices. This hegemonic imaginary has also seeped into a global set of assumptions about the efficacy of evidence-based policy and practice, without interrogation of the methodologies that produce 'evidence' within particular socio-cultural contexts, political dynamics and power relations. The regime of truth that 'evidence' is value-free, apolitical, and objective is so powerful as to rely increasingly on large-scale data collection as the primary (and often only) source for solutions to a range of complex and deeply political socio-cultural issues, of which entrenched inequalities are entwined but mostly ignored. This 'truth' is interwoven with the forms of polarisation, populism, and plutocracies that subtly (and sometimes not so subtly) undermine scientific forms of knowledge and knowing, making feminist and decolonial critiques of science particularly troubling. These epistemological contestations challenge us to question and to create sPace to meet the urgencies of our times without unwittingly doing further harm by blindly trusting in 'evidence' to simply fix what are complex temporal/spatial entanglements of social, material, and cultural differences. How can we stay with the trouble? By troubling evidence-based hegemonies, as well as counter-hegemonic certainties, PPoEMs turn attention to epistemological, ontological, and ethical reframings that centre transformative equity and social justice praxis. A key aim is to consider how evidence-based hegemonies conceal the methodological contestations that determine what is seen to count as evidence and who is privileged to determine this. What then are the institutionalised practices of validation, inclusion, and exclusion that produce bodies of evidence used to determine presumed effective equity policy and practice? Who participates in such processes and who is excluded? What does evidence do to bodies of people and knowledge that have been, and continue to be, marginalised, devalued, pathologised, and/or excluded? What are the underpinning methodologies that create the conditions for some bodies of evidence to be valued, validated, and institutionally recognised, whilst others are cast aside? These are some of the questions that underpin the focus of this chapter and that have led us to create PPoEMs as an ongoing reflexive sPace for reframing for transformative equity praxis.

The hegemony of 'evidence' and data analytics

Part of the hegemonic practice of equity research and evaluation is to focus primarily on method, skipping over the underpinning methodological dimensions that frame what kinds of methods are prioritised, why, with what effects, and for whom. We consider methods as sets of tools – and the kinds of tools chosen, and the ways these are put to work, matter. Methods are inextricably tied to the methodological frameworks that guide their practice. The methodology we understand as an ethical-political-epistemological-ontological complex which frames the ways that method becomes animated in space-time. However, methodological consideration is increasingly absent from the field of equity in higher education, and this we argue has significant implications for the reproduction of inequalities through equity interventions. We understand 'equity interventions' as encompassing activities aiming to progress equity aims, including research, evaluation, teaching, and professional practice, all of which tend to focus on the method in the pursuit of 'evidence' to inform the development of equity interventions. Indeed, there appears to be an assumption around 'evidence-based policy and practice' that methods are outside of the scope of concerns with epistemology, ontology, and ethics; a decontextualisation that is so fiercely apolitical as to deny that evidence inevitably carries heavy consequences for humans and more-than-humans, most particularly those subjected to multidimensional injustices.

Twenty-first-century forms of knowledge production are invested in large-scale data analytics and algorithms, driven by methodologies related to that which is seen to be purely logical, computational, and calculable. "The spatiality of the logic of algorithms is most commonly figured as a series of programmable steps, a sequence, or a 'recipe'" and "each step in a calculative procedure is defined by its position in a finite series" (Amoore, 2016: 11). Yet this "overlooks the extent to which algorithms modify themselves in and through their nonlinear iterative relations to input data" (ibid.). Inevitably, who inputs that data and with what intentions matter for equity and social justice. A prime example of the machinery of data analytics impacting knowledge and communities differently is Cambridge Analytica's motto that "data drives all that we do" in the aim to "change audience behaviour" (Amoore, 2016: 6). A scandal was uncovered in 2018 involving Cambridge Analytica and Facebook in which data analytics were mobilised to influence voting behaviour in the Brexit referendum and 2016 US election, targeting communities with particular political profiles (e.g. Cadwalladr, 2017a, 2017b; Osborne, 2018; Rosenberg et al, 2018 cited in Burke et al, 2022: 4). Although not an example of data analytics in higher education, the eventual impact on policy and practice of both the Brexit referendum and the Trump election has broader implications for equity and social justice in higher education.

Yet, the complexities of human and more-than-human socio-cultural-political relations, power dynamics, ethical concerns, and inequalities are viewed largely as irrelevant to such data-driven methods. Equity is fundamentally a *social* problem outside of calculable logics; one that requires developing methodologies that enable a sensitivity, response-ability, and deeply ethical reorientation to how higher education as a social institution is entwined with wider socio-cultural-political dynamics. This requires close attention to the ethical-political-epistemological-ontological complex that frames equity knowledge and practice and demands critical, sustained, reflexive engagement with ethics and the political nature of equity. After all, equity – when not taken superficially – is fundamentally about understanding the history and enduring nature of oppression, exclusion, marginalisation, injustice and inequality, higher education's role in producing and sustaining inequalities and ways that higher education might transform (or sustain) unequal relations. This is about struggle, contestation, representation, participation, and redistribution. Method without full consideration of methodology does not have the capacity to deal with such complex concerns. In response to such considerations, we put the language of 'dynamic' to work methodologically. With historical links to musical notation, this term and its attendant meanings also provide new possibility of conceiving and discussing the way that social dynamics 'crescendo' or 'diminuendo' in terms of their amplification in close concert with contextual conditions. Dynamics are not mechanical, nor are they predictable. Dynamics might help us to engage questions of power and difference, as always becoming, always fluid, always shifting. This is a way to trouble the hegemonic methodologies underpinning the dominant discourse of 'evidence-based policy and practice' that prioritises measurability, and by necessity that which is observable, and large-scale data production.

In the context of higher education, the digital revolution has rapidly moved towards large-scale data analytics as a major source for evidence-based policy and practice. A primary example is the growing use of learning analytics in higher education and its increasing application to equity interventions. The deficit imaginary that is so deeply engrained in equity frameworks is ever-present in the mobilisation of learning analytics. A key question driving the use of these datafication technologies is: Which students are at risk and how can that risk be managed? The attraction of such technologies in the neoliberal timescapes of higher education is both the scale in which 'equity' can supposedly be addressed and the rapid pace in which solutions can be put in place, with an emphasis on (cost-)efficiency rather than ethics. Learning analytics can help to quickly identify the students not attending lectures, not using the library, missing assessment deadlines and can utilise a small team of support staff to reach out to these students in a transactional, customer-oriented context; redirecting students to student services where this is deemed to be useful. The underlying inequalities that students are navigating, which are affecting the quantifiable patterns of participation that can be easily observed via such technologies, are left unexamined. Thus, a surface-level, decontextualised approach, directed at diagnoses and remediation of the individual student, is put into play, without any care to the structural, institutional, and systemic power dynamics that unequally impact students navigating multidimensional socio-cultural-political injustices. The hegemonic imaginary then puts into effect the machinery of a range of data analytics, underpinned by objectivist and dehumanising ontological framings, which appear on the surface to have utility in the context of global neoliberalism, in which humans (and students) are reduced to customers, resources, or capital. There is little sPace within such conditions for sustainable, long-term systemic-level transformation towards equity and social justice, leaving solidly in place the intersecting foundations of neocolonial, neopatriarchal and neoliberal ways of knowing and doing 'equity'.

The effect of such machinations is multiple but one important feature is the unequal dynamics shaping pedagogical relations; circling back to a system of banking education, in which professional and academic staff 'know' what is best for all students. Although *diversity* is valued in the market university, not least as students from every background carry a funding load contributing to the institution's income generation, *difference* is a problem to be regulated and controlled (Burke, 2015). Students who participate differently from the hegemonic expectations built into institutional systems and structures are seen to require transformation at the individual level, through equity interventions, so that they might fit into the dominant framework/way of being (Archer, 2003: 23). The methods underpinning the evidence produced through data analytics about difference serve as a kind of panopticon, in which students grappling with complex inequalities, traumas, and challenges become visible without knowing when, how, or by whom they are being viewed – and yet are intensely aware of their visibility in terms of sensibilities of not fitting in, not being the right kind of student, not belonging, being an outsider in higher education time-space. This is commonly framed as 'imposter syndrome' – an individualising, pathologising discourse that requires students to 'overcome' this supposed disorder. Indeed, it is often recognised that everyone in some ways experiences a mild form of 'imposter syndrome', normalising this sensibility while further concealing the underlying structures of inequality from view in the unequal cultural value order of the institution of higher education.

Through large-scale methods, such as surveys, the discursive framing of the problem (such as measuring quantitative, measurable, observable forms of participation) is already embedded in the research or evaluation instrument, and thus there is little sPace to 'stay with the trouble' of the institutionalised misrecognition that is rooted in structures of inequality. Ethics in a methods-centric framework, become instrumentalised as a stage in the process of gaining ethical approval. The institutional approach to ethics approval is imperative and has provided a broader scope to engage with ethical consideration; we are not arguing against it. However, when methodology is not central to sustained, reflexive, response-able and careful ethical engagement, profounder questions are ignored about who determines what 'equity' is, who is subjected to the gaze of equity intervention and how these interventions, including research and evaluation, produce knowledge, knowing, and evidence about equity, often in ways that are harmful to those navigating complex inequalities. Amoore (2016), in her important interrogation of the ethics of algorithms, makes a key distinction between ethics as a code of practice and "ethics as the inescapably political formation of the relation of oneself to oneself and to others" (2016: 7). Although she locates this in the composite of 'human-algorithm relations' – the ethico-politics she points to has broader significance for the field of equity across the range of its scope, reach, practice, and impact. We explored the limitations of the method in Chapter 6, when we examine processes of equity evaluation that are grounded in the desire to find 'what works', without ethical attention to the contested values at play in e-valu-ation. In this chapter, we are concerned with the ethical-political-epistemological-ontological complex of methodology, pointing to the need to move to counter-hegemonic methodologies for transformative equity praxis.

Counter-hegemonic methodologies for transformative equity praxis

Moving away from the hegemonic imaginaries of evidence-based policy and practice, we offer a methodological framework oriented to collective forms of praxis, by weaving together the rich bodies of feminist, decolonial, critical, post/structural, and sociological theory and methodology. PPoEMs understands research, evaluation, teaching, and professional practice as pedagogical sPace in which participants collaborate across and with differences to co-create the ethical conditions for 'knowing-with' (Mbembe, 2023) and 'making-with' (Haraway, 2016). PPoEMs is grounded in a commitment to the redistribution of the privilege of being a researcher in recognition that we are all researchers and have a 'right to research' (Appadurai, 2006). PPoEMs theorise "the relationship among the pedagogical, the affective, the political and the ethical sensibilities in educational practices that attempt to instill critical hope and transformation" (Bozalek, Carolissen and Leibowitz, 2014: 4). PPoEMs' orientation to critical hope vis-a-vis praxis recognises the richness of critical research, theories, and methodologies in making sense of entrenched inequalities that insidiously shape pedagogical relations, experiences, embodiments, and subjectivities. This generates possibilities for moving dominant and myopic foci from research products (in hegemonic terms represented as 'evidence') towards methodologies concerned with generating equity and social justice transformations through praxis. Moving away from fixed notions of tangible evidence, PPoEMs draw on critical, feminist, decolonial, and post/structural theories of embodiment, subjectivity, and practice to draw attention to the ways inequalities are lived, experienced and felt through complex formations of knowing, being and doing (Burke, 2012). This post-Freirean framework of critical hope weaves in the critiques of feminist scholars, to embrace postures of *un/knowing* and *un/learning* the (neo)colonial, masculinist authoritarian dis/positions that are at the heart of oppressive relations. We embrace a more-than-humanism that is committed to the participation in equity knowing and action of those regularly denied representation in such processes. PPoEMs follows Haraway's invitation to stay with the trouble by learning to be truly present as beings "entwined in myriad unfinished configurations of places, times, matters, meanings" (Haraway, 2016: 1–2) and takes heed of the "colonial temptation to build hierarchies between beings, cultures and things" (Mbembe, 2022: 12).

PPoEMs resists hierarchies and authoritarianism, striving towards solidarities in taking up dis/positions of reparation through epistemic justice. Disrupting the positioning of the social scientist as the dispassionate researcher measuring the world as it is, difference is seen as a resource for *knowing-with* and *making-with*. There is no one 'truth' to be discovered or claimed by a sole detached researcher; rather, there are multiple 'truths', which are contested and tied to complex relations of power, difference, and inequality (Rich, 1979; Lather, 2004) and which can be collectively reimagined through communities of praxis. The community of re-searchers pay particular attention to the truths of those who have been silenced, excluded and pathologised through the colonising, regulating, normalising, and paternalistic gaze of hegemonic forms of social science research and policy (Harding, 1986).

It is important that higher education institutions collect data that identifies and reveals unequal patterns of access to, participation in, impact of, and outcomes through, higher education. We are not disputing the value of this work. However, data needs to be gathered and analysed within broader methodological frameworks that seek to capture the contextual, intersecting, multiple and often contradictory layers of inequality. PPoEMs are attuned not only to concrete and measurable barriers but also to intersecting inequalities that unwittingly reproduce inequalities through taken-for-granted methods, values, practices, or assumptions otherwise ignored (Burke, 2012). Generating knowledge and insight about the ways that insidious inequalities impact access and participation in higher education requires methodologies underpinned by praxis, in which a dialogic dynamic across action and reflection is sustained (Freire, 1972). Attention to the different and contradictory ways that inequalities play out in local, institutional, disciplinary, subject-based, regional, national, and global contexts is key to such approaches.

Uncovering the values of those producing and validating evidence, PPoEMs aim to uncover contested values and generate knowledge through a sustained commitment to qualitative forms of parity of participation. Narismulu (2016) explains:

> Challenging assumptions about the assignment of value is central to tackling the chauvinisms and bigotry that are still rife in our society and the world.
> *(2016: 88)*

Sayer (2011), in *Why Things Matter to People*, argues for a new conception of social science that takes into account the ways in which normative reasoning might complement critical theory's attempts to provide adequate accounts of human capacity, vulnerability, and flourishing. We acknowledge that an endless 'making the familiar strange' can be both difficult-to-achieve and exhausting. Yet we also promote that redistributing access to conceptual tools via widening participation in theory-driven research and evaluation will produce more nuanced and response-able reflection/action in relation to social-cultural-political relations and contexts. This requires a form of ethical reflexivity that turns methodological consideration back onto itself.

Meta-moments, movements, and metaphors

The term *meta* connotes a turn towards the self-referential. It signals an interrogation of genre or convention 'from within' a genre or convention, through bending a subject back onto itself. PPoEMs is a form of meta-methodology; an approach that supports sustained interrogation of different methodologies of equity research, practice, evaluation, and policymaking. This 'bending back on itself' is a key aspect of the methodology, not as an individualised process of self-reflection to improve one's human capital but as a collective process of knowing-with and making-with differently with a deep commitment to an ethic of care. Drawing in the critical, feminist, post/structural, and sociological conceptual ensemble of previous chapters, this is a praxis committed to researching research, evaluating evaluation, practising on practice. Freirean-inspired dialogic praxis is unstable, critical, and self-referential (Lumb and Roberts, 2017).

The reflective *meta-moment* has a long history in theories of learning (e.g. Brockbank and McGill, 2007). The opportunity to metaphorically 'step back' and relate to an experience or phenomenon is considered in many of these frameworks a key tool for learning. A fundamental pedagogical aspect of PPoEMs is about creating contexts in which cooperatively constructed meta-moments can survive and, importantly, be considered valuable 'assets' for a project or team. The discomfort created by learning across different social positions is a key currency of the context created. Critical pedagogy brings an analysis of power at play, and this is where the instability lives. Feminist praxis, inspired by Freirean insight, is a commitment to bringing theorising and action together in ongoing dialogue and refusing to separate processes of critical reflection and practice. Reflexivity is thus central, with a sustained engagement with the ethics of knowing and doing. The conceptual resources of feminist epistemologies provide some of the tools needed to make visible the largely invisible; to bring to light the gendered, classed, and racialised inequalities that profoundly shape how we frame knowledge, who is seen as a knower and how higher education practices such as research, writing, and publication are entangled in these power dynamics of knowledge, knowing, and doing.

Building critical reflection into methodology as a mode of ethical participation is part of the *Pedagogical* aspect of PPoEMs. If social justice praxis is
about learning and acting across difference, then critical reflection, in a context
of connection with others and to difference, plays a key role in the possibility
of this learning. Indeed, critical reflection situates experience as data (Denzin
and Lincoln, 2017) and provides the possibility of breaking with established
norms, conventions, understandings, and scaffolded necessarily from our existing norms, conventions, and understandings.

Patti Lather in tracing how she became a methodologist researching research focuses on the importance of apprehending what frames our
knowledge-making process, as part of an advocacy for 'critical frames in education research':

> What is sought is a reflexive process that focuses on our too easy use of
> accepted forms, a process that might lead us toward a science capable of
> continually demystifying the realities it serves to create. What I am talk-
> ing about, in Lincoln's (1990) wonderful word play, is not "your father's"
> paradigm. It is an altogether different approach to doing empirical inquiry
> that suggests that the most useful work in the present crisis of representa-
> tion "is that which uses form to disrupt received forms and undermines an
> objective, disinterested stance (Spanos, 1987: 271).
>
> *(Lather, 2004: 235)*

PPoEMs draws on histories of deconstructing the fiction of the frames that
guide our approach to research, practice, evaluation, and policymaking in
higher education. This demands a non-linear commitment to movement,
rejecting the hegemonic narrative of linear 'progress' engrained in neocolonial
imaginaries that are often reactionary and that seek remedies that are vacuous
of an ethic of care. Such reactionary postures are incapable of apprehending
the harm done to those whose interests are ignored; those who are regularly
misrepresented on the basis of hegemonic forms of 'evidence'. The forms of
movement we advocate for then are not reactions but responses. Responses
that are grounded in an ethic of care to the experiences, values, and knowledges
of marginalised bodies; that are response-able through engaging in sustained
processes of reflection/action, action/reflection in the context of histories of
institutionalised inequality. PPoEMs demands sPace for patience, care, and
deep listening whilst recognising the need to act response-ably in the moment,
being truly present in knowing-with and making with Others. This requires a
patience that takes account of the accounts of those ordinarily excluded from
participating fully in processes of power. This is a new movement that is collective and is about the human capacity to be moved in dialogue with others
(Ahmed, 2017: 5). It is a feminist movement driven by "the growing connections between those who recognise something – power relations, gender

violence, gender as violence – as being what they are up against, even if they have different words for what that what is" (Ahmed, 2017: 3).

Difference is thus imperative to moving-with others. Through recognising difference as valuable, solidarity is generated through a sense of *resemblance* to a recognisable context, experience or emotion that is moving to others. The resemblance relates to the explanatory potential of histories of social theory and action. It creates re-cognition of our connection to ourselves and other beings. It moves at the level of the e-motion-al, the affective domain that is otherwise excluded from hegemonic imaginaries of equity. The *resemblance*, a resonance of sorts with experience and/or observation, if we are open to it and to discomfort, can lead to a form of *re-assembling* – a new orientation to the world emerging, shifted by the insight of the reading and questioning with other voices and an inability to see it the same way again.

A multidimensional methodology for reconceptualising participation

Across different higher education contexts, people participate in a "dynamic regime of ongoing struggles for recognition" (Fraser, 2003: 57), mostly without adequate attention to the unequal resources available to differently positioned participants (maldistribution) and the cultural value order that reinforces the status and authority of privileged bodies (of knowledge and people) while subordinating Others (misrecognition). These insidious relations of inequality shape the political dynamics of representation; who has an author/itative voice and whose experiences and interests are marginalised and disregarded (misrepresentation). As we have argued in Chapter 2, Nancy Fraser's social justice framework provides a powerful set of conceptual tools in relation to the multidimensions and intersections of redistribution, recognition, and representation. Her conceptual framework is particularly fruitful for reconceptualising 'participation', as participation has largely been taken for granted as apolitical in evidence-based policy and practice.

PPoEMs invites researcher-practitioners and practitioner-researchers to grapple with the tensions and dilemmas posed by the imperatives of equity policy and practice, which commonly attempt to treat persons 'equitably' through standardised mechanisms devised on notions of 'sameness'. A methodological framework that foregrounds critical praxis provides the tools to recognise and represent 'difference' in ways that pay close attention to complex power relations as an inevitable and valuable part of social life. Critical praxis troubles regulatory technologies that exclude those who do not conform to the hegemonic way of being (Chawla and Rodriguez, 2007) to interrogate hegemonic concepts of 'participation', most often couched in a quantitative framing, as a form of social inclusion that transforms the individual student through the hegemonic discourses of 'aspiration', 'confidence', 'resilience' and 'potential'. Without critical praxis, this form of 'inclusion' reproduces mis-recognition; for example, the idea that the problem of equity lies with students diagnosed with deficiencies and disorders (lack of confidence and imposter syndrome are two key examples).

Without praxis-based methodologies to interrogate multidimensional injus-tices, a vicious circle is unwittingly put into place in which resources that have been specifically intended to create greater equity become complicit in mald-istribution, misrecognition, and misrepresentation. PPoEMs instead creates sPace to examine technologies of categorisation, including the ways catego-risation homogenises and narrows complex relations through monodimen-sional logics (e.g. through over-simplified equity categories such as 'Regional, Rural and Remote'). We are not denying that categorisations are sometimes necessary devices to produce targeting methods, datasets, and evidence, thus providing some of the tools needed to formulate equity policy and practice. However, categorisations, when devoid of reflexive, ethical forms of praxis, are problematic in the constructions that they produce – narrowing, reduc-ing, over-simplifying, and decontextualising. Categorisations simultaneously enable and constrain the ways we think about questions of access, equity, and participation. PPoEMs offers a range of critical concepts and tools to engage categorisations whilst deconstructing and problematising them.

Redistributive equity requires intricate and critical attention to the target-ing methodologies through which equity groups and institutional categorisa-tions are produced as technologies for intervention. Praxis-based principles guide targeting to focus on redistributing resources to those groups who have suffered long-standing forms of social-cultural-political inequality. When put to work within communities of praxis (see later), a more nuanced approach to decision-making is enabled, grounded in the principle of redistribution. This facilitates a dialogic (rather than data-driven) approach to reflexively considering structural and material inequalities, such as those which oper-ate through socio-economic status, and to examine these in relation to sym-bolic and cultural formations of (mis)recognition. This nuancing of targeting methodologies considers how structural and material inequalities are inter-secting, embodied formations that are entwined with cultural and political inequalities that work at material, discursive, and affective layers of experience. PPoEMs, woven with Fraserian social justice theory (see Chapter 2), is designed to prompt the development of methods for redistribution of equity resources that engage analysis of the intimate relationship of socio-economic inequali-ties to formations of difference, tied to misrecognition and misrepresenta-tion. Methodological considerations and developments are vital to address these complexities and to generate frameworks and mechanisms committed to equity and social justice processes and practices. This encourages ongoing, collective processes of reflexivity framed by an ethic of care. This multidimen-sional methodology engages participants in sense-making of the institutional structures and practices that are implicated in reproducing inequalities at multiple and intersecting cultural, symbolic, discursive, and material levels.

This pedagogical, praxis-based approach to equity research, evaluation, and practice opens spaces for analysis of the "forms and levels of economic dependence and inequality that impede parity of participation" (Fraser, 2003: 36) and emphasises the importance of a dialogical approach to participation, in a "democratic process of public deliberation" (Fraser, 2003: 43). There is however a dilemma in the circularity of this argument, as Skeggs cautions:

> To make a recognition claim one must first have a recognizable identity, and this identity must be 'proper': that is, it must have recognizable public value. This immediately presents a problem for those who are not considered to have 'proper' identities and are continually misrecognized; it also presents a problem for those who are forced to inhabit an identity category not of their own making, as well as those who are forced to be visible in order to be seen to have a recognizable identity.
>
> *(Skeggs, 2004: 178)*

Such cautions lead us back to the importance of exercising an ethic of care in engaging in equity work. Our critical hope is that PPoEMs offer the analytic tools (as described earlier) to illuminate such ethical dilemmas and challenges, which inevitably emerge when occupying a position of response-ability and troubling counter-hegemonic positions of certainty (as well as hegemonic ones). This draws on Haraway's imperative to stay with the trouble – to do so we must abandon the desire for certainty – we require social justice conceptual resources that enable a deep, ethically oriented form of mindfulness that is dialogically formed with Others and unsettles the insatiable need for certitude.

The imperative of praxis-based methodologies is to illuminate how actions are always shaped by particular representations and understandings of the world, although "the visible, that which is immediately given, hides the invisible which determines it" (Bourdieu, 1990: 126–127 in McNay, 2008: 181). PPoEMs aims to enable the more subtle, sometimes invisible, and insidious inequalities at play in higher education (which are always connected to wider social relations and contexts) to be linked to the level of subjectivity, emotion, and the embodied context of action and practice.

In this way, the concept of parity of participation, grounded in a quantitative framing of action and practice, requires troubling. Equity policy and practice has been characterised by a commitment to parity of participation (in various articulations across different geopolitical timescapes). However, conceptions of parity are too often monodimensional, strongly framed by a deficit imaginary and distracted by what is measurable and observable. This relies on measures such as counting numbers of people within one-dimensional policy categorisations – driven by questions such as 'how many from [an equity categorisation] enrolled in higher education in a particular year?'

The equity categorisation takes further hold in deficit imaginations, convincing those with the power to make policy decisions that the problem lies in raising the aspiration or resilience of people identified within the homogenising categorisation.

We lose sight of the root problem:

- What are the social and economic structures that reproduce the conditions in which there are growing inequalities that affect educational access and participation?
- What are the relations of maldistribution that perpetuate inequality and educational disadvantage?
- How do these social and economic inequalities affect how different people are unequally recognised, valued and represented in society and in higher education?

In short, we need a reframing of notions of parity of participation to challenge deficit imaginaries and to support higher education development for equity and sustainability. As we argued, drawing on Fraser, a social justice reimagining of parity of participation substantially deepens engagement with equity by examining the implications of *who participates* and *on what terms*. This shifts towards qualitative conceptions of 'participation' in which the participant is 'on a par with others', bringing attention to power dynamics and unequal relations hidden in the taken-for-granted hierarchies of higher education.

PPoEMs centres Fraser's critique of hegemonic constructions of participation. Rather the aim is to "empower those involved in change" (Lather, 1991: 3) engaging in meaning-making in the sPace of collaboration. As Lather (1991: 11–12) explains, the "requirements of praxis are theory both relevant to the world and nurtured by actions in it; theory that emerges from 'practical political grounding'". PPoEMs aims to create challenging, imaginative, and creative spaces for participants to know-with and make-with, within communities of praxis. Praxis underscores the urgency of creating spaces of dialogue to inspire methodological and pedagogical imagination in ways that explicitly challenge socioeconomic inequalities, cultural misrecognitions, and political misrepresentations. In this way, praxis enables critical hope – not in an overly idealistic or naive way but hope that transformation is possible through praxis – that is, collective and critical thinking and action. Praxis refuses the position that there is no alternative to the hegemonic systems and practices. It rejects the regimes of truth that benefit only a small group of people, their values, interests, and perspectives. Praxis refuses the regime of truth that higher education and its purpose is determined by narrow market-oriented, commercialised, industry-centric, and corporate goals and argues for a broader articulation of higher education's potential contribution to human and more-than-human flourishing.

Communities of praxis

The concept of communities of practice is a salient feature of educational discourse that originally emerged from the work of Lave and Wenger (1991). The concept emphasises that learning is always a situated, social, and relational process, considering learning

> not as a process of socially shared cognition that results in the end in the internalization of knowledge by individuals, but as a process of becoming a member of a sustained community of practice. Developing an identity as a member of a community and becoming knowledgeably skilful are part of the same process, with the former motivating, shaping, and giving meaning to the latter, which it subsumes.
>
> *(Lave, 1991: 65)*

Lave further elaborates that "we should not lose sight of the fact that institutional and individual successes and failures of learning are interdependent and are the product of the same historical processes" (Lave, 1991: 64). The social and contextual nature of learning is central in the forming of "groups of people who share a concern or a passion for something they do and learn how to do it better as they interact regularly" (Wenger-Trayner and Wenger-Trayner, 2015: 2). Key dimensions of communities of practice include: a shared domain of interest; a community in which shared exchange, learning, understanding and values underpin a sense of belonging in that group; and a set of shared practices that characterise the connection amongst the community in term of ways of doing and ways of being. Importantly then, concept recognises that we do not engage in practice as *individuals* only but in *wider social contexts and practices*. Further, it highlights that our practices, what we do and how we do it, are shaped by particular histories – *recognisable* ways of doing and being in *particular* communities of practice; shared values and perspectives, which foster a sense of belonging and identity; a common set of interests, concerns, knowledge, and passions; and a sense of collective identity.

PPoEMs build on this but emphasise the imperative of exercising an ethical reflexivity by opening time and space for communities of practice to engage in critical interrogation of the shared assumptions, values and perspectives that are collectively revalidated. When those shared understandings are taken uncritically as a way of structuring academic and/or professional practice, there is potential for exclusion, marginalisation, and the reproduction of multidimensional injustices. It is crucial then to create the conditions for participants to critically engage the diversity, difference, and contestation *within* and *across* communities of practice. When left uninterrogated, communities of practice become trapped in a kind of circularity in which shared values and interests are continuously reproduced and become entrenched methodologies framing practice. This circularity perpetuates the exclusion of the values, interests, and perspectives (the misrepresentation) of those outside of, or on the peripheries of, the core participants. For those who are outside of the community of practice, a sense of not belonging, alienation or disconnection can become a way of understanding difference. This is a form of misrecognition, in which the cultural patterns of value become internalised in a body (of knowledge or people) through a pathologising notion of difference as 'Other'. When the politics of difference are not named or articulated, and the emphasis is only on what is (assumed as) shared, a sense of alienation and shame is often the lived experience of the outsider position. As communities of practice are often underpinned by implicit sets of assumptions and taken-for-granted practices, this energetic, collective sense of belonging also then works to exclude or denigrate others who do not fit in socially, culturally, politically, or discursively. Power relations, which are not always visible, are at the heart of the exclusionary dynamics of communities of practice, even when the experience of core participants is felt as inclusive and legitimating.

In these ways, our educational practices require ethical, reflexive praxis to bring to light unwittingly produced exclusions and discourses of denigration and pathologisation for those positioned as outside, Other and/or different. In reimagining communities of practice as communities of praxis our collective efforts are invested in bringing to light hidden sets of values, assumptions, and interrogating power relations at play through cycles of *collective, critical* reflection-action and action-reflection. Communities of praxis foreground the need for *sustained reflexivity* to question taken-for-granted practices and recognise difference. Communities of praxis aim to foster a sense of connection and belonging across the diversity and difference of participants who work collectively to interrogate, to make explicit, and to trouble the shared and contested values and principles articulated by participants. Through this, Communities of praxis aim to develop inclusive practices for equity and social justice through processes of ongoing exchange to create greater sensitivity to diversity and difference; thus promoting an ethic of care.

In Chapter 2, we illustrated 'misrecognition' through the case study of *Art for a Few* and the ways communities of praxis can bring insidious inequalities to light and create sPace for generating counter-hegemonic practices. *Art for a Few* illuminates how power works within communities of practice where key participants, in this case, the admissions tutors, draw from shared values, assumptions and perspectives to assert judgment on a person positioned as different from, and inevitably excluded from, that the community of practice. The shared judgment of a community of practice is reproduced in relation to what counts as legitimate forms of experience and knowledge without questioning the assumptions underpinning those judgements. The subtle processes of difference and inequality that play out in the misrecognition of the Other are not observable in any straightforward, measurable, or quantifiable way.

Art for a Few was disseminated widely across the UK to art educators engaged in selection processes. The research resonated with the programme team of one of the most selective fine arts degree programmes in the country, as they realised year-on-year their student intake was formed of white, middle-class young people from across and outside the country, with no representation from local schools and colleges (the University was in a relatively impoverished and ethnically diverse local community). The programme team formed a community of praxis, engaging deeply with the research and analysis and broadening the scope of participation to equity practitioners and representatives of local schools and colleges. Generating sPace through communities of praxis, participants collectively transformed: (1) the relation between the university programme and the local schools, colleges, and communities, (2) the programme team's admissions and pedagogical practices, (3) the constitution of the student cohort from a monocultural to a highly diverse student community, and (4) the inclusion and recognition of Other art forms previously excluded.

The aim of PPoEMs, which opens sPace for communities of praxis, is for *research to become a pedagogical time-space* in which diverse communities of participants engage in a collaborative process to generate new ways of knowing and doing. The purpose is to create collective, dialogical, and participatory methodologies, temporalities, and spatialities, which engage participants in processes of knowing-with and making with Others for transformative equity and social justice. Pedagogies are conceptualised not as methods of teaching and learning but as relational spaces beyond formal classroom spaces through which we engage the politics of difference (Weedon, 1999) and the circle of knowledge (Freire, 2009). Through the circle of knowledge, participants co-produce meaning and explicitly examine the values circulating across and within particular pedagogical, research and evaluative spaces, time/frames and contexts. It is our aim that communities of praxis can provide the sPace for hopeful theorisation/action about the possibility of channelling resources, relationships and decision-making processes that have the capacity to move towards sustained change underpinned by a collective sense of value, whilst engaging questions of difference.

Towards praxis-based methodologies for equity and social justice

Methodology is increasingly situated outside of the hegemonic discourse of 'evidence-based policy and practice' and research is similarly detached from the rapid pace in which new digital technologies and large-scale data production are the grammars underpinning the hegemonic methods for the development of equity in higher education. The bodies of critical, feminist, and decolonial research, theory, and methodology that provide crucial knowledge for challenging the reproduction of inequalities are rendered obsolete, and/or located in academic spaces and seen as irrelevant to institutional equity strategies and operations. Simultaneously, significant insight emerging from years of lived and professional experience is institutionally invalidated through the exclusion of practitioner- and student-knowledge. Communities most impacted by equity interventions through methodologies prioritising measurement of variables deemed to be important by those privileged to decide, are misrepresented by decontextualised data and 'evidence'. This we argue is ir-response-able and fails to engage the complex entanglements of decades of injustice and inequality for which higher education is part. The separation of critical research, practitioner insights, and lived experiences of inequality from the development of equity policy and practice is detrimental to generating social justice forms of social, cultural, and institutional transformation in, through, and beyond higher education.

Building on Chapter 5, we have argued that the politics of time are central to these exclusions, with the spatio-temporalities in which new digital technologies offer computation, calculable but profoundly dehumanising data analytics for which higher education turns for answers. Further, the appeal of skipping over methodological considerations is part of the certainty invested in hegemonic frameworks for producing 'evidence' and forming policy and practice on this basis. This is exacerbated by neoliberal forms of austerity, in moves away from public funding to student loans, casualisation, and increasingly intensified workloads, all of which offer little time and space for critical reflection/action and collaborative knowing-with and making-with communities that have suffered decades of misrepresentation. A quantitative framework for 'parity of participation' renders concerns with the quality of participation irrelevant, leaving hegemonic methods of measurement of participation solidly in place as the primary source of decision-making. Thus, a vicious circle operates in which aims for equity are continually undermined by the timescapes of higher education and hegemonic methodologies, which are not interrogated in relation to ethical concerns with care, response-ability and representation due to pressures on time, space and resources. The white, masculinist desire for size is insatiable – size matters and paying attention to local context is seen as an extravagance – time-consuming and too small to matter. Rather large-scale data is the preferred framing, with a neoliberal focus on efficiency and a narrative that critical research methodologies are outdated and outmoded, largely as these are not seen to be cost-effective. This is likely to be further entrenched by the marketisation and commercialisation of higher education, in which students are increasingly valued in terms of income-generation, and thus situated as customers, rather than in the context of developing meaningful pedagogical relations with students, as part of higher education's capacity to contribute to human and more-than-human flourishing and well-being. The ethical-political-epistemological-ontological complex that shapes how method/ology is put to work in space-time matters for commitments to dismantle inequalities yet is brushed aside in the pursuit of measurement, data production, evidence, and efficiency. A social justice praxis reframing is critical for transformative reorientations to higher education equity, away from neoliberal imperatives, and towards redressing the colonial and patriarchal histories embedded in contemporary higher education structures, systems and practices.

We have introduced a praxis-based methodological framework, PPoEMs, to counter hegemonic assumptions that research and evaluation are only valid if they aim for efficiency, generalisability, measurability, and neutrality. Equity research, evaluation, and practice, when response-ably and ethically committed to examining, revealing and challenging maldistribution, misrecognition and misrepresentation, must then work to dislodge unequal relations of power that perpetuate injustice. This requires analyses of how higher education not only is complicit in the reproduction of inequality but also plays an active role in sustaining multidimensional injustice. Representations of higher education as a neutral, apolitical site of knowledge production and teaching must therefore be questioned. Praxis-based methodologies expose the ways knowledge and power are inextricably connected and are not reducible to measurable facts or information. PPoEMs is offered to get beneath hegemonic assumptions that sustain the unequal order and to reveal that methods represented as decontextualised and apolitical actually privilege the values and interests of those in powerful institutional positions, whilst Others are misrecognised and discounted. PPoEMs, and the generation of collective sPace through communities of praxis, involve differently situated participants in processes of reflexive re/consideration of the different and contested values at play across heterogeneous participant communities. An aim is to generate 'knowledge commons' (Mbembe, 2022) about the field(s) in which participants are differently and unequally located, positioned, and represented. This requires acknowledging and addressing differences as part of the process of equity research, evaluation, and practice.

By introducing the concept of sPace as part of reframing higher education timescapes, we aim to contribute to the dismantling of the colonising, objectifying, and dehumanising discourses of evidence-based policy and practice that are influenced by hegemonic versions of what and who is seen to count. We understand the contemporary neoliberal, neocolonial, neopatriarchal timescapes of higher education as another iteration of Freire's (critique of) banking education. Thus, we argue for a shift in temporal orientation to deep praxis – one that reveals the insidious ways that certain values seep into our pedagogical and methodological imaginations, leading us to believe there is no alternative, and reproducing value through methods assumed to be neutral and value free. Rather, PPoEMs involve processes of re-searching research, evaluating evaluation and practising on practice to engage with the 'world-making', constructive quality of research, evaluation, and practice, through shifting our dis/positionality towards reflexive, iterative, care-full, response-able cycles of participatory meaning-making across difference. We build on these considerations in Chapter 8, by offering examples of how PPoEMs creates new programmatic possibilities, focusing on the practices of equity.

References

Ahmed, S. (2017) *Living a Feminist Life*. Durham, NC: Duke University Press.

Amoore, L. (2016) *Cloud Ethics*. Durham, NC: Duke University Press.

Appadurai, A. (2006) 'The right to research', *Globalisation, Societies and Education*, 4(2), 167–177.

Archer, L. (2003) *Race, Masculinity and Schooling: Muslim Boys and Education*. Berkshire: Open University Press.

Bozalek, V., Carolissen, R., and Leibowitz, B. (2014) 'A pedagogy of critical hope in South African higher education', in Bozalek, B., Leibowitz, R., Carolissen, B., and Boler, M. (Eds) *Discerning Critical Hope in Educational Practices*. Oxford and New York: Routledge.

Brockbank, A., and McGill, I. (2007) *Facilitating Reflective Learning in Higher Education*. Maidenhead: McGraw-Hill Education.

Burke, P.J. (2012). *The Right to Higher Education: Beyond Widening Participation*. London: Routledge.

Burke, P.J. (2015) 'Re/imagining higher education pedagogies: Gender, emotion and difference', *Teaching in Higher Education*, 20, 388–401.

Burke, P.J., Coffey, J., Gill, R., and Kanai, A. (Eds) (2022) *Gender in an Era of Post-Truth Populism: Pedagogies, Challenges and Strategies*. London: Bloomsbury Academic.

Cadwalladr, C. (2017a) 'Mark Zuckerberg says change the world, yet he sets the rules', *The Guardian*. www.theguardian.com/commentisfree/2017/feb/19/mark-zuckerberg-says-change-world-he-sets-rules

Cadwalladr, C. (2017b) 'The great British Brexit robbery: How our democracy was hijacked', *The Guardian*. www.theguardian.com/technology/2017/may/07/the-great-british-brexit-robbery-hijacked-democracy

Chawla, D., and Rodriguez, A. (2007) 'New imaginations of difference: On teaching, writing, and culturing', *Teaching in Higher Education*, 12(5), 697–708.

Denzin, N.K., and Lincoln, Y.S. (2017) 'Introduction: The discipline and practice of qualitative research', in Denzin, N.K., and Lincoln, Y.S. (Eds) *The Sage Handbook of Qualitative Research* (5th ed.). Thousand Oaks, CA: Sage, 1–26.

Fraser, N. (2003) 'Social justice in the age of identity politics: Redistribution, recognition and participation', in Fraser, N., and Honneth, A. (Eds) *Redistribution or Recognition? A Political-Philosophical Exchange*. London and New York: Verso.

Freire, P. (1972) *Pedagogy of the Oppressed*. Harmondsworth: Penguin Books.

Freire, P. (2009) *Pedagogy of Hope*. London, UK: Bloomsbury.

Haraway, D. (2016) *Staying with the Trouble: Making Kin in the Chthulucene*. Durham, NC: Duke University Press.

Harding, S. (1986) *The Science Question in Feminism*. Ithaca and London: Cornell.

Lather, P. (1991) *Getting Smart: Feminist Research and Pedagogy with/in the Postmodern*. New York and London: Routledge.

Lather, P. (2004) 'Critical enquiry in qualitative research: Feminist and post-structural perspectives, science after truth', in de Marrais, K., and Lapan, S. (Eds) *Foundations for Research: Methods of Inquiry in Education and the Social Services*. Mahwah, NJ: Lawrence Erlbaum Associates, 203–216.

Lave, J. (1991) 'Perspectives on socially shared cognition', in *Situating Learning in Communities of Practice*. Pittsburgh: American Psychological Association, 62–83.

Lave, J., and Wenger, E. (1991) *Situated Learning: Legitimate Peripheral Participation*. Cambridge: University of Cambridge Press.

Lumb, M., and Roberts, S. (2017) 'The inedito viavel (untested feasibility) of practitioner imaginations: Reflections on the challenges and possibilities of dialogic praxis for equity and widening participation', *International Studies in Widening Participation*, 4(1), 18–33.

Mbembe, A. (2023) *Transforming Knowledge for UNITWIN/UNESCO Chairs Programme 3–4 November 2022*. Paris, France: UNESCO Headquarters, UNESCO.

McNay, L. (2008) *Against Recognition*. Cambridge: Polity.

Narismulu, P. (2016) 'A heuristic for analyzing and teaching literature dealing with the challenges of social justice', in Burke, P.J., and Shay, S. (Eds) *Making Sense of Teaching in Difficult Times*. London and New York: Routledge.

Osborne, H. (2018) 'Tory donors among investors in Cambridge Analytica parent firm', *The Guardian*. www.theguardian.com/politics/2018/mar/21/tory-donors-among-investors-in-cambridge-analytica-parent-firm-scl-group

Rich, A. (1979) *On Lies, Secrets and Silence*. New York: W.W. Norton.

Sayer, A. (2011) *Why Things Matter to People: Social Science, Values and Ethical Life*. New York: Cambridge University Press.

Skeggs, B. (2004) *Class, Self, Culture*. London and New York: Routledge.

Weedon, C. (1999) *Feminism, Theory and the Politics of Difference*. Hoboken, NJ: Wiley-Blackwell.

Wenger-Trayner, E., and Wenger-Trayner, B. (2015) *An Introduction to Communities of Practice: A Brief Overview of the Concept and Its Uses*. www.wenger-trayner.com/introduction-to-communities-of-practice

PART THREE

Social justice transformation through equity praxis

Throughout this book, we have argued against monodimensional, deficit imaginaries, which contribute to a vicious cycle of equity interventions unwittingly perpetuating insidious inequalities. We have interrogated the certainties invested in hegemonic, and sometimes counter-hegemonic, positions that lead us to believe there is no alternative. The vicious cycle is perpetuated through the politics of e-motion; the ways we are moved in space and time to take certain directions, and not others, through the feelings surrounding multidimensional injustice that are ignored or concealed from view. We fall into a state of overwhelm or despair, or we accept the status quo and collude in the hegemonic order. We refuse to recognise the power of higher education to be a force for equity and social justice and instead accept a narrow, limiting, and monodimensional view that equity is a problem of fixing 'the disadvantaged' to conform to the cultural values of the hegemonic order, entrenched in neoliberalism and its intersection with neocolonial and neopatriarchal orientations.

Against these conditions of the hegemonic order, Part Three strongly reasserts our position; our collective imagination is powerful in generating alternative frameworks. We articulate the possibilities for creating transformative equity praxis through weaving together the tapestry of social justice theories, concepts and methodologies. We offer the idea of an 'equity spectrum'; ways of thinking/doing 'equity work' that overlap, meld, contradict, and connect across reflective/active dialogic processes. *What we think matters*, and we consider this spectrum as a way to think with and against various positionalities of different response-abilities.

In Part Three, we bring attention to the different, contested, and often overlapping perspectives that come to play in the complex timescapes of higher education, as an institution that has the capacity to both reproduce

DOI: 10.4324/9781003257165-11

and transform unequal relations. We reiterate the imperative of continuously thinking-with the challenges and dynamics we are negotiating, and this might mean navigating different positionalities across the spectrum at any one time, or at different times in which we are working-with others across and with relational difference. We show how ethical methodological frameworks can engage participants across difference and power in the research/practice nexus, opening up access to theoretical, methodological, and conceptual tools to illuminate and examine social, cultural and political inequalities, as well as then translate these insights for transformative equity praxis. We argue that praxis-based approaches can generate critical time, space, and resources for collaborative, reciprocal, reflexive, and ethical ways of reframing equity and widening participation around broadly valued social purposes.

Part Three identifies and demonstrates that transformative equity praxis is possible using case studies from work co-developed in the Australian context at the CEEHE. We present two case studies to illustrate how we, in the CEEHE, put these ideas to work through ongoing reflection/action as part of our sustained, collective, social justice praxis. The first case study details a praxis-based project, situated within the UNESCO Chair in Equity, Social Justice and Higher Education at the CEEHE; a project attending to the overlooked question of how experiences of GBV over the life course impact higher education equity. The knowledge of victim-survivors, when brought together with the expertise of community partners and the insights of feminist research, is contributing to the broader aim for higher education to become a force for gender justice and against GBV. The second case study details a praxis-based project of counter-hegemonic evaluation at the CEEHE, whereby methods of evaluation practice are animated with and through a sustained focus on methodology, responding to the ethical dilemma of valuing across difference, adopting sPaces of *care-full* evaluation. These case studies reach beyond superficial, one-dimensional, and decontextualised solutions, instead digging into the challenge of higher education equity work in often overwhelming times.

8

BEYOND DEFICIT IMAGINARIES, TOWARDS PRAXIS

Introduction

Throughout this book, we have argued against monodimensional deficit imaginaries that contribute to a vicious cycle of equity interventions, unwittingly perpetuating insidious inequalities. We have woven together the theoretical and conceptual threads from across a wide body of critical, feminist, decolonial, post/structural and sociological material to offer instead a multidimensional, social justice tapestry, a new framing for transformative equity. In this chapter, we offer two case studies to illustrate how we at the CEEHE put this multidimensional framework into ongoing reflection/action as part of our sustained, collective, social justice praxis.

In the first part of this chapter, we continue to unpack the multidimensional framework, looking more closely at the different threads woven through it. The threads have different tones, textures, and shapes, but when woven together, these differences provide nuance, richness, and depth for sustaining engagement with the complexity of questions of equity and social justice. Our aim is always to reach beyond utilitarian, superficial, one-dimensional and decontextualised solutions and to instead dig deep into the challenge of staying with the trouble of equity. In response to this challenge, we offer the idea of an 'equity spectrum'; ways of thinking/doing 'equity work' that overlap, meld, contradict, and connect across reflective/active dialogic processes. *What we think matters*, and we consider this spectrum to think with and against various positionalities of different response-abilities. Haraway draws on the ethnographic 'thinking practices' of Marilyn Strathern to argue "it matters what ideas we use to think other ideas" with (Haraway, 2016: 11). In bringing to life what we see as a spectrum of equity thinking practices, we echo this point, emphasising

DOI: 10.4324/9781003257165-12

that ideas not only matter for policy and practice but also have real-world social-cultural-political-material affects/effects on bodies of knowledge and people who have been systematically subjugated by and through higher education practices in all of their worldly – and institutional – contexts. That is, the practices within higher education – including but not only those deemed as 'equity practice' – have wider implications because higher education is always an institution in relation to the broader human and more-than-human world(s). Thus, in offering the idea of the spectrum, we are inviting readers to engage a more expansive conception of equity – one that matters in, through and beyond higher education. Relationality is more than the relationships we form; indeed, as Haraway (2016) suggests, "We become-with each other or not at all" (2016: 4). This includes understanding that wherever we might place ourselves on a spectrum "we know both too much and too little, and so we succumb to despair or to hope, and neither is a sensible attitude. Neither despair nor hope is tuned to the senses, to mindful matter, to material semiotics, to mortal earthlings in thick copresence" (Haraway, 2016: 4). It is this 'thick copresence' that we strive towards in this book, inviting readers into this copresence with us and within their communities of praxis for equity and social justice.

We recognise that staying with the trouble can often become reconstituted as being a 'troublemaker'. It feels troublesome, in the context of neoliberal imperatives to suggest the need to problematise, consider complexity and to bring theory into a marketised, corporatised context that is looking to 'fix' the problem of equity. Becoming visible as the 'feminist killjoy' (Ahmed, 2010) is an ongoing risk of taking up multidimensional, social justice praxis, thus perpetuating misrepresentation even in situations that appear to be representative. The neoliberal expropriation of feminist notions of 'voice' loses all meaning in, for example, a committee context in which different voices in the room are unequally positioned by the explicit hierarchical positions of the chair, the minute-taker, the executive, senior and mid-level leaders, and other staff and student representatives. Less easy to see though are the related and more insidious power dynamics by which the intersecting forces of neoliberalism, neocolonialism and neopatriarchies, as well as institutionalised ableisms, misogynies, racisms, classisms, transphobias, and heterosexisms produce capillary power just about impossible to name, speak, or act upon. Thus, we recognise the invitation to stay with the trouble is challenging, for us all. We hope then that offering the idea of an equity spectrum enables enriched access to the multidimensional nature of equity and social justice, most especially for readers engaged in thinking-with and making-with these ideas in ways that matter within communities of praxis.

A spectrum of equity

We have introduced a range of different contexts, positions, and perspectives in relation to the contested timescapes of equity in higher education. We have attempted to make our own position explicit throughout this book – that is, we are endeavouring to create sPace for reflection/action for counter-hegemonic, social justice praxis to reframe equity in, through, and beyond higher education. However, we have also emphasised the importance of uncertainty, unknowing, response-ability, thinking-with and making-with; processes that refuse to settle on a final, fixed, or rigid position, solution or intervention. Rather our (critical, anticolonial) hope is to be responsive to context, including the dynamic nature of power in our messy, more-than-human relations. In considering equity as a spectrum, and in relation to multidimensionality, we aim to outline the different, contested, and often overlapping perspectives that come to play in the complex timescapes of higher education, an institution that both reproduces and transforms unequal relations. We recognise that in reflection and in action, we need to continuously think-with the challenges and dynamics we are negotiating, and this might mean navigating different positionalities across the spectrum at any one time, or at different times in which we are working-with others across and with relational differences. In this way, difference is imperative to moving-with others.

We understand the equity spectrum through a lens of movement; movement in the political sense of a collective commitment to social change (as in 'feminist movement' or 'Access Movement' – see Chapter 1). More broadly, this is about the human capacity to be moved in dialogue with others (Ahmed, 2017: 5), an idea central to the forming communities of praxis for social justice transformation possibilities. This is about our sense of connection to a social problem that matters to and beyond ourselves – to recognise that our human capacity is about extending the world beyond the self and thus breaking free of the bounded individualism that neoliberal imperatives demand. We see little chance for transformative equity in a context that understands freedom as only the aspiration of the individual to succeed in a framework of neoliberal-bounded individualism. This can only reproduce the widening of inequalities in which only some are winners, and others lose. In this iteration, disadvantage is reconstructed as the responsibility of the disadvantaged person, losing sight of the need to move together with our differences as a resource for thinking and doing equity. Thus, movement is about the connected sense of self to others; extending notions of success to understand that personal flourishing is inter-dependent on the capacity of the person to contribute to more-than-human flourishing for which participation in higher education might facilitate. This requires the sPace to create "connections between those who recognise something . . . even if they have different words for what that" is (Ahmed, 2017: 3). This brings attention to affective dimensions, and to recognising how e-motion matters because it moves us to work with others for collective movement. The e-motion-al thus contributes to change. We have argued in Chapter 7 that this can lead to re-assembling – working with others to create new positionalities and orientations, and seeing together differently. Our spectrum therefore is offered as a dynamic tapestry of positionings that move across, between, against, and with each other, but also offer insight into the taken-for-granted discourses that inevitably shape how equity is constructed, developed, and made, and who participates in such processes.

Equity is not just a site of political contestation; it is also a political site of feeling, largely hidden by the hegemonic imperative for objectivity, measurement and datafication. Lived experiences of inequities are inextricably connected to sensibilities of fear, (not) belonging, dis/connection, in/security, un/safety, and shame. The deficit imaginary framing, with its gaze on bodies marked by equity categorisations, renders invisible the structures, relations, and positions of power, authority, and privilege. However, feminist post/structuralism understands power as fluid and dynamic, troubling binary and static conceptions, whilst recognising that structural inequalities matter in producing homogenising, monodimensional, binarising logics. Attending to the emotional layers of equity brings out the struggles, contradictions, and discomforts commonly unacknowledged yet so key in knowledge-making, policy-formation, and the generation of practice. The fear of loss of socioeconomic resource, cultural status, and/or authority is rarely made explicit in considerations of equity but is an undercurrent of the politics of decision-making in relation to distribution, recognition, and representation. The sense of shame associated with the gaze of equity creates absences and silences around what equity should or should not encompass; we bring attention to this later in this chapter through the case of GBV. The sense of joy that can be felt in doing equity hides the unequal power dynamics in which the recipient of equity interventions is often misrepresented. The sense of despair attached to the feeling that equity work is overwhelming can sometimes lead to stagnation and/or an unwillingness to engage the complexities equity raises, not least because those complexities are entangled with emotion.

The politics of emotion then moves through bodies as feelings to sustain or transform unequal relations of power. Emotion moves decisions in particular directions, often without a trace, but with powerful effects on the communities directly impacted by those decisions. This is the affective power of the emotional; often psychologised as personal issues to be overcome, ignoring that the affective dimension of power is always tied to the social. Shame is a poignant example that perpetuates misrecognition through locating shame in the bodies of individuals marked by deficit, leaving residues felt at the level of personhood as not belonging, not being good enough, not having value. Yet shame is a social emotion that reinforces structures of inequality and relations of subordination. The case of GBV helps illuminate how these politics of emotion put shame in social motion to denigrate the bodies of people subjected to gender injustice (Burke et al, 2023).

Feminist post/structural theory illuminates that we are all always complicit in complex power relations, situated by the structural, material, discursive, and emotional inequalities at play. This is regardless of how committed we might be to equity agendas and where we might situate ourselves on the equity spectrum. We are all necessarily socially situated – we cannot move outside of relations of power – but these are dynamic and multidimensional relations. This knowledge of our inevitable complicity and situatedness in unequal power dynamics and the intersecting political forces shaping social institutions (including neoliberalism, neocolonialism, neoconservatism, neopatriarchy, and more) provokes emotion; feelings of guilt, shame, despair, anger, resentment and fear. These emotions, felt at the level of the personal but manifesting in social inequalities, matter in what we think and what we do and the directions we take – or do not take. The politics of the e-motion-al – how we move in relation to the social, discursive, and material formations of which we are part – is why we argue so strongly for exercising collective uncertainties and critical reflexivity. The form of reflexivity we argue for resists the seduction of neoliberal revalorisations of self-centricity. It is a reflexivity embedded in praxis and an ethics of care for and with others.

The equity spectrum spans deficit imaginaries to counter-hegemonic certainties – positions that demand sustained reflexivity within communities of praxis. Inevitably, we all move across the full range of the spectrum, and thus the transformative equity praxis reframing we offer is intended to engage critically with these two ends of the equity spectrum, whilst actively countering hegemonic equity. We position ourselves and the book in relation to transformative equity praxis, as a countering of hegemonic approaches that are regularly produced through neoliberal framings of equity. However, we strive to avoid becoming certain in our own dis/position towards transformative equity praxis, by engaging an ongoing questioning and re-searching approach to what we think we know. This can be a painful process, and it requires a kind of patience with ourselves in connection to others, and is always best done in conversation-with.

Next, we set out some of the threads aligned to two positionings within this spectrum: *hegemonic equity* and *transformative equity praxis*. We offer this not as a static typology but as material to think-with and make-with in the sPace of our communities of praxis. That is, we suggest a re-search reorientation to equity in which we are engaged together in "sustaining creativity of people who care and act" (Haraway, 2016: 5) to animate the reflection/action dialogic processes of transformative equity praxis.

Hegemonic equity tends to accept social categorisation (e.g. Low SES), facilitating their (mis)representational effects through unquestioning use. Hierarchy is welcome and necessary. A deficit imaginary runs rampant via historically formed relations of power/knowledge uncritically adopted as normal and natural. This readily locates 'the problem' equity work is responding to in the bodies and behaviours of the historically excluded, adjudicating value using prefigured notions of what 'success' is. Hegemonic equity relies on the bounded human individualism of dominant neoliberal imaginaries, with students and staff imagined as discrete units of human capital to be supported/exploited, ultimately in the service of financial capital. A form of accountability linked to audit cultures and new managerialism reigns under hegemonic equity, with transactional interaction and underrepresented groups the ones forced to give accounts of themselves under a critical and colluding gaze. Being "productive" is about mobilities that support neoliberal markets and nation-states in contemporary economic warfare. Superficial celebrations of diversity help to hold in place structural inequalities related to race, class, gender, preferring instead new 'common sense' neoliberalised notions such as a diverse staff being more financially effective/productive. With hegemonic equity, marginalised/colonised knowledge, ways of knowing, and knowers are 'included' in an assimilatory system of neocolonialism. Language is only a tool of communication, propagandising 'opportunities' for belonging to dominant orders. Spatio-temporalities are produced by those in positions of authority with short time/frames, transactional interpersonal relationships, and legalistic 'partnerships' the norm. Hegemonic equity tends towards an ethics of moral panic *for* Others. In this formation of equity, difference is not only difficult but also dangerous, and the patronising glare of pastoral power is the ready response to Others.

Transformative equity praxis acknowledges social categorisation but resists the judgements commonly attached to these, recognising the attending dangers of homogenisation and misrecognition. Instead, this is a praxis of working with care through the dilemma of how categorisation plays a role in the redistribution of resources. *Transformative equity praxis* tends towards 'flattening' hierarchies, making new relations of power/knowledge possible. A critical imaginary interrogates historically formed relations of power/knowledge, seeing them as arbitrary, problematic, yet durable social constructions. 'The problem' that equity work is responding to in this orientation is the structures and practices and value-systems of those re/authorised to ex/collude in and through higher education. Transformative equity praxis moves beyond the bounded human individualism of the neoliberal imaginary to a relational view of knowledge and social reality. Response-ability is the focus: the desire and capability to respond, in reciprocating relations, with Others. Those in positions of higher education hierarchies are the ones held to account by interrogating complicity in sustaining oppressive power relations of domination, whether that be explicit, insidious, or unintended. Nation-state economic productivity is not seen as the guiding purpose of higher education. A bigger vision of higher education's role in building just and sustainable societies is generated. Difference is understood as a necessary and valuable difficulty. Transformative equity praxis takes epistemic justice seriously, implementing long-term anti-colonial efforts, led by those who have suffered the effects of colonisation. In this context, language is an endless opportunity to problematise power relations and build new language as new hope for new realities.

Equity space-time (sPace) is co-produced through response-able pedagogical relations with conduct characterised by feminist care ethics. With transformative equity praxis, parity of participation in its fullest sense becomes a possibility.

To reiterate, we do not present the two positions (*hegemonic equity* and *transformative equity praxis*) as a binary classification. These are articulated and shared as orientations within a spectrum of positions in relation to the notion of equity in higher education. Clearly, however, we advocate for striving towards the latter; imperfectly, yes; in the bind of complicitous and capillary relation, absolutely. But we believe these orientations are important and have worked with colleagues to demonstrate their empirical possibility. In the following sections, we now share two separate yet linked case studies from the CEEHE at the University of Newcastle in NSW, Australia, where we have been working together for nearly a decade, working with colleagues to create what we see as the conditions for transformative equity praxis.

Case 1 – mobilising higher education for gender justice and to challenge Gender-Based Violence

GBV is an insidious social problem of epidemic proportions across the world, rooted in multidimensional gender injustice (Fraser, 2013). Globally, one in three women experience GBV in their lifetime, with detrimental effects on health, education, and overall well-being, extending beyond individuals to encompass families, communities and societies at large (WHO, 2021). The impact of GBV on higher education access and participation, and the crucial role that higher education could play in challenging GBV as part of its commitment to gender equality, is widely ignored.

In this section, we set out the transformative potential of higher education to progress equity and gender justice and to contribute to the work of eliminating GBV through the knowledge and insights of student victim-survivors of GBV. We set out the case study of a praxis-based project, situated within the UNESCO Chair in Equity, Social Justice and Higher Education at the CEEHE. This is sustained, iterative collaborative work with students and community partners and within our project team. Members of the project team are Penny Jane Burke, Julia Coffey, Jean Parker, Stephanie Hardacre, Felicity Cocuzzoli, Julia Shaw, and Adriana Haro (for further information, see www.newcastle.edu.au/research/centre/ceehe/research-project-gender-based-violence-and-higher-education).

The project attends to the overlooked question of how experiences of GBV over the life course impact higher education equity. The project team's long-term aspiration is to enable the transformative potential of higher education to uncover and help dismantle the multidimensional gender injustice that reproduces and sustains the global pandemic of GBV. We draw on this project to demonstrate how fostering research/theory/practice praxis can significantly deepen the collaboration necessary to generate equity and gender justice in, through and beyond higher education. The project team is developing a gender justice hub of transformative equity praxis, guided by PPoEMs (see Chapter 7), strategically designed to facilitate collaboration among higher education researcher-practitioners, student victim-survivors and community organisations. This collaborative agenda aligns with the 2030 United Nations Agenda for Sustainable Development, particularly the ambitious goal to eradicate all forms of GBV (WHO, 2021). The project points to the potential of higher education to acknowledge and actively combat the systemic challenges posed by GBV, thus advancing the global pursuit of equitable, peaceful societies rooted in the multidimensions of social, cultural, political, and planetary justice.

The project foregrounds the experiences of student victim-survivors to break the silencing of the voices of those with lived experiences of GBV, voices crucial to developing knowledge and strategies for gender equity. This silencing is another layer of institutionalised misrecognition that is then internalised in a sense of subordinated value but diagnosed as an individual problem through the discourse of 'imposter syndrome'. This insidious injustice, violence, and trauma that are turned back onto the bodies of victim-survivors are intolerable and must be struggled against. The misrepresentation of the GBV experience is entwined with problematic linear conceptions of time embedded in higher education systems and structures (Bennett and Burke, 2018; Burke and Manathunga, 2020) and individualised constructions of trauma. The hegemonic construction of a 'traumatological timeline'– a "temporal imaginary that assigns a linear trajectory to the experience of trauma" (Wieskamp and Smith, 2020: 74) – imposes institutionalised expectation on individual GBV victim-survivors to 'overcome' what is a social relation of gender injustice (Burke et al, 2023: 4). This constructs GBV associated trauma as "something one can (and should) avoid, leave behind, or cure" (King, 2012: 38). In this sense, the notion of linear temporality assigns a progressive aspect to trauma recovery – a straight, step-by-step journey towards a positive outcome (that is, recovery) (Burke et al, 2023: 4).

> This is the "privatisation of trauma" (Thompson, 2020, p, 106), which individualises, desocialises and depoliticises traumatic experiences of GBV that are then pathologised through medicalised forms of diagnosis that are "linear, mechanistic and mono-causal".
> *(Marecek, 1999, p. 165 cited in Thompson, 2020, p. 106)*
> *(Burke et al, 2023: 4)*

The project team has conducted research with 430 students in the Australian Hunter and New England region (Burke et al, 2023; Coffey et al, 2023), with a long-term research agenda to extend the project to Ghana, where a collaborative foundation has been formed over a decade (e.g. Burke, Gyamera and the Ghanaian Feminist Collective, 2023; Gyamera and Burke, 2018; Gyamera, 2013). This is the first research of its kind that explores the continuum of GBV and its impact on higher education access and participation. Drawing from Kelly's germinal work (1988), gender injustice takes an array of expressions, events, and behaviours on a continuum of violence, from sexual banter to rape and intimate partner violence, in which the "everyday expressions and behaviours scaffold a culture of gender inequalities that sustains and enables the rarer acts" (Anitha and Lewis, 2018: 1). The project reveals that GBV is an expression of gender injustice (Fraser, 2013); maldistribution, profoundly exacerbated by GBV, and the devaluing and subordination of bodies of knowledge and people associated with femininities.

The project[1] involves conventional data collection and analysis methods but is also designed to generate non-hierarchical communities of praxis (see Chapters Two and Seven), through the CEEHE's arts-based programmes,[2] student advocacy platforms, and community partnership. The research involved a comprehensive, mixed-methods survey, for which an email was circulated to all students at a large regional university in Australia inviting them to anonymously complete a survey designed to obtain demographics, information, and qualitative responses relating to the temporality, spatiality, and incidence of the forms of GBV they had experienced throughout their lifetime. Four hundred and thirty students[3] participated in the survey, which found that most student-participants had first experienced GBV at age 13 and that most experienced GBV in their own or someone else's private residence. Students recognised the value of higher education study for their personal and family's wellbeing but they also aspired to use their degrees to help other victim-survivors and to make a difference to their communities and to others. In-depth interviews were conducted with 48 student victim-survivors to explore: experiences of accessing university study; expectations, experiences, and perspectives of higher education, its value and purpose; sense of safety, connection, and belonging at university; and student perspectives on how higher education might better address GBV (Burke et al, 2023; Coffey et al, 2023).

The qualitative data from the surveys and interviews were analysed thematically, with the project team bringing feminist qualitative, quantitative and equity practitioner perspectives to the analysis. The analysis was iterative, collective, and supported by discussions with students participating in the arts-based programme, 'Claim Our Place' and community partners, from the domestic, family, and sexual violence (DFSV) sector, engaging with a series of project workshops. The student-participants often expressed the high value they placed on having a voice through the project, as one student-participant explains:

> When I saw that this study was happening, I was like, yes, interview me . . . change needs to happen. I just really want to be a part of making that happen . . . so I just really wanted to help.
>
> *(student quote from Burke et al, 2023: 9)*

The students perceived higher education as a life-changing opportunity, as well as a chance to help others, but this was countered by profound sensibilities of alienation, shame, not belonging, unworthiness and isolation. This is a form of "insidious trauma"; the "traumatogenic effects of oppression that are not necessarily overtly violent or threatening to bodily well-being at the given moment but that do violence to the soul and spirit" (Brown, 1995 cited in Bertram and Crowley, 2012: 64). Insidious trauma is exacerbated by a politics of shame that is moved into individual bodies through institutionalised misrecognition: the combined impact of victim stigmatisation with deficit imaginaries, powerfully illustrated in the words of different student-participants (all following student quotes are drawn from the project survey and interview data):

> *Why am I studying this degree? Like why? How could I be of any use to anyone?*
>
> *The after-effects of abuse lowered my self-confidence and esteem so that I felt I did not deserve a better life.*
>
> *My ex said I was too stupid and too dumb to go to uni. I believed him for a long time.*
>
> *You can't get over this feeling of you're not worthy, you don't even deserve to be here.*

The violence and insidious trauma that students faced combined with profound forms of resource deprivation had detrimental effects on their studies:

> *Violence right before exams made me unable to participate in them due to distress. I failed courses I would never have otherwise. I have countless withdrawals due to being unable to cope.*
>
> *My partner made it impossible for me to study by behaving in a violent and controlling way. This prevented me from being able to meet assessment deadlines. I felt extremely afraid and isolated and was not able to access student support. I was deeply afraid that my partner would find the letters or emails and become violent. This resulted in a huge [student] debt.*
>
> *After I experienced [domestic violence] I was homeless, living in my car and I did my first ever final exams at university the day after sleeping in my car.*

Students suffered profound financial deprivation as well as restrictions on their freedom. Rigid policies such as compulsory attendance as well as the burden of large student debt exacerbated by severe disruption to their studies were a major theme emerging from the survey data. Students made important recommendations to the university on this basis as illustrated in the following extracts from the anonymised qualitative survey responses:

> *I fell through the cracks. This is how distance education is a massive disadvantage to people in difficult situations. I feel that better progression rules and wellness checks would have potentially benefited me.*
>
> *Access to consistent and quality psychological services would help.*
>
> *We carry such a heavy burden already, the ever-growing financial burden [of student debt] is scary.*
>
> *Please excuse our attendance rates for compulsory tutorials. We are so often going through wars at home that no-one knows about, attendance in the middle of one of those wars could mean additional violence for us, as well as a waste of time in class while we can't concentrate anyway.*

The students' provided key insights about how higher education can recover a social justice orientation to equity. One student explains this eloquently:

> *Education itself provides the freedom, focus and escape to a better future for women and children. It's not rocket science. Free education. Opportunity to thrive leads to contributing citizens. The hidden women numbers are huge.*

The range of recommendations students offered across the survey and interview data included:

- raising awareness, building capacity and new forms of expertise;
- higher education institutions taking an explicit stance against all forms of injustice, including GBV;
- policymakers, community services, and institutions ensuring the costs of study are covered, safe accommodation is available, and free healthcare, wellbeing, and legal services are provided;
- higher education institutions enabling greater flexibility, including students being able to study from home to accommodate caring commitments and to avoid punishing students suffering from restrictions on their mobility;
- reforming policies that are unfairly punitive for students and that create the conditions for excessive debt, withdrawal and poor educational profiles.

The project team has formed communities of praxis with student victim-survivors and DFSV community organisations to build a new gender justice hub involving a suite of co-developed initiatives in response to the students' recommendations. The Hub aims to develop and sustain inter-agency collaboration; promote awareness and build knowledge about gender injustice and its manifestation in GBV; and produce education, training, and continuing professional learning to generate expertise and capacity within higher education and across academic, professional, and policy fields.

A key insight emerging from the student-participants was the need for navigational support. However navigational support is too often embedded in neoliberal framings that perpetuate deficit and stigmatising imaginaries (Burke et al, 2021). In the CEEHE, and through our suite of equity programmes, we have developed a relational approach to navigation, grounded in critical, feminist, and decolonial praxis. The 'Relational Navigator' framework (Burke et al, 2021) draws from Freirean forms of pedagogical praxis (Freire, 1972), in which unequal power relations are redressed, reciprocal, iterative processes of critical reflection/action are sustained, and an ethics of care is a key part of equity practice. 'Caring for' and 'caring about' the student is foregrounded and underpinned by social justice principles. The Relational Navigator walks alongside students in the context of their lives, as a partner navigating unwieldy and fragmented domains of social, community, and student services. The student is the primary navigator in this power dynamic but has the support and care of the Relational Navigator team to ensure that the resources and supports available (e.g. educational, financial, legal, healthcare, and housing) are accessible and appropriate. There is ongoing and active co-advocacy to raise awareness of the gaps in services and the implications of these absences for the wellbeing and flourishing of people and communities most affected by multidimensional inequalities. This is further strengthened by a foundation of community partnership, working together to trouble problematic assumptions around who is seen as having the right to higher education and who is not (Burke, 2012).

The overarching aim of the Relational Navigator framework in the context of the gender justice hub is to ensure that (1) victim-survivors have access to the quality resources, opportunities, expertise and support required to enable them to thrive in, through and beyond higher education; (2) social justice forms of parity of participation are enabled through multidimensional transformative equity praxis; (3) insidious trauma is alleviated at the systemic and structural levels, including by removing 'cold' disclosure to myriad organisations, people and services; and (4) the knowledge, insight, and capacity of student victim-survivors is recognised and represented to contribute to transformation for equity and gender justice. The location of the Relational Navigator in the wider project, including ongoing research situated in the project's communities of praxis, enables a sustained questioning, re-search stance, with practice informing the research processes and research informing the programmatic co-development.

Case 2 – striving for counter-hegemonic evaluation ('Reclaiming My Place' evaluative research)

Earlier in this book (Chapter 6) we looked in detail at policy and programme evaluation, taking account of how ubiquitous a phenomenon it has become, with a reminder that its current formations are only relatively recent, and related to the rise of NPM and new managerial accountabilities. Our analysis drew on work showing that policy and programme evaluation approaches have themselves been increasingly 'neoliberalised' whilst, simultaneously, these processes help to embed neoliberal imaginaries into the constant reformation of higher education. In this context, we argued that a focus of social justice praxis must be how ethically problematic the evaluation of equity-oriented policy and programme has become. If the values and interests driving much policy or programme evaluation do not readily correspond to the values and interests of underrepresented communities and individuals, these are conditions suited to the ongoing subjugation of ways of knowing, being, and doing that are different to the prevailing cultural hegemony.

Evaluation is an imperative increasingly, albeit often chaotically, attached to most equity policies and programmes. Much evaluation in the field of equity and widening participation is tied to methodological frameworks underpinned by and reproductive of deficit imaginaries. This does not however need to be the case. Histories of thought in the social sciences drawing on notions such as participation, empowerment, and justice have themselves been drawn upon to create different approaches to evaluation. Guba and Lincoln's important work *Fourth Generation Evaluation* foregrounds, for example, how evaluation has a "fundamentally social, political, and value-oriented character" (Guba and Lincoln, 1989: 7). Perspectives such as these are important for social justice praxis, and they have helped produce an array of approaches including but not limited to *empowerment* evaluation (Fetterman, 1994); *culturally competent/sensitive* evaluation (e.g. Lafrance, 2004; SenGupta et al, 2004; NSWT DET, 2023); forms of *responsive* evaluation (e.g. Abma, 2005); *feminist* evaluation (e.g. Mertens, 2005; Podems, 2010), *sustainability-ready* evaluation (Rowe, 2021), even *anti-capitalist* evaluation (Mathison, 2016).

With colleagues at the CEEHE, we have sought to articulate and produce contexts capable of recognising how evaluation is an explicit process of valuing (Burke and Lumb, 2018), and, given our advocacy for social justice praxis, we have sought to bring counter-hegemonic commitments into policy and programme evaluation (Gordon et al, 2022). The contexts we continue to seek are restive spatio-temporalities (sPaces) that can destabilise and resist some of the worst effects of the processes rearticulated earlier, that is, how evaluation often reproduces dominant value frameworks and power relations whilst facilitating the ongoing 'neoliberalisation' of higher education contexts and practices. In this section, we offer a brief description of an effort with colleagues to bring the critical, feminist, anti-colonial, post/structural, and sociological commitments of PPoEMs into an embedded and ongoing process of pro-gramme evaluation. The description of this effort with colleagues can only, in the space afforded to us here, begin to introduce a complicated context we continue to work through and will continue to publish from. For those wanting a more detailed and systematic account of the methods and prac-tices, we invite you to engage with the already published work (Gordon and Lumb, 2021; Cocuzzoli et al, 2023; Lumb and Gordon, 2023). This is not perhaps a typical 'case study' in that we want to focus more so on how meth-odology mattered in this context: how the commitments of PPoEMs pushed and pulled on the methods, animating them in ways we believe are important for questions of social justice; methods made restive with counter-hegemonic possibility through a sustained focus on methodology, anticipating different futures; practising in ways that acknowledge how every evaluation process is *situated* (Gordon and Lumb, 2021) and is thrust into ethical dilemmas of valuing across difference, and, in this case, navigated by producing sPaces of *care-full* evaluation (Lumb and Gordon, 2023).

We have already in this chapter recognised how GBV is an insidious social problem of epidemic proportions, rooted in multidimensional gender injustice (Fraser, 2013). In the case study above, we detailed a response to the impact of GBV on higher education access and participation, and the crucial role that higher education could play in challenging GBV as part of its commitment to gender equality. One aspect of this social justice praxis context is 'Reclaim-ing My Place' (RMP), a programme developed by CEEHE in partnership with community-based service providers. The arts-based programme engages with women who have lived experiences of GBV and stalled (formal) educa-tion histories. RMP seeks to create a context for participants to have positive learning experiences whilst developing opportunities for engagement in for-mal education and lifelong learning. RMP was developed by our CEEHE col-league Felicity Cocuzzoli, an artist/practitioner who has worked across child, family and community spaces in the Hunter, Newcastle and Port Stephens areas of NSW, Australia for more than 25 years. A proud descendent of the Wiradjuri Nation, Felicity is committed to engaging with communities in and through art.

RMP aims to generate relationships of learning and support between the participants, the practitioners (who also participate), the visual art, the facilita-tor, and the timescape created by the programme. The intent built into RMP is that it provides a supportive context for exploring the role education can play in participants' lives. Women are encouraged and supported to acquire confidence in their work with diverse mediums, colour, and design. All partici-pants' work is valued regardless of art-based experience. This support comes from the facilitator, practitioner participants and from the women themselves to each other. At the conclusion of RMP, a community-based exhibition of participating artists' work is held and is also curated online. Formal education pathways are a quiet backdrop to the programmatic practices and, with human services and education agency partners, opportunities for education to play a greater role in the context of the lives of women can emerge.

As we argued in Chapter 6 of this book, key moments of misframing in policy and programme evaluation are decisions relating to what sort of knowledge is to be created during an evaluation process. There is almost guaranteed misframing well beforehand too of course, when programmes are designed in response to policy and funding signals, which then commonly have evaluation bolted on to recoup the stats and story that will show whether the initiative 'worked' or not. Programme logics and theories of change are developed as 'best-practice' as part of this design. These logics and programme theories are not often enough interrogated to uncover who or what is being valued, and why. When an evaluative research effort was initiated in relation to RMP, rather than trying to understand if the programme logic driving the initiative 'worked', instead the aim was to explore the experiences and impact of RMP, both for the practitioners of the family services and for the women who have completed the programme. To be clear, it is our position that programme logics do have a place in equity programme design and evaluation. It is also our position that one of the most useful aspects of programme logic development is the opportunity to collectively interrogate the valuing at play in any programmatic initiative. Dr Rhyall Gordon is a colleague at the CEEHE whose work involves developing sPace to support the exchange between theory and practice in the context of equity projects both within the University of Newcastle and in the wider community. Rhyall has over 20 years of experience in community development and has carried out community-based research projects in the areas of homelessness, affordable housing, food security, refugee policy, and the youth sector. One of the key roles Rhyall plays is supporting a process of critical reflection and interrogation of the assumptions that guide programme logics/programme theories that have been developed by relatively more privileged equity practitioners with whom we either work or by whom we have been commissioned. It is here in the interrogation of assumptions through high-quality critical questioning that we can start to apprehend, resist, and reorient dominant notions, value-systems, and epistemic injustices. This we see as one aspect, one moment, of counter-hegemonic evaluation practice when animating methods with PPoEMs.

As Cocuzzoli et al (2023) have described in their summary of the RMP evaluation process, each method moment developed in the evaluation of RMP was designed to echo RMP stylings. Art was used to support conversation and to share ideas. For example, in the early stages of the work by using audio recordings of art-making sessions to produce tentative and preliminary rounds of analysis that were brought back to the practitioners and participants for further interrogation and development. These types of efforts were about rigorous knowledge creation; a conception of rigour that aims to ensure 'excellence' through forms of participation imbued with an ethic of care. Previously, with colleagues, we have shown how the terminological devices that drive evaluation, including notions of 'participation', need to be treated with great caution. A methodology that aims to refuse hierarchy needs to take up practices that name current hegemonic approaches whereby the privileging of some knowledges or ways of knowing eclipse Others. We see this as one way to think about PPoEMs, as making more democratic possibilities and redistributing access to political processes rather than facilitating the endless 'political death' of misframing for individuals and communities who are commonly the focus of these evaluation processes (Gordon et al, 2022). This is arguably linked with the problem of performativity in evaluation.

> Performativity [works to] produce the very phenomenon that it anticipates (Butler, 2011: 35) whereby the assumed expertise of the evaluators allows for an exclusive decision on key questions and consequently their privilege (and privileged knowledge) is continued and the 'disadvantage'/lack of expertise/lack of knowledge of others is reproduced.
>
> *(Gordon et al, 2022: 284)*

The RMP evaluation sought to resist this dynamic by explicitly valuing the development of ongoing reflexivity through feminist praxis that did not seek 'distance' and 'independence' from the process but instead recognised how "an evaluator has experiences, sensitivities, awareness, and perspectives that lead to a particular standpoint. In other words, feminist evaluators recognise that they bring who they are into the evaluation process" (Podems, 2010: 5). As Cocuzzoli et al (2023) identify, it was important to recognise how critical reflection was already embedded in RMP programmatic practice. Being a programme designed by drawing on the commitments of PPoEMS, with activities designed for reflection undertaken by both practitioners and participants, sPaces were available for different participation in evaluation, prefiguring dispositions towards reflection and making different spatio-temporalities possible. During RMP, whether it be focused on the art practices, on the experiences of learning new skills, on support offered to others, or on how life outside the workshop is being managed, all participants are supported to reflect on their role and capacity to explore who they are and want to be in the world. The programmatic contexts of RMP view this type of critical reflection as a key tool to creating and building imagined futures. With such a foundation, those involved with RMP (the women participants, the practitioner participants, and the facilitators) were in a strong position to participate in more formal evaluative research looking at the programme and sectoral context.

As Lumb and Gordon (2023) have articulated, the evaluation of RMP was designed to generate new knowledge but also to acknowledge practices that may (even unintentionally) limit the development of new knowledge. This involved trying to make more explicit the political dimensions of evaluation as part of methodology; naming the unavoidable contestations of any context, and the power dynamics making ourselves and relations possible. This was not to create 'level playing fields of knowledges', but to create sPace for the hitherto invisible knowledges of participants. This potential rests on relational practices that prioritise participation. We moved with Tronto's ethic of care to build participatory evaluation methods and guide practice towards avoiding patronising or hierarchical forms of care that can play out in evaluation (Abma et al, 2020). This is an ethic that seeks to avoid over-reification and reproduction of categorisations that are exclusive, exploitative, pathologising, or framed by deficit. It is an ethic that seeks to critically examine relations of power, influence, and difference in relation to evaluation design and methods. It is an ethic in which evaluators see themselves in reciprocal relation and response-able with the communities the programme is designed to serve. In the context of the RMP evaluation, it was *attentiveness, responsibility, competence*, and *responsiveness* (Tronto's ethical elements of care) that helped to guide the development of shared participatory evaluation space to support critical reflection, including a foundation for learning about evaluation technologies such as 'evidence', 'rigour', and 'accountability' (Lumb and Gordon, 2023). Exploring these aspects of evaluation, by privileging the perspectives of participants, produces pedagogical moments for all and the possibility of co-constructing knowledge in ways that are guided by those the programme is supposed to benefit. It is an approach which is more aligned with deconstructive efforts rather than the preconstructed certainties. As reported by Cocuzzoli et al (2023), the process produced the following insights in relation to RMP programmatic contexts:

1) RMP creates spaces where there is no agenda to try to "fix" something in the participants; 2) Exploring and learning through the art and other workshop practices enabled participants to let go of prior categorisations and self judgements to develop a new sense of themselves and their capability and potential; 3) The learning and reflection practice of RMP allows for positive learning/education experiences. The transformative potential of positive learning experiences was identified by the participants as one of the most important successes of RMP; 4) The workshops create space and time for self-care and group-care. As the program progresses the sense of support, care and connection steadily develops in the participants; 5) Practitioners were exposed to (and mostly embraced) new forms of social work practice that challenge traditional notions of hierarchy, boundaries, vulnerability, risk and strengths based approaches; 6) Art is a key aspect of RMP's success. It is both a means and end in itself. It facilitates many other processes of positive learning and reflection as well as providing an end point through an art piece that gets celebrated; 7) Life-long learning and access to diverse

forms of education is a crucial part of rebuilding the lives of women who have a history of gender-based violence.

(Cocuzzoli et al, 2023: np)

This is an evaluative research effort that has refracted existing programmatic commitments that seek to refuse hierarchical formations prefiguring contexts. And it has not always been comfortable. Sector worker/practitioners have been key in developing the insight above that their own professional subjectivities are challenged by a less pathologising context in which no one is there to be 'fixed' or seen as 'the problem'. Earlier in this case study we discussed how much equity evaluation in the field of equity and widening participation is tied to methodological frameworks underpinned by and reproductive of deficit imaginaries, holding the evaluative 'gaze' firmly on students and community members rather than on structures and practices of exclusion, marginalisation, and oppression. The important insights developed by the sector worker/practitioners, we argue, is only possible when the gaze of an evaluation shifts away from a deficit imaginary imbued with the bounded individualism of neoliberalism and allowing the performative effect of seeking/confirming a pre-ordained 'truth' to run rampant. Instead, the gaze can turn towards structures of oppression that include the complicity of the relatively more privileged or 'powerful' in each context. This is what PPoEMs seeks to facilitate; embedding counter-hegemonic sPace that is embedded in programmes to generate mutually valuable learning across differences. When an evaluation is pedagogical in this way, it opens possibilities for multidimensional revision and refinement of a programmatic context by all involved through understandings that emerge from care-full participation.

The creative contexts of the RMP evaluation, drawing on and reflecting the art-based contexts of the RMP programme, make possible e-motion-al dimensions of sPace. PPoEMs animates methods so that different movements are possible, producing contexts in which affect is recognised as an aspect of our embodied subjectivities, shifting in relation to the material and social context we inhabit. This is evaluation *as* social movement, seeking to resist hegemonic rule, striving for different feeling spaces and different temporalities than the objectifying, dehumanising glare of a new managerial accountability guided by transaction and financial audit imaginary.

This description of an ongoing effort with colleagues Flic and Rhyall can only begin to scratch the surface of a rich and complicated context, one we are still working through and from which we will continue to publish. We invite you to engage with the already published work (Gordon and Lumb, 2021; Cocuzzoli et al, 2023; Lumb and Gordon, 2023) for a more detailed and systematic account of the methods and practices that mattered in this case. We also encourage you to maintain contact with the CEEHE who are using the PPoEMs framework to provoke a growing number of contexts in concert with colleagues and community members to reimagine evaluation *for* equity.

Conclusion

Throughout this book, we have argued for the urgency of turning to the significant insights of feminist, anti-colonial, post/structural, and sociological material which over decades and across the world has generated theories, concepts, and methodologies crucial to staying with the trouble of equity. In this chapter, we have woven these threads to further elaborate our offering of *transformative equity praxis* as a reframing to counter the toxic effects of deficit imaginaries, rooted in histories of multidimensional injustice and the sedimentation of neoliberalism. In conceptualising equity as a spectrum, we have argued that the challenge of creating terminology to guide equity work is to resist the hegemonic logics that fix power in homogenising, polarising and binarising ways. Those positions aligned with a politics of counter-hegemony are also vulnerable though to reasserting postures of certainty, imposing authority on Others and creating new regimes of truth. Instead, we argue that power, in all of its fluidity and contextuality, requires troubling our desire for mastery over knowledge/power and practice and that we might instead engage in the iterative, non-linear work of seriously engaging differences, uncertainties, imperfections, and the shifting dynamics, emotions, and contexts that animate movement in time-space. This is not an invitation to just accept the hegemonic order that is grounded in an ignore-ance that as much as we claim commitment to equity we collude in the ongoing production of deeply embedded inequity. Rather we have intricately traced through the characteristics of what we have termed 'hegemonic equity' and 'transformative equity praxis' to bring to the surface the contesting power relations at play in institutions and the ways we might stay with the trouble of equity. We insist that it matters what ideas we think-with and make-with, and similarly that the affective dimensions of social-cultural-political dynamics matter too. Thus, we have brought a politics of emotion into the spectrum to illustrate that feelings shape the movements we take – or do not take. In drawing on two case studies grounded in a transformative equity praxis reframing, we have shared how we put these ideas to work in the making-with others, through deep collaborative and social justice participatory formations of equity praxis. In our final chapter, we consider how the foundations of bodies of social justice theorisation and methodological framing enable us to move towards futures for human and more-than-human flourishing by reimagining higher education *for* equity.

Notes

1 The project was conducted in accordance with ethics approval from the University of Newcastle Human Research Ethics Committee (approval number H-2021–0110).
2 The programs, developed and led by Felicity Cocuzzoli with the team, are 'Reclaiming My Place', a community-based programme for women victim-survivors of GBV to engage in lifelong learning processes, and 'Claim Our Place', a programme for student victim-survivors.

3 The students were provided a list of services available to them within and beyond the university, including free access to counselling services via a community partner organisation.

References

Abma, T.A. (2005) 'Responsive evaluation: Its meaning and special contribution to health promotion', *Evaluation and Program Planning*, 28(3), 279–289. https://doi.org/10.1016/j.evalprogplan.2005.04.003

Abma, T.A., Visse, M., Hanberger, A., Simons, H., and Greene, J.C. (2020) 'Enriching evaluation practice through care ethics', *Evaluation*, 26(2), 131–146. https://doi.org/10.1177/1356389019893402

Ahmed, S. (2010) 'Killing joy: Feminism and the history of happiness', *Signs*, 35(3), 571–594. https://doi.org/10.1086/648513

Ahmed, S. (2017) *Living a Feminist Life*. Durham, NC: Duke University Press.

Anitha, S., and Lewis, R. (2018) 'Introduction: Some reflections in these promising and challenging times', In Anitha, S., and Lewis, R. (Eds) *Gender Based Violence in University Communities: Policy, Prevention and Educational Initiatives*. Bristol: Policy Press.

Bennett, A., and Burke, P.J. (2018) 'Re/conceptualising time and temporality: An exploration of time in higher education', *Discourse: Studies in the Cultural Politics of Education*, 39(6), 913–925. https://doi.org/10.1080/01596306.2017.1312285

Bertram, C.C., and Crowley, M.S. (2012) 'Teaching about sexual violence in higher education: Moving from concern to conscious resistance', *Frontiers: A Journal of Women Studies*, 33(1), 63–82. https://doi.org/10.5250/fronjwomestud.33.1.0063

Burke, P.J. (2012) *The Right to Higher Education: Beyond Widening Participation*. London and New York: Routledge.

Burke, P.J., Cameron, C., and Fuller, E. (2021) 'The relational navigator: A pedagogical reframing of widening educational participation for care-experienced young people', *IJSP*, 10(1). https://doi.org/10.14324/111.444.ijsp.2021.v10.x.015

Burke, P.J., Coffey, J., Parker, J., Hardacre, S., Cocuzzoli, F., Shaw, J., and Haro, A. (2023) '"It's a lot of shame"': Understanding the impact of gender-based violence on higher education access and participation', *Teaching in Higher Education*. www.tandfonline.com/doi/full/10.1080/13562517.2023.2243449

Burke, P.J., Gyamera, G.O., and the Ghanaian Feminist Collective (2023) 'Examining the gendered timescapes of higher education: Reflections through letter writing as feminist praxis', *Gender and Education*, 35(3), 267–281. https://doi.org/10.1080/09540253.2022.2151982

Burke, P.J., and Lumb, M. (2018) 'Researching and evaluating equity and widening participation: Praxis-based frameworks', in Burke, P.J., Hayton, A., and Stevenson, J. (Eds) *Evaluating Equity and Widening Participation in Higher Education*. London: Trentham Books Limited, 11–32.

Burke, P.J., and Manathunga, C. (2020) 'The timescapes of teaching in higher education', *Teaching in Higher Education*, 25(6), 663–668. https://doi.org/10.1080/13562517.2020.1784618

Cocuzzoli, F., Gordon, R., Burke, P.J., and Lumb, M. (2023) *Reclaiming My Place Evaluation Summary*. Centre of Excellence for Equity in Higher Education, University of Newcastle. www.newcastle.edu.au/__data/assets/pdf_file/0005/940766/RMP-Evaluation-Summary_Digital.pdf

Coffey, J., Burke, P.J., Hardacre, S., Parker, J., Coccuzoli, F., and Shaw, J. (2023) 'Students as victim-survivors: The enduring impacts of gender-based violence for students in higher education', *Gender and Education*, 35(6–7), 623–637. https://doi.org/10.1080/09540253.2023.2242879

Fetterman, D. (1994) 'Empowerment evaluation', *Evaluation Practice*, 15(1), 1–15. https://doi.org/10.1016/0886-1633(94)90055-8

Fraser, N. (2013) *Fortunes of Feminism: From State-Managed Capitalism to Neoliberal Crisis*. New York: Verso Books.

Freire, P. (1972/1968) *Pedagogy of the Oppressed*. New York: Continuum.

Gordon, R., and Lumb, M. (2021) 'The situated evaluation and re-imagining methods', *AARE Conference 2021: Reimagining Education Research*, Melbourne, VIC, 28 November–2 December. http://hdl.handle.net/1959.13/1495925

Gordon, R.B., Lumb, M., Bunn, M., and Burke, P.J. (2022) 'Evaluation for equity: Reclaiming evaluation by striving towards counter-hegemonic democratic practices', *Journal of Educational Administration and History*, 54(3), 277–290. https://doi.org/10.1080/00220620.2021.1931059

Guba, E.G., and Lincoln, Y. (1989) *Fourth Generation Evaluation*. Thousand Oaks, CA: Sage.

Gyamera, G.O. (2013) 'Education and social justice in the era of globalization: Perspectives from India and the UK', *Journal of Education Policy*, 28(4), 536–537. https://doi.org/10.1080/02680939.2012.756556

Gyamera, G.O., and Burke, P.J. (2018) 'Neoliberalism and curriculum in higher education: A post-colonial analyses', *Teaching in Higher Education*, 23(4), 450–467. https://doi.org/10.1080/13562517.2017.1414782

Haraway, D. (2016) *Staying with the Trouble: Making Kin in the Chthulucene*. Durham, NC: Duke University Press.

Kelly, L. (1988) *Surviving Sexual Violence*. Minneapolis: University of Minnesota Press.

King, C.S. (2012) *Washed in Blood: Male Sacrifice, Trauma, and the Cinema*. New Brunswick, NJ: Rutgers University Press.

Lumb, M., and Gordon, R. (2023) 'Care-full evaluation: Navigating ethical challenges in evaluation with an ethics of care', *2023 SRHE International Research Conference Higher Education Research, Practice, and Policy: Connections & Complexities*, Birmingham, December. http://hdl.handle.net/1959.13/1495923

LaFrance, J. (2004) 'Culturally competent evaluation in Indian country', *New Directions for Evaluation*, 102, 39–50. https://onlinelibrary.wiley.com/doi/pdf/10.1002/ev.114

Mathison, S. (2016) 'Confronting capitalism: Evaluation that fosters social equity', in Donaldson, S.S., and Picciotto, R. (Eds) *Evaluating for an Equitable Society*. Charlotte, NC: Information Age Publishing, 83–107.

Mertens, D. (2005) 'Feminism', in Mathison, S. (Ed) *Encyclopedia of Evaluation*. Thousand Oaks, CA: Sage.

NSW DET (NSW Department of Education) (2023). *Re-Imagining Evaluation: A Culturally Responsive Evaluation Framework for the NSW Department of Education*. https://education.nsw.gov.au/content/dam/maineducation/teaching-and-learning/aec/media/documents/Re-imagining_Evaluation_Framework_-_FINAL.PDF

Podems, D.R. (2010) 'Feminist evaluation and gender approaches: There's a difference?', *Journal of Multidisciplinary Evaluation*, 6(14), 1–17.

Rowe, A. (2021) 'Evaluation at the Nexus: Evaluating sustainable development in the 2020s', in Uitto, J.I. (Ed) *Evaluating Environment in International Development*. London: Routledge. https://doi.org/10.4324/9781003094821

SenGupta, S., Hopson, R., and Thompson-Robinson, M. (2004) 'Cultural competence in evaluation: An overview', *New Directions for Evaluation*, 5–19. https://doi.org/10.1002/ev.112

Thompson, L. (2020) Toward a feminist psychological theory of "institutional trauma". *Feminism & Psychology*, 31(1), 99–118. https://doi.org/10.1177/0959353520968374

WHO (2021) *Violence Against Women*. World Health Organisation. www.who.int/news-room/fact-sheets/detail/violence-against-women

Wieskamp, V.N., and Smith, C. (2020) ' "What to do when you're raped": Indigenous women critiquing and coping through a rhetoric of survivance', *Quarterly Journal of Speech*, 106(1), 72–94. https://doi.org/10.1080/00335630.2019.1706189

9

GENERATING CHANGE THROUGH EQUITY PRAXIS

Foundations and futures

Introduction

We have argued for a new imaginary of higher education equity; against the colonising, marketising, corporatising, and commercialising forces of neo-liberal capitalism that, far from building equitable systems, reproduce the injustices of the inter-related dimensions of maldistribution, misrecognition, and misrepresentation. Neoliberalism works in concert with neocolonialisms, neopatriarchies, and neoconservatisms (and other inequitable global forces such as post-truth populisms and plutocracies) in the sustained exploitation of human and more-than-human resources, ultimately widening inequalities and contributing to multidimensional planetary crises. We have pointed to the insidious nature of the cycle of injustice, subordination, and exclusion in which higher education is complicit, producing a dynamic of collusion in sustaining and increasing inequality. As a powerful social institution of knowledge formation, deeply entwined with the orientations that shape our present and future directions, we see higher education as entangled in the complex social relations that, when left unchallenged, contribute to the multi-scaler crises of our times; including the deepening of inequalities and societal divisions, instabilities, conflict, violence, global pandemics, disease and viruses, climate change and environmental degradation, and ongoing ignore-ance of the harm of colonial histories and neocolonial dis/positions. Simultane-ously, we recognise that higher education generates knowledge to address these crises (albeit in fragmented ways through individual research agendas rather than a mobilisation of institutional power for social justice-oriented transformations) and so we resist falling into the trap of polarising think-ing. With a more holistic response-ability of higher education to challenge

DOI: 10.4324/9781003257165-13

multidimensional social injustice in mind, we reject the decontextualisation of higher education from these urgent societal concerns and we understand equity in higher education as entangled in the complicated dynamics in which these crises have emerged.

We therefore challenge narrow constructions of equity that reduce it only to proportional parity of participation – the datafication of people from disadvantaged backgrounds enrolled, retained and 'successful' in higher education. We have argued that such narrowly framed ideas are steeped in deficit imaginaries that individualise what are social, cultural, political, and ethical concerns; and we have shown how this demands our long-term, sustained, collective, and methodologically rigorous response. Our book thus argues for a substantially expanded vision of equity through the concept of *transformative equity praxis*. This contrasts with hegemonic versions of equity, which construct the problem of equity as developing interventions to raise aspirations, or provide individual remediation strategies, or develop 'inclusive education' based only on assimilation. This hegemonic equity *misframing* constructs higher education as a neutral site, outside of social-cultural-political relations and positions equity as peripheral to the main purpose of higher education: to produce 'employable' graduates through teaching excellence, and commercialised products through research innovation, with the aim to benefit economic markets and increase nation-state competitiveness in the neoliberal global order.

The peripheral positioning of equity as outside of the 'core business' of higher education ensures that teaching and research (the key mechanisms in which the politics of knowledge and knowing are produced in the interests of hegemonic orders) are left unchallenged and unexamined. Equity is kept firmly away from feminist, decolonial, post/structural, and critical analyses, facilitating postures of ignore-ance to be perpetuated in which a depoliticised notion of 'fairness' is the focus, while histories, systems and practices of social injustice, inequality and marginalisation are seen as irrelevant. Higher education itself is constructed as a neutral site, largely unaffected by, and protected from, the insidious forces of inequality. Thus, the grammar and vocabulary afforded by social justice praxis (with its in-depth ethico-political concern with power and dismantling injustice) rarely enters the hegemonic discourse of equity, inclusion, and widening participation. The rare exception is through areas of more challenging academic scholarship, which is invested in the publication machine to service prestige cultures, with no system to ensure insights from such work influence the national and institutional policy-formation of equity and widening participation. The discourse of 'evidence-based' lends itself well to the politics of hegemonic equity frameworks. The separation of this more challenging academic scholarship from equity practice ensures that institutional equity strategies are hollowed out, not to be contaminated by the 'ideologies' of feminist, decolonial or critical theory.

Feminist, decolonial, and critical scholarly work built over decades of theorisation, analysis, knowledge-formation, and activism is thus mostly disregarded, or at least marginalised, in the context of hegemonic equity. Instead, what equity becomes is a corporate strategy for institutions to recruit and retain bodies marked as 'diverse' and then to celebrate diversity in the prestige economies that fuel the global market rankings of higher education. Throughout this book, we have argued that the neoliberal equity agenda further entrenches social-cultural-political injustice and the multidimensional, multi-scale crises that most immediately threaten the wellbeing and flourishing of those confronted by the intensification of inequality. This is continuously covered up by the manipulative discourses of neoliberal equity that invest in the assurances of measurement, calculability, and algorithms to build 'evidence' to progress equity agendas. Ultimately, we have argued, equity becomes trapped in a vicious cycle of re/producing inequity.

As we noted in Chapter 1, an important discourse within hegemonic neoliberal equity is EDI. Although a broader discourse across a range of contemporary contexts (i.e. not unique to higher education), that the EDI discourse has taken hold in higher education transnationally, and appears to have taken a hegemonic position, suggests an alignment with neoliberal political forces which underpin contemporary higher education. The EDI discourse is highly seductive in its implication that action is being taken, yet this is an example of where our vigilance towards, for example, 'decolonising the curriculum' must guard against the potential of 'the nonperformative' (Ahmed, 2006). The rise of EDI as the reason/able formation of contemporary equity in organisations, including universities, presents more critical formations of equity with serious and challenging questions. How to ensure EDI does not only imply action, relying on vacuous discursive posturing related largely to the marketisation, corporatisation and commercialisation of contemporary higher education? How to prevent EDI becoming a technology of datafication for the purposes of the corporate university? How to respond to another moment in which social movements underpinned by years of detailed critical work can be reworked and manipulated for hegemonic gains? These questions lead to other questions, including: What happens as new discursive regimes come to play against, alongside, and/or in parallel with other discursive regimes, already extensively critiqued by social justice scholars and activists but with those critiques largely ignored within the hegemonies of institutional spaces? For example, how do discourses of widening participation relate to discourses of EDI? Does this matter and if so in what ways? How are new institutional hierarchies produced in and through these different discursive regimes? EDI as a hegemonic discourse tends to gloss over the significant contestations in and beyond the field. There are different meanings, positions, and values at play in and against EDI; how do these matter in institutional policy and practice formations; and who is represented in these debates and in what ways and through what mechanisms (and in what ways does this contribute to ongoing distortions and misrepresentations)? These are questions we challenge the reader to continue to contemplate at the closing moments of this book. We see an aspect of transformative equity praxis being an ongoing close consideration of whether and how rich and critical theorisations of inequality, power, and difference become part of, or are made absent from, institutional efforts around EDI. Whether and how do slippages between research, theory, evidence, and measurement dismiss or dismantle these rich theorisations, or whether and how do we make time and space to sustain transformative equity praxis?

We make these arguments in the context that higher education matters beyond the realms of its perceived borders; we understand it as a powerful social institution that plays a key role in reproducing social-cultural-political inequalities, hierarchies, and stratification. However, with that power and through reimagining equity as a site of praxis comes the possibility of higher education contributing to personal, institutional, social, and planetary flourishing and wellbeing. This is what our book is concerned to enable by pointing to social justice methodologies for *transformative equity praxis*.

A multidimensional reimagining of higher education for equity

We have offered a multidimensional equity reframing by introducing *PPoEMs*. This multidimensional framework weaves feminist, decolonial, critical, post/structural, and sociological material through a tapestry of higher education for equity and social justice. This reimagining of higher education's role in generating equity beyond utilitarian discourses of widening participation (Burke, 2012) expands the scope of equity to address social-cultural-political, and entwined ecological, injustices that would be difficult to disentangle without the insights afforded through this multidimensional reframing.

The tapestry we have woven featured redistribution-recognition-representation as crucial dimensions for reimaging higher education for equity, and through our analysis, we have identified two distinctive positions within an equity spectrum: deficit imaginaries, embedded in *hegemonic equity* (aligned with neoliberal capitalism and its intersection with other unjust social forces) and *transformative equity praxis* (aligned with bodies of social justice theory/action) that seeks to avoid producing counter-hegemonic certainties through sustained reflection/action, action/reflection. By analysing at length these two positions throughout the book, we have attempted to unearth insidious inequalities that are otherwise ignored or overlooked, produced through, and concealed by hegemonic equity, deficit imaginaries, and counter-hegemonic certainties. Throughout the book, we have emphasised that we are all situated within complex power dynamics, and this demands that we stay with the trouble of meaning-making. The production of new regimes of truth through counter-hegemonic posturing will only generate new forms of inequality, exclusion, and oppression. Rather transformative equity praxis brings participants together through collective questioning, relinquishing the desire to master bodies of knowledge and people. Exercising uncertainty and care-full, caring, and compassionate forms of response-ability for human and more-than-human others is valued as an ethical refusal to settle on a final, fixed or rigid position, solution or intervention. If we have any chance of understanding the role of complicity and collusion higher education plays in reproducing social-cultural-political inequalities, and to nurture its capacity to contribute to dismantling these, an ethical reflexivity grounded in an ethics of care and exercised within participatory communities of praxis is paramount.

In offering this idea of an equity spectrum, in which we bring to light the differently textured threads shaping hegemonic equity and transformative equity praxis, our aim therefore is to move beyond static typology and instead to create material to think-with and make-with in the sPace of communities of praxis, engaged over time and space in processes of reflection/action, action/reflection. PPoEMs engages co-participants in a re-search reorientation to higher education for equity in which collaborative formations emerge that question the hegemonic and counter-hegemonic certainties that block our view of the possibilities for new ways of thinking and doing. This re-search process is pedagogical in that it is about learning-with one another from different standpoints, experiences, values, and personhoods to generate new ecologies of meaning (Mbembe, 2023: 13). We understand that this can be a painful process, and it requires a kind of patience with ourselves and one another.

Central to this possibility is acknowledging that equity work is tied to the politics of emotion, feelings that are covered up by the objectivist, disembodied discourse of evidence-based policy and practice. Feelings matter just as ideas do; we thus need sPace to acknowledge the feelings that move bodies to re/act or to act response-ably. Fear of loss of power is one such emotion that can reinforce an unwillingness to dig into the complexity of inequality, often interconnected with feelings of guilt. The shame that is associated with being marked by disadvantage or being seen as a victim of injustice or inequality holds bodies at the margins; silenced by the power of those with author/ity to re/present what the problem of equity is through the mobilisation of data and evidence, claimed to be objective and value-free. Thus, the e-motion-al is critical to moving, or not, in transformative ways, to produce and/or counter the harms of hegemonic neoliberal misframings of equity. We have pointed to the messiness of countering, which can also become embroiled with regimes of truth, and a new common sense about what and who counts, again requiring a sustained orientation to collective praxis. We have also pointed to the problematic of transformation – a concept that requires staying with the trouble, recognising that transformation is complex, multidirectional, and contested.

The concept *transformative equity praxis* signals a commitment to transformation influenced by a multidimensional social justice re/conceptualisation of higher education for equity in an advocacy for approaches and practices that can engage, disrupt, and shift deeply rooted systemic inequalities. Transformative equity praxis recognises the capacity of higher education to play a substantial role in invigorating frameworks, imaginaries, and ways of thinking-with and acting-with for our collective well-being and flourishing.

This book has encouraged readers to create communities of praxis, mobilising sPace that can stay with the trouble of insidious inequalities cultivated through hegemonic equity, embedded as they are in toxic deficit imaginaries. Aligned to what we call transformative equity praxis is the necessity of dislodging monodimensional, deficit imaginaries, which we have argued profoundly narrow, limit and ultimately sabotage commitments to develop higher education for equity. Deficit imaginaries are entrenched in hegemonic equity frameworks and manipulate 'evidence' in favour of regulating the bodies of 'the disadvantaged'. The focus of hegemonic equity is on transforming individuals suffering from a range of supposed deficiencies and disorders so that they can fit in, and be 'included', in the dominant order, including the cultural value order that perpetuates the status subordination of marginalised bodies of knowledge and people. An example of this, provided through a case study in Chapter 8, is the status subordination of knowledge and people associated with femininities, which together with gendered maldistribution, manifests in a continuum of GBV. However, within a framework of hegemonic equity, gender injustice expressed through GBV is regularly constructed as outside the realm of higher education equity agendas. This further marginalises the knowledge of victim-survivors, who must both overcome the injustice and trauma of GBV, to fit into higher education, and contributes to the institutional silencing of GBV to avoid the stigmatisation attached to being constructed as a victim. This tragically overlooks the knowledge student victim-survivors bring to higher education, which could provide significant insight into building strategies to build gender equity and, ultimately, to end GBV. This vicious cycle of injustice contributes to the ongoing social epidemic of GBV (Burke et al, 2023). This is all compounded by the peripherisation of equity, in which gender equity is treated as separate from the core practices in higher education. Thus, teaching and curriculum development, which could enable engagement with questions of gender injustice and relatedly to GBV, is not considered to be relevant.

We understand *hegemonic equity* and *transformative equity praxis* as different to neatly typed positions within a spectrum. Rather, we recognise that all of us move in and out of the positionings of the equity spectrum because inequalities and injustices are insidious – that is they are baked into the histories of social institutions and thus almost impossible to see without the tools to bring them to light. While we are concerned with structures of inequality, which are less malleable and more static in formation, we argue that a more 'capillary' conception of power helps us see how patriarchy is reformed fluidly across time and space, and in relation to political forces such as colonialism, capitalism, neoliberalism, globalisation, and neoconservatism, which themselves are not monolithic but dynamic forces (Burke, 2012). We have argued, with this understanding of 'capillary power', drawing on post-Foucauldian scholarship, that it is in the everyday inter/actions that reflection/action can matter intensely. In this conceptualisation of social power, it is at the capillary levels, that is, at the extremities of the social body, where in everyday actions of higher education sPaces, our conduct with each other reproduces inequalities and arguably therefore this too is where transformative equity praxis can go to work in apprehending and refusing. Ethical reflexivity – that is a position of questioning that puts an ethics of care for more than ourselves at the heart of the process – is like a magnifying glass that helps participants to collaboratively examine the almost invisible manifestations of generations of oppression, violence, and injustice that are part of the fabric of our social institutions, including higher education, even while we claim higher education to be a central producer of objective, value-free, universal knowledge.

This book has thus been more concerned with the *methodologies* that enable praxis and less so with the methods that put praxis to work. This is not to say that methods are insignificant – *what we do matters*. However, it is to counter the preoccupation with methods, that over-emphasise the tools available (survey or interview, workshop, or forum, online or in person) without connecting questions of method to the ethical-political-epistemological-ontological complex that significantly frames how the method is animated in time-space. We have argued strongly that it is the way we approach what we do that makes a difference and this must always be grounded in a rigorous methodological framework; one formed by social justice ethical-political-epistemological-ontological commitments. It is our critical hope that the PPoEMs framework will enable readers to engage their own methods in their own contexts, guided by a commitment to parity of participation, grounded in the multidimensional, intersecting principles of redistribution-recognition-representation. More broadly, we aim for PPoEMs to contribute to an expanded vision of equity; one that positions higher education as a response-able and significant partner with other social institutions/organisations/agencies in addressing urgent societal crises and helping to transform the conditions towards human and more-than-human flourishing for social and planetary justice. Dismantling multidimensional inequalities is key to this and higher education has a crucial role to play, demanding a reimagining of its purpose, beyond widening participation to benefit the neoliberal order.

This massive project of transformative equity praxis can feel overwhelming, sometimes throwing us into a state of lethargy or even despair. We feel this too and it weighs heavily. However, our orientation to this expanded vision of equity in higher education we believe is thinkable and doable in the context of everyday thinking and doing differently *together*. This is not the work of a sole person appointed to a senior role in EDI – nor is it the work of a director or manager of an equity and widening participation unit. It is not the work of a lone executive leader. No one person can create the transformative conditions we are pointing towards. Transformative equity praxis requires a different form of *redistributed leadership* committed to deep and sustained forms of collaboration across and with differences as a resource for thinking and doing higher education differently, inclusively, and equitably.

Redistributed leadership engages all participants together in processes of making a difference; of thinking-with and making-with others. This is not a problem of method; it is guided by a broader methodological framework that offers the ethical-political-epistemological-ontological complex needed to co-create the methods that will support participatory, pedagogical, reciprocal, and response-able processes. We are not denying that leadership matters here but are pointing to a leadership framework embedded in transformative equity praxis – guided by PPoEMs and enabling participants the sPace to take part in collective action/reflection, reflection/action. This form of leadership counters the competitive, self-centric, resource-managerialist, and corporate forms that tend to be privileged by masculinist-neoliberal-neocolonial leadership 'styles'. Instead redistributed leadership demands the vulnerability of the leader to learn-with, think-with, and make-with others who are recognised as equal peers by and through a collaborative process. It prioritises reciprocity, co-response-ability, care-full, and caring dis/positions and a sense of being together for a project beyond ourselves. It requires ongoing re-working of the relationalities that form collaborative sPace, recognising that collaboration is imperfect and embedded in power dynamics that require troubling through reflexive processes of collective reflection/action, action/reflection. Redistributed leadership is framed by PPoEMs, guided by the ethical-political-epistemological-ontological complex of feminist, decolonial, post/structural, critical, and sociological commitments to equity and social justice.

All of this requires a sustained troubling of the dominant structures of time-space in higher education – structures that privilege a neutral, depoliticised, and decontextualised view of time and space through discourses of management. The concept of sPace has been offered as part of the PPoEMs framework to pay attention to the politics of space-time otherwise ignored and to shift in temporal orientation to deep, collective praxis – one that reveals the insidious ways that certain values seep into our pedagogical and methodological imaginations, leading us to believe there is no alternative. sPace is a reframing that shifts our dis/positionality in time and space towards reflexive, iterative, care-full, response-able cycles of participatory meaning-making

204 Social justice transformation through equity praxis

across and with difference. These are contexts for re-searching research, evaluating evaluation, and practising on practice to engage with the 'world-making', constructive quality of research, evaluation, and practice. sPace facilitates participation that resists and refuses the 'political death' of mis/framing through counter-hegemonic moments: that is, reflexive efforts to generate awareness of power relations that are both producing and playing out within, space and time. The 'counter' moment refuses the hegemonic ir/rationalities guiding conduct in material and social space, and 'Pace' involves care-full refusal of the flow of power relations in time through different rhythms of practice, whether that be a collective, ethically oriented 'speeding up' or 'slowing down'. Countering is not about managing space and time but practicing together with an ethics that places dialogic relations, with each other, with material and pedagogical space, and with time, at the heart of social justice praxis.

References

Ahmed, S. (2006) 'The nonperformativity of antiracism', *Meridians*, 7(1), 104–126. www.jstor.org/stable/40338719

Burke, P.J. (2012) *The Right to Higher Education: Beyond Widening Participation*. London and New York: Routledge.

Burke, P.J., Coffey, J., Parker, J., Hardacre, S., Cocuzzoli, F., Shaw, J., and Haro, A. (2023) ' "It's a lot of shame": Understanding the impact of gender-based violence on higher education access and participation', *Teaching in Higher Education*, 1–16. https://doi.org/10.1080/13562517.2023.2243449

Mbembe, A. (2023) *Transforming Knowledge for UNITWIN/UNESCO Chairs Programme 3–4 November 2022*. Paris, France: UNESCO Headquarters, UNESCO.

INDEX

9 781032 189703